Friends and Enemies in Organizations

Friends and Enemies in Organizations

A Work Psychology Perspective

Edited by

Rachel L. Morrison

and

Sarah L. Wright

palgrave
macmillan

First published 2009 by
PALGRAVE MACMILLAN

Palgrave Macmillan in the UK is an imprint of Macmillan Publishers Limited, registered in England, company number 785998, of Houndmills, Basingstoke, Hampshire RG21 6XS.

Palgrave Macmillan in the US is a division of St Martin's Press LLC, 175 Fifth Avenue, New York, NY 10010.

Palgrave Macmillan is the global academic imprint of the above companies and has companies and representatives throughout the world.

Palgrave® and Macmillan® are registered trademarks in the United States, the United Kingdom, Europe and other countries

ISBN-13: 978-0-230-53876-4   hardback

This book is printed on paper suitable for recycling and made from fully managed and sustained forest sources. Logging, pulping and manufacturing processes are expected to conform to the environmental regulations of the country of origin.

A catalogue record for this book is available from the British Library.

A catalogue record for this book is available from the Library of Congress.

10   9   8   7   6   5   4   3   2   1
18   17   16   15   14   13   12   11   10   09

Printed and bound in Great Britain by
CPI Antony Rowe, Chippenham and Eastbourne

To Thomas (Sarah's son) and Olive (Rachel's daughter),
both of whom were conceived after, but born before, this book.

Contents

List of Tables and Figures

Tables

Figures

List of Contributors

Rachel Morrison Ph.D. runs the Organizational Behaviour programme within the Faculty of Business at AUT University (NZ). She has published articles in a variety of academic Management and Psychology journals. Dr Morrison's research interests include gender and equity issues in the workplace, social identity, relationships in the workplace, work-life balance and friendship formation.

Sarah Wright Ph.D. is a lecturer in Organisational Development and Leadership at the University of Canterbury, New Zealand. She teaches courses on organizational behaviour and diversity on organizations. Her research interests include social relationships in the workplace, loneliness, emotions in organizations, employee selection, assessment and validation, emotional climate in organizations, and employee retention. Sarah is currently working on a longitudinal project on employee retention with a Government organization and has an ongoing research programme looking into loneliness at work. Prior to her current academic role, Sarah worked as an organizational psychologist for international and local management consulting firms.

Helena Cooper-Thomas Ph.D. lectures at the University of Auckland in Industrial, Work and Organizational Psychology; in particular organizational socialization, person-organization fit, psychological contract, and performance competencies. Her research interests are in Industrial Work and Organizational Psychology, in particular organizational socialization, person-organization fit, psychological contract, and performance competencies.

Terry Nolan Ph.D. is a senior lecturer at AUT University, New Zealand. He currently teaches Information Systems within the Business School at Auckland University of Technology. His research reflects an interdisciplinary approach to the study of management, organizations and society. He is interested in the effects of power and influence upon discourse, human and business relationships, and information systems.

Wendelin Küpers Ph.D. is affiliated with the Department of Management and International Business at Massey University, Auckland, New

Zealand. He is a member of the Integral Leadership Review's Integral Leadership Council and is its Bureau Chief for New Zealand. His publications in peer reviewed journals tend to focus on integral leadership and/or phenomenology.

Patricia M. Sias Ph.D. is Professor of Communication in the Edward R. Murrow College of Communication at Washington State University. Her research centres on workplace relationships. She has published articles in and served on the editorial boards of a variety of academic journals including Communication Monographs, Human Communication Research, Management Communication Quarterly, Western Journal of Communication, Communication Quarterly, and Journal of Applied Communication Research. She has won numerous awards for her research including the W. Charles Redding Outstanding Dissertation in Organizational Communication Award from the International Communication Association, several Top Paper awards from the National Communication Association, and the Distinguished Faculty Achievement Award from the Washington State University College of Liberal Arts.

Erin B. Gallagher M.A. is a Doctoral Candidate in the Edward R. Murrow College of Communication at Washington State University. Her research focuses on organizational socialization processes. She has published in the *Western Journal of Communication*.

Karin Sanders Ph.D. is the Head of the Organizational Psychology and Human Resource Development Department at the University of Twente. Her main research interests include the effects of Human Resource Management on attitudes and behaviours, in terms of cooperative behaviour, commitment, knowledge sharing and absenteeism of employees within teams. She is particularly interested in the effects of alignment between line managers and HRM/HRD managers on organizational climate.

Barbara Winstead Ph.D. is a professor at Old Dominion University. Her research focuses on relationships, gender, and individuals who are HIV+. She is particularly interested in how gender influences relationships, how relationships influence coping, and how relationships influence individual health and safety behaviours (e.g., medical adherence and condom use). She is also interested in how individuals cope with multiple roles.

Valerie Morganson M.S. is a student in the Industrial and Organizational Psychology Doctoral Program at Old Dominion University. Her research focuses on gender issues in career development and workplace interventions to promote work-life balance.

Janie Harden Fritz Ph.D. conducts research on communication in problematic workplace relationships, organizational communication ethics, and communication pedagogy. She has published in numerous com-munication journals, is co-editor of Problematic Relationships in the Workplace (Peter Lang), and is the current 2nd vice-president of the Eastern Communication Association. Dr Fritz is an Associate Professor in the Department of Communication and Rhetorical Studies, McAnulty College and Graduate School of Liberal Arts at Duquesne University. She specializes in interpersonal and intercultural communication.

Adrian Furnham Ph.D. is a Professor of Psychology at University College London. His research interests include organizational psychology; psychometrics, especially personality assessment; complementary medicine; cross-cultural psychology, especially mental health and migration and economic socialization. He has over 500 publications.

Giles St. J. Burch Ph.D. is a Senior Lecturer in HRM in the Department of Management and International Business, The University of Auckland. He is a Registered Psychologist (NZ), Chartered Occupational Psychologist and Associate Fellow of the British Psychological Society, and a Chartered Scientist (UK). He is also an elected member of the American Psychological Association (Society of Consulting Psychology) and a founding member of the British Psychological Society's Special Group in Coaching Psychology. He has a particular expertise in personality profiling, psychological coaching, career counselling, team facilitation and leadership development. Prior to practising as a consulting psychologist, Giles worked for a number of years in the mental health field.

Iain McCormick Ph.D. is a leading Asia Pacific management consultant and business coach who recently returned to New Zealand after a decade in Hong Kong. He is the author of over 100 practical and academic articles in a wide range of psychological and business topics.

He heads the Executive Coaching Centre Limited in New Zealand and coaches a range of boards of directors, chief executives and other senior managers in New Zealand and Australia.

Acknowledgements

Sarah and I would like to acknowledge all of our extraordinary contributing authors, both for their own chapters and also for engaging so positively and helpfully in the peer review of other's contributions. The book could not have happened without you.

Thanks also to our departments and colleagues at Canterbury University and AUT University for the support we have received during the process of creating this book. Special thanks to Professor Stuart Carr (Massey University) whose encouragement and know-how got this project off the ground. Thanks also to Keith Mackey for his guidance and Yehuda Baruch for providing timely advice regarding editorial procedure. His wise counsel was very much appreciated.

Last but not least, thanks to our families and especially to our husbands, Justin and John, for their love, support and unfailing encouragement.

1
The Organizational Chart's 'White Spaces'

Rachel L. Morrison and Sarah L. Wright

Jo is the practice manager at a small accounting firm. She has been the cause of a great deal of trouble in the past few years. Several secretarial staff resigned primarily because of her bullying, political and self-interested behaviour.

Holly and Cate are good friends; they were recruited from University and joined the firm within a few weeks of each other. Over a relatively short time their relationship developed from a positive, collegial working relationship into a close friendship, based on a similar work ethic. They provide each other with social support in what is often a very stressful work environment. On being hired they had expectations that they were on a similar career path in terms of promotion and career opportunities.

Over the last six months Holly and Cate have been working closely on a large and complex audit. They are beginning to get behind and Jo is increasingly concerned that the project will run over budget. Jo has a tendency to be quite abrasive towards others when things do not go to plan and has been putting pressure on Holly and Cate to work extensive overtime. Although initially compliant with Jo's requests, Cate announces that she is pregnant and asks that her hours be reduced to a normal, full time load. In spite of demands from Jo, Cate continues to insist that her hours be kept within those agreed in her employment contract. During a staff meeting Cate makes a public request for her hours to be reduced, suggesting solutions to get the audit finished, which overrides Jo's proposal of simply having most staff stay late every night. Jo comments snidely 'Well Cate... if you really feel that you can't handle this job you're more than welcome to stay home and start your new career as a housewife... I'm sure you can use your mediocre accountancy skills to balance the family budget'. No one, including the partners, said anything to support

Cate, even though they knew the comment was extremely uncalled for and very unfair.

Although devastated by the attack from Jo and the lack of support from the senior partners, Cate stands up to Jo, refusing to be bullied. She tries to find a feasible solution to enable the audit to be completed within normal working hours. Jo is enraged at Cate's audacity in questioning her during a meeting and determines to make her a target. Jo has insinuated to senior partners that Holly and Cate's close friendship has compromised their productivity, implying that both have been lazy and they have been engaging in gossip, internet surfing and other off-task behaviour. As a result of Jo's back stabbing, Holly is promoted at the next promotion round to senior accountant and Cate is not, even though, in most respects their performance is equal. The partners should have made promotion decision on merit alone but feared retribution from Jo, knowing that Jo would only want Holly promoted. Most of the staff know that Jo makes the decisions around the firm; the partners remain very conciliatory towards Jo and struggle with taking hard decisions and 'being the boss' when leadership is clearly required.

Jo engineers circumstances so that Cate has to assist Holly (and is under her direct control). Cate feels undermined and resents being asked to support Holly in her work. Cate's attitude towards her work and colleagues deteriorates. She has taken to making snide remarks, giving silent treatment and sending bitchy emails. Cate and Holly have several mutual friends. Cate has always been the one to organize social events but has recently stopped inviting Holly along. Holly knows that she really deserved her promotion and becomes angry that Cate is not supportive. On the other hand, Cate believes that her career and salary have been compromised. Ill feeling and animosity quickly develop between the two friends. Without the constraint of relational loyalty, Holly starts to take credit for work Cate does in her assistant role. Holly and Cate now only talk about work matters. Because Holly is no longer included in social events she feels increasingly ostracized and starts to become lonely. She feels alienated from her colleagues and no one seems to understand things from her perspective. Her only supporter is Jo, who she does not like as a person but knows she has to keep on her 'good side.'

Because of these issues a constant undercurrent of tension surges through the office. Over time, quite serious performance issues begin to emerge. None of the issues are in any way directly related to the technical aspects of accounting or client management; however the issues have a significant impact on the practice. Clients have noticed the

*tension between the accountants at the firm and have become increasingly
uncomfortable; several have even gone to other firms.*

This short vignette demonstrates how easily relationships at work
can turn from mutual friendships into toxic relationships, affecting the
entire working environment and organizational climate. A relationship
which started out as a loyal and supportive friendship between Holly
and Cate, quickly moved into enemy territory, creating a tense emotional climate. Jo, a sub-clinical psychopath, whose character traits and
behaviours are not uncommon in many workplaces, has created a divi-
sive and tension-filled working environment with everyone fearing her
retribution. Not surprisingly, the majority of people dislike turning up
to work in these environments. The simple answer would be for management to confront the cause of the problems, i.e., Jo's inappropriate and
bullying behaviour. However in many workplaces the obvious solutions
are not always the most feasible and so the situation often gets much
worse. Leaving the situation as it is often results in unacceptable levels of
turnover, with good performers leaving the organization, worsening
the morale of those who remain. Given that we cannot often choose
who we work with, work-based relationships need attention, not only
to realize the many benefits they can bring to the work environment,
but to avoid the negative consequences of relationship deterioration.

This book stems, in part, from our belief that all organizational activities
take place in the context of interpersonal relationships, and these relationships are, in fact, the basis *for* organization. Humans are social animals
and, as such, the relationships that we have with those in our work environment are an extraordinarily salient aspect of our happiness and wellbeing. As Holly and Cate did on joining the accounting practice in our
opening vignette, many people *expect* social relationships to form within
their work environment and to provide a much-needed source of friendship and companionship. On the other hand, when workplace relationships degrade and turn sour we usually have to continue to interact.
Within the organization we may be 'forced' into potentially negative and
toxic relationships with those (such as Jo, from the vignette above) who,
in other circumstances, we would avoid.

'Friends and Enemies in Organizations: A Work Psychology Perspective'
is an exploration into the current world of relationships in the workplace.
The book focuses on the ways in which friendship, isolation and enemy-
ships influence and affect our experience of work. The theme of the
research volume is 'Alienation to Suffocation'; canvassing issues from isolation and loneliness (when true friendships are wholly absent) through

to the positive aspects of a friendly workplace and how these relationships might be maintained or managed, and finally delving into the 'dark side' of negative and destructive social interactions in the workplace. There has been much written about both romance at work (e.g., Bowes-Sperry & Powell, 1999; Mano & Gabriel, 2006; Pierce & Aguinis, 2001; Powell & Foley, 1998) and formal organizational relationships, such as the relationship between supervisors and their subordinates (e.g., Aryee, Chen, Sun & Debrah, 2007; Glomb & Hulin, 1997; Lapierre, 2007; Murphy & Ensher, 1999; Paglis & Green, 2002). So, while relationships in organizations have not been completely ignored, they have certainly received relatively little attention given their centrality to organizational functioning and the everyday experiences of organizational life. This book therefore fills a gap by narrowing the focus specifically to friends and enemies at work and the ways in which people develop and maintain their relationships with one another. The role the workplace and organizational climate plays and the extent to which cooperative behaviours impact on collegial relationships are also covered.

This book represents a broad development in Organizational Psychology in addressing workplace social relationships. Its purpose is simply to begin concentrating on a number of key aspects of work-based relationships and how they affect organizational life, both positively and negatively. In the next chapter, Sarah Wright looks at the issue of how individuals can feel lonely in the work environment. She argues that loneliness in the workplace has received relatively little attention in the literature and that, historically, research has tended to focus almost exclusively on personal characteristics as the primary determinant of the experience, and largely ignores the workplace as a potential trigger. This chapter argues that personality tends to be overestimated as the reason for loneliness and only modest emphasis is given to environmental factors, such as the organizational climate, friendship development and social support. This chapter queries such conclusions and argues that it is also important to look carefully at the organizational environment to determine how contextual factors can affect an individual's experience of loneliness.

In Chapter 3, Helena Cooper-Thomas examines how the organizational socialization process can affect relationships in an organization. Organizational socialization is the process by which a new employee (newcomer) gets up to speed in their new role and organization. In order to function successfully in his or her new environment, the newcomer needs to understand the informal, inescapably social side of the organization. For example, experienced insiders know what good role performance really looks like, beyond the job description, but may not share this information with a newcomer until or unless they come to like and accept them as a friend. Hence, while relationships with newcomers are of little value to insiders, they can be critical in enabling newcomers to adapt successfully. Dr Cooper-Thomas' argument in this chapter is that successful socialization is fundamentally about relationships and becoming part of the social fabric that defines an organization. To illustrate this argument, she explores research on how newcomers develop and depend on relationships with insiders (peers, manager, mentor, and other newcomers) to achieve successful socialization, with success defined along five dimensions ranging from individual role performance to external representation of the organization. Dr Cooper-Thomas will also briefly present the pitfalls of having ineffective relationships for organizational socialization, using examples of isolation and enemy-ships. Last, she suggests practical strategies for newcomers to achieve successful socialization.

Chapter 4 explores the interplay between three interdependent concepts – climate, culture and interpersonal relationships. Terry Nolan and Wendelin Küpers present organizations as 'worlds' in which climate and culture have a reciprocally influencing relationship which, in turn, impact upon workplace peer relationships. The chapter explores the conceptual differences between culture and climate, and the various ways to approach organizational climate. The authors explore the notion of ethical and emotional climates and the impact these environments can have on peer relationships. They conclude their chapter with ideas to cultivate a 'wise climate' in an attempt to sustain positive relations in the organization.

Patricia Sias and Erin Gallagher address the question of how friendships within a workplace are formed, maintained and ended. Throughout Chapter 5 they focus on why and how workplace friendships develop, deteriorate and maintain stability. Peer friendships have been found to go through three primary transitions: from co-worker/acquaintance-to-friend, friend-to-close friend, and close friend-to-almost best friend. Each of these transitions is characterized by different antecedents and communication styles, moving from the superficial to the intimate. The authors also note the effects of unfair supervision in the workplace, explaining that differential treatment from a supervisor to his or her subordinates influences co-worker communication, sometimes creating friendships in times of adversity or driving a wedge that ultimately ends the relationship. The chapter provides insight into the role of communication in the joint construction of relationship perceptions and highlights the impact of the workplace context on friendship development, maintenance and dissolution.

In Chapter 6, Karin Sanders explores the notion of cooperative behaviour in relationships. Although this topic is well recognized in the academic literature, seemingly little empirical work has been conducted on reciprocity in workplace relationships. Cooperative behaviour involves at least two parties and therefore is affected by the quality of the relationship between the parties. This chapter aims to expand on this idea and focuses on reciprocity within relationships to explain trust, conflict and cooperative behaviour within organizations. Throughout the chapter Dr Sanders illustrates that supervisors play a key role in eliciting cooperative behaviours from their subordinates, while also playing an important role in developing reciprocity amongst co-workers.

On the topic of friendship, Rachel Morrison presents an analysis of the organizational outcomes of workplace friendships. The foundation for Chapter 7 is that research generally supports the notion that a friendly workplace has positive organizational outcomes. The impact of close personal friendships at work is less clear-cut however. Given the numerous forms and functions of friendships in the workplace, the soundness of conceptualizing friendships as uniformly positive is queried. Dr Morrison agues that while some friendships will be valuable both for employees and at the organizational level, factors such as maintenance difficulty, dual-role tension, boundary violations and distraction from work mean that having close friends within the workplace can create numerous difficulties for employees. Individuals will utilize their workplace friendships in quite different ways, and the various functions and forms of workplace friendship mean that it is not a phenomenon with clear organizational outcomes. While friendship relationships for men and women are similar in many respects, there have been consistent findings in both the social psychology and organizational psychology literature of gender differences in friendships. Thus differences in the way that men and women conceptualize and rely on friends in times of stress and adversity are explored within a workplace context. In all probability the organizational correlates of friendships will be different for various types of friends, for the various functions friendships have, for the degree of closeness in the friendship, and for the difficulty experienced maintaining the relationship in the workplace.

In Chapter 8, Barbara Winstead and Valerie Morganson address the issues surrounding gender and relationships. To understand gender and relationships in the workplace the authors begin with a discussion of how best to understand gender. Gender has been used to represent biological categories, socialization processes, sociocultural stereotypes, or an interactional performance (i.e., 'doing gender', West & Zimmerman, 1987). Thus, the first section is a discussion of the complexities of studying gender, gender and relationships, and gender and relationships in the workplace. The subsequent sections present research on gender and workplace friendships, mentoring and social networks. They then consider the special status of cross-sex relationships in the workplace and negative relationships. In conclusion they discuss the need for additional research and fresh perspectives on the study of gender and personal relationships in the workplace.

Janie Fritz, in Chapter 9, discusses the notion of incivility in the workplace. Incivility may be defined as low intensity, deviant behaviour that violates workplace norms for mutual respect. Dr Fritz argues that the effects of intra-organizational incivility are considerable and resolving conflicts among co-workers can account for as much as 13% of managers' time. This chapter details the nature of incivility and its consequences. Dr Fritz provides keys to recognizing and dealing with habitual instigators, and remedies that are being used effectively by organizations to curtail and correct employee-to-employee incivility.

How does vanity affect workplace relationships? In Chapter 10, Adrian Furnham explores the research on vanity and narcissism. He provides a thorough review of the literature and research on narcissism, pointing out that, while highly self-confident narcissists may at first be beneficial at work or in social relationships, a problem arises when self-confidence 'spills over' into arrogance and narcissism. Professor Furnham also reflects upon how this personality disorder can help and hinder business relationships and team performance. He explores the nature of the narcissistic employee and how their behaviour of grandiosity, need for admiration, and lack of empathy can influence peer relationships and commercial transactions.

Finally, in Chapter 11, Iain McCormick and Giles Burch consider the implications of psychopathic personalities in the workplace, the impact that such a personality may have on relationships with colleagues, and how they can be managed by colleagues. This chapter provides an intriguing insight into the behaviours of these individuals which can have a major impact on colleagues and staff around them, for example: pathological lying, manipulation of others and bullying. This, coupled with their lack of conscience, guilt and low empathy makes it difficult to have a constructive relationship with these people in the workplace. The authors outline that there are a range of workplace problems associated with psychopathy including, for example, blackmail, discrimination, extortion and violence. The authors also point out that dealing with psychopathic personalities is difficult as they do not respond well to therapy or coaching, and therefore it is difficult to facilitate more constructive working relationships through changes in their own work-related behaviours. The authors go on to discuss how colleagues can manage their relations in such a way as to minimize the risk of becoming 'victims' of their psychopathic colleagues.

This collection of chapters represents the first attempt to pull together a wide range of ideas about, and approaches to, informal workplace relationships and organizational life. Our focus throughout the book has been towards constructive ideas to improve workplace processes and practices to ensure relationships are positive, constructive and promote healthy organizations.

As Patricia Sias and Erin Gallagher assert in Chapter 5 *'the "organizing" in organizations occurs primarily in the context of informal relationships; those that are invisible in an organizational chart, but exist in the chart's "white spaces". Among the most ubiquitous and powerful of these informal relationships are workplace friendships.'*

References

Aryee, S., Chen, Z. X., Sun, L. Y. & Debrah, Y. A. (2007). Antecedents and outcomes of abusive supervision: Test of a trickle-down model. *Journal of Applied Psychology, 92*(1), 191–201.

Bowes-Sperry, L. & Powell, G. N. (1999). Observers' reactions to social-sexual behavior at work: An ethical decision making perspective. *Journal of Management, 25*(6), 779–802.

Glomb, T. M. & Hulin, C. L. (1997). Anger and gender effects in observed supervisor-subordinate dyadic interactions. *Organizational Behavior and Human Decision Processes, 72*(3), 281–307.

Lapierre, L. M. (2007). Supervisor trustworthiness and subordinates' willingness to provide extra-role efforts. *Journal of Applied Social Psychology, 37*(2), 272–297.

Mano, R. & Gabriel, Y. (2006). Workplace romances in cold and hot organizational climates: The experience of Israel and Taiwan. *Human Relations, 59*(1), 7–35.

Murphy, S. E. & Ensher, E. A. (1999). The effects of leader and subordinate characteristics in the development of leader-member exchange quality. *Journal of Applied Social Psychology, 29*(7), 1371–1394.

Paglis, L. L. & Green, S. G. (2002). Both sides now: Supervisor and subordinate perspectives on relationship quality. *Journal of Applied Social Psychology, 32*(2), 250–276.

Pierce, C. A. & Aguinis, H. (2001). A framework for investigating the link between workplace romance and sexual harassment. *Group & Organization Management, 26*(2), 206–229.

Powell, G. N. & Foley, S. (1998). Something to talk about: Romantic relation-ships in organizational settings. *Journal of Management, 24*(3), 421–448.
West, C. & Zimmerman, D. H. (1987). Doing gender. *Gender and Society, 1*(2), 125–151.

2
In a Lonely Place: The Experience of Loneliness in the Workplace

Sarah L. Wright

British business leaders suffer from office politics and loneliness

British business leaders battle against office politics and loneliness, according to results of a survey announced today for the International Leadership Summit Leaders in London ... Asked to indicate the worst elements of business leadership 43 per cent of respondents answered politics, while 31 per cent indicated that loneliness was the most unpleasant aspect of the job ... just 8% of respondents said responsibility was the worst part of their job and a tiny 6% said they disliked being criticised as part of the role ... 'Loneliness is an unavoidable by-product of effective people management' said Gary Fitzgibbon, chartered occupational psychologist. 'A good leader must exhibit fairness, objectivity and emotional detachment – this last quality in particular prevents the development of special relationships with colleagues and therefore renders the leader isolated and alone in the work environment'...[1]

If we are to believe anecdotal literature and media reports, loneliness bedevils many successful executives and business leaders. However, it is puzzling that a phenomenon already reported as a current experience by so many organizational leaders should receive so little attention by researchers. Several commentators have argued that the availability and quality of social relationships in the workplace is diminishing (e.g. Joyce, 2004), however loneliness in the workplace has been curiously

---

[1]Retrieved from the WWW on 18 November 2008 from http://www.heartmath-report.com/index.php/weblog/2004/06/

neglected in the literature. Loneliness is not a new phenomenon to study empirically, nor is loneliness at work a new concept for journalists to report on. For instance, the words 'loneliness' and 'isolation' are often mentioned in the popular media when a leader or senior executive is estranged because of his or her business or political dealings. However, the area of workplace loneliness remains a nebulous and under-examined construct, both empirically and theoretically. The research surrounding loneliness tends to focus almost exclusively on personal characteristics as the primary determinant of the experience, and largely ignores the workplace as a potential trigger. As such, personality tends to be overestimated as the reason for loneliness and virtually no attention is given to environmental factors, such as organizational climate, friendship and camaraderie, social support, community spirit or person-organization fit, as the potential causes of loneliness. This chapter queries such conclusions and argues that it is also important to look at the organizational environment to determine how contextual factors can affect an individual's experience of loneliness.

Whilst other chapters in this book discuss the benefits and rewards of social relationships in the workplace, this chapter attempts to understand the experience of those who lack functional workplace relationships and the factors which may impact on loneliness. This chapter introduces and explores the construct of loneliness at work. It reviews the theoretical and empirical literature related to the topic and builds towards a discussion of how an individual's social environment can operate to create feelings of loneliness. The chapter concludes with a section on interventions to manage loneliness.

Work and social interaction

In most organizations, work consists of more than simply technological and intellectual processes. For many, the act of 'working' is considered a social institution which requires the continual fostering of human cooperation (Berman, West & Richter, 2002; see also Chapter 6 in this book). As such, work settings can provide an environment where an individual's social and emotional needs are fulfilled. For instance, an employee may ask for the opinion of another employee, or request their help on a project, allowing both individuals to maintain their self-esteem and reassurance of worth. Further, a co-worker may extend to a fellow co-worker an invitation to lunch or acknowledge another's achievements, which again fulfils the individual's needs for attachment, approval or social integration, and provides a sense of belonging. However, for numerous individuals the social reality of working is not so rosy. In many organizations the attention is often focused on productivity, competition, decisions, deadlines, and reports, and less focused on the human element of organization and productivity (Riesman, 1961). In many ways, human interaction is often perceived as 'getting in the way' of work productivity.

Humans, whether they are at home or at work, are social animals, so much so that a basic need to belong is a fundamental motivator in human existence (Flanders, 1982). Further, the need to belong and attach to others does not cease to exist upon entering the workplace. Rather, the need for interpersonal affiliation appears to be essential for physical and psychological wellbeing across the life span, including life at work (Cacioppo, 2008; Cacioppo, Hawkley & Bernston, 2003). Positive interpersonal relationships, whether they are at work or not, are 'good medicine', and are fundamental for a sense of community (Peplau, 1985). People can have a range of relationships at work, ranging from a superficial greeting in the corridor, to the development of an intimate relational tie leading to marriage. For some employees however, they may feel they have a host of acquaintances at work but no one who really understands them.

Defining loneliness at work

The words 'lonely' and 'loneliness' have been given both objective and subjective meanings in their common everyday usage. They are often used in the media to refer to isolation, aloneness, solitude or social dysfunction. Strictly speaking however, loneliness is a subjective construct; a self-perceived interpersonal deficiency revealing how an individual experiences the discrepancy between their personal relationships and their social environment (Peplau & Perlman, 1982). Loneliness reflects a breakdown in social interaction and poor quality interpersonal relationships. In an article on the experiential nature of loneliness, Killeen (1998, p. 763) comments that loneliness 'can make you feel as though you are the only person in the world ... it can make you feel totally isolated and useless ... [Loneliness] is as individual as your every thought ... one moment you are feeling alone but comfortable; the next minute you feel like you are the only person in the world ...'. These descriptions suggest there are many subjective clusters of feelings, thoughts and behaviours which lead a person to conclude 'I am feeling lonely'.

Additionally, the experience of feeling lonely has little to do with the number of social relationships an individual may have, but rather lies with the quality and meaningfulness of those relationships (e.g. Gaev, 1976).

Recognizing therefore that loneliness is not synonymous with actual social contact, loneliness at work can be defined as the *distress caused by the perceived lack of good quality interpersonal relationships between employees in a work environment*. This deficiency between the individual's actual and desired interpersonal relationships at work, and the inability to rectify such discrepancy may engender feelings of loneliness.

Distinguishing loneliness at work from similar psychological constructs

When people think about loneliness at work, they are often referring to, or associating it with interpersonal isolation. Loneliness tends to highlight the feeling of being alone, either emotionally, socially or geographically. However, without the *desire* to be with another individual, or group of individuals (real or imaginary), aloneness and isolation do not qualify as true loneliness (Hartog, Audy & Cohen, 1980). For instance, when an individual is spending time with a friend, the individual is neither lonely nor alone. According to Mijuskovic (1979) whenever genuine feelings of friendship are present, then loneliness is muted in consciousness.

Because of the complexity of loneliness, its everyday usage is often confused with other terms such as aloneness, isolation, alienation, solitude, lack of social support and depression. Although loneliness shares characteristics with other emotional states and the terminology is often used interchangeably, loneliness is a unique construct.

Aloneness

Aloneness is the objective condition of being by oneself. People's perception of, and reactions to, aloneness can vary considerably, ranging from contentment to loneliness (Burger, 1995). Spending time working alone is not invariably associated with loneliness, as people can be very productive, concentrate for longer and therefore be content in their seclusion (Larson, Csikszentmihalyi & Graef, 1982). In contrast to loneliness, aloneness can indicate a certain degree of choice in wanting to be by oneself, and the ability to control one's personal space in their work environment. As such, choosing to work alone is often the preferred choice over-working in public situations, and does not imply the pain associated with loneliness. However, long periods of aloneness can lead to individuals feeling less happy, less cheerful, less sociable and less excited when they are alone than when they were with others. Being alone during daily life is correlated with sadness, irritability, boredom and loneliness (Larson et al., 1982). In general, it would be expected that employees are more likely to feel lonely when they are by themselves for extended periods of time (Killeen, 1998).

Isolation

Isolation is similar to aloneness, except the circumstances in which one is isolated are not under one's control. In the literature, isolation usually refers to the restriction of social relationships due to the physical environment. Rather than being perceptually based, isolation refers to the objective condition of having few social ties, a lack of integration into current social networks, the diminution of communication with others and being cut off from social ties for an extended period of time (Rook, 1984). As such, isolation is more of an objective condition than it is a subjective experience. Therefore being alone or isolated is not equivalent to being lonely. Although isolation is one of the strongest predictors of feeling lonely in daily life, isolation is a separate construct from the experience of loneliness (Ernst & Cacioppo, 1998). One can be isolated without feeling lonely, and one can feel lonely without being isolated. As people move into more isolated working conditions however, there is typically a concomitant rise in feelings of loneliness.

Alienation

Alienation refers to a form of powerless self-estrangement (Hancock, 1986). When people are alienated they feel like they don't belong to the social world. Alienation is the separation from social institutions and feeling powerless and normless (Bell, 1985). There is no necessary connection between the alienation one experiences at work and one's levels of loneliness, and as such the concepts are quite distinct. However, similarly to aloneness and isolation, the experience of unwelcome alienation from colleagues could well lead to an associated increase in feelings of loneliness.

Solitude

According to Gotesky (1965, p. 236) solitude is 'that state or condition of living or working alone ... without the pain of loneliness or isolation being an intrinsic component of that state or condition'. Solitude is often a refreshing experience in a normally social work environment, more so than mere aloneness, and has a more optimistic, incubating, creative effect. In contrast to loneliness, solitude indicates the freedom to be alone. Many people who are in intellectually challenging or demanding roles often appreciate solitude and find fulfilment in it, whereas fulfilment is not often used to describe loneliness. The experience of solitude is perceptually based, in that solitude for one person might mean loneliness for another.

Lack of social support

In contrasting social support with loneliness Rook (1984) purported that, unlike a lack of social support, loneliness is characterized by negative emotions such as sadness, anxiety, boredom, self-deprecation and feelings of marginality. Social support comes from any social experiences in the work environment, whether positive or negative, that support physical and psychological wellbeing. As such, a lack of social support is part of the developmental process of loneliness rather than being synonymous with it (Murphy & Kupshik, 1992). Loneliness refers to the subjective experience of deficits in interpersonal relationships, whereas a lack of social support refers to the limited availability of social resources (Perlman & Peplau, 1984). However, social support is often inaccurately referred to as the direct opposite of loneliness. From an experiential perspective social support is not always received positively. Receiving help from a fellow colleague does not always produce positive feelings of being supported. Helping tends to be perceived as supportive only if the helper conveys an attitude of caring toward the recipient, rather than helping out of obligation (i.e. the boss told them to) or indifference (Caplan, Cobb, French, Van Harrison & Pinneau, 1975).

Depression

Loneliness, while similar to depression, can be differentiated from it. According to Weiss (1973) there is a need to rid oneself of the distress of loneliness by integrating into new relationships. With depression, there is a drive to surrender to it. As such, the lonely are 'driven to find others and, if they find the right others, they change and are no longer lonely' (Weiss, 1973, p. 15). Even though there are strong correlations between loneliness and depression, there is some evidence to suggest that loneliness is more than simply negative emotional arousal. Bragg (1979) for instance, compared university students who were lonely and depressed, lonely but not depressed, or neither lonely nor depressed. The research suggests that respondents who were lonely without being depressed tended to be distressed specifically about the interpersonal and social aspects of their lives, whereas those students who were both lonely and depressed tended to be distressed over a wider range of personal issues. Conceptually therefore, loneliness is a more specific experience of relationship dissatisfaction than depression (Horowitz, French & Anderson, 1982).

General literature related to loneliness in the workplace

In the 1970s an American sociological theorist, Philip Slater, recognized that cultural values and social institutions could exacerbate loneliness. Slater (1976) argued that social institutions such as schools and private corporations emphasize individualism and personal success through competition and independence, which he argued tends to go against the basic human needs for belonging, community and engagement with others. He argues (p. 34):

> Individualism is rooted in the attempt to deny the reality of human interdependence. One of the major goals of technology in America is to 'free' us from the necessity of relating to, submitting to, depending upon, or controlling other people. Unfortunately, the more we have succeeded in doing this, the more we have felt disconnected, bored, and lonely.

Rather than classifying loneliness as abnormal, Salter described it as a normal and common by-product of social forces. In essence, he strongly believed that the competitive life is disconnected and lonely, and its satisfactions short-lived. Similarly, Seidenberg (1980, p. 186) argued that 'corporate men are lonely both in their travels and in their offices ... they secretly yearn for more trust and genuine friendship, which are absent both from competitors on the outside and inside from the organisation'. In 1982 Peplau and Perlman also suggested that social institutions which emphasize 'rugged individualism and success through competition' might foster loneliness (p. 9).

Literature on occupational stress also touches on isolation and loneliness as both a cause and consequence of stress at work. For instance, Cooper (1981) described the problem of isolation as being a factor that adds to the strain of the executive. Not surprisingly, being higher in the organization results in fewer opportunities for feedback and social dialogue from others, simply because the top is not a very crowded place. As such, there are fewer people around at that level to provide support and feedback. Cooper suggests that 'at highly competitive managerial levels ... it is likely that problem-solving will be inhibited for fear of appearing weak. Much of the American literature (particularly) mentions the isolated life of the top executive as an added source of strain' (Cooper, 1981, p. 281).

There is also some evidence in the literature to suggest that personal communication is not reciprocal in situations where the parties have unequal status. As such, there is more willingness to self-disclose up the status hierarchy (i.e. from subordinate to boss) than down it (Earle, Giuliano & Archer, 1983). Business research from Adamson and Axmith (2003) suggests that for two-thirds of Chief Executive Officers (CEOs) the most difficult issue they face is feeling disconnected from others at work. This feeling of disconnection is thought to be attributable to their ongoing responsibility and preoccupation with business matters, being isolated from family and friends, and experiencing a sense of alienation from aspects of their personality. It would seem from this research that wearing a mask while in the CEO position is necessary to respond to expectations of organizational stakeholders. Such masking can create feelings of existential distress, heightened anxiety, impatience, emotional withdrawal and abusive outburst (Adamson & Axmith, 2003). Nevertheless, there is often little sympathy for the likes of CEOs who can earn up to 500 times what some of their employees earn (Kirk, 2003)!

Contrary to the conceptual links between individualism, seniority and loneliness, empirical research by Page and Cole (1991) on the demographic predictors of loneliness in an adult population, report that managers and those with professional occupations tend to experience less loneliness than other occupational groups, such as technicians, sales and clerical staff. Interestingly, the research indicates that service workers experienced the most loneliness amongst those surveyed. This finding is worthy of note as service workers may in fact encounter the most human contact during their working day out of all the jobs surveyed, yet the human contact may be more emotionally taxing because of the nature of the role. However, this finding corresponds with Page and Cole's contention that economic status influences loneliness, in that reduced income and poorer education status are influential factors in reported loneliness. Those in professional or managerial occupations who typically have a higher income and more advanced education are, according to Page and Cole, less likely to be lonely due to their economic and social wellbeing. This conclusion runs counter to previous claims that the role of senior manager tends to be isolating and potentially lonely. However, individual differences may account for such discrepancies in that, for some managers or professionals, status and income may be sufficient to remedy the isolating factors of the job, while for others the isolation may be so burdensome that high income does not compensate for the pain associated with loneliness.

Empirical studies on workplace loneliness

Few studies have investigated the interaction between the situational and personal factors that promote loneliness, and even fewer studies have focused on loneliness in the workplace. Only a small handful of published empirical studies have specifically examined the nature of loneliness in the workplace, and it is to this research that this chapter now turns.

Research carried out by Gumpert and Boyd (1984) suggests that small business owners frequently feel lonely, a problem which the authors attribute to excessive workloads and stress. In their survey of 249 small business owners, respondents were asked a series of questions regarding their relationships at work and involvement with others outside of their business, their health status and several open-ended questions regarding the psychological aspects of business ownership. The authors also conducted semi-structured interviews with 12 business owners to discuss the causes and possible remedies for their isolation. In general, the respondents who experienced the most loneliness were those who had transitioned from a corporate environment to a small business environment. On the whole, they experienced loneliness due to a general lack of colleagues with whom to share experiences, explore ideas and commiserate. Among the respondents, 68% reported that they had no confidant with whom they could share their concerns regarding their business. Many respondents felt they were unable to converse with their competitors, as this could pose problems for business development and maintaining a competitive advantage. In other words, an individual cannot easily develop meaningful relationships with those who are in competition with them.

Gumpert and Boyd's (1984) research does however suffer from several methodological issues. Firstly, loneliness was not quantifiably assessed as such. Rather, it was gauged using open-ended, unstructured questions, which ranged from defining loneliness as isolation or aloneness, through to the term meaning loneliness 'at the top'. Further, although open-ended questions provide rich information, the data do not provide standardized comparison amongst the respondents, inhibiting generalizations drawn from the study. Secondly, the authors did not study a comparison group of employees who were not self-employed. It is therefore not possible to determine if small business owners are especially vulnerable to loneliness or whether their levels of loneliness are in fact different to other employees. Subsequent research by Bell, Roloff, Van Camp and Karol (1990) found no support for the author's claim that individuals who are self-employed are more likely to be lonely than those employed by others.

Bell et al.'s (1990) research sought to address the hypothesis that people who are successful in their jobs are more likely to consider themselves lonely than people who are less successful. The research, conducted by researchers in the field of communication, questioned whether senior-ranked employees had fewer friends and spent less time with their family and were consequently lonely, or whether greater economic remuneration for those in higher organizational levels (and the corresponding social opportunities such remuneration can purchase) offset job demands and feelings of loneliness. Interestingly, the correlation between organizational level and loneliness was small but negative (–.12), indicating that loneliness is associated with those at the bottom of the hierarchy. This correlation remained even after commitment, hours worked per week, job satisfaction, age, education, and family income were controlled for. A one-way analysis of variance revealed that people near the top of their organizations reported being less lonely than those at or near the bottom, despite those higher up in the organization working longer hours and sharing fewer hours with family. In explanation, the researchers argued that people at higher levels of their organizations may differ on individual or interpersonal dimensions, such as social skills, marital satisfaction and interpersonal orientation. In essence, it may be that the social skills that lead these individuals to advance the organization's ladder, may also be responsible for their lower levels of loneliness. Members towards the top of the organization also have greater access to resources which makes them attractive social associates. Gender and marital status did not affect the respondents' reports of loneliness. In a subsequent regression analysis, workgroup cohesion was the best predictor of loneliness. Interestingly, there was a strong positive relationship between hours worked and loneliness but only for those who thought their workgroup was not close. The authors reasonably argue that if the work environment is oppressive working long hours will more likely contribute to loneliness. Not surprisingly, the number of hours worked is irrelevant to loneliness if the work environment is cohesive and supportive and the employee has high job satisfaction. Bell et al.'s (1990) study does however suffer from methodological weaknesses. For example, they concede that it is unlikely that the top and the bottom of the organization mean the same thing for employees from different organizations. In other words, it is hardly likely that being at the top of the hierarchy in a small retail shop is comparable to being at the top of a large corporation.

In remedying these methodological limitations, Reinking and Bell (1991) conducted a field study to examine how one's career situation interacts with his or her communication competence to influence the person's level of loneliness. The researchers proposed the hypothesis that individuals who occupy low positions in organizational hierarchies would be more prone to loneliness. They also sought to address whether the negative correlation between organizational level and loneliness was a result of communication competence at more senior levels. Similar to previous findings (Bell et al., 1990; Page & Cole, 1991), Reinking and Bell (1991) found that loneliness was associated with those respondents in lower level positions, even when communication competence was controlled for. In an explanation for this finding, the authors argue that success in the workplace may be more important for many people than closeness to others. Moreover, an individual may not see a deficit in personal relationships when achievement at work fulfils primary goals.

Reinking and Bell's (1991) follow-up study exhibits some methodological limitations, largely in relation to the generalizability of the results. The research was conducted with respondents from a civil service organization. It is therefore questionable whether those respondents at the top carried the same burdens, uncertainty and sacrifices that accompany senior level positions in private industry. As the authors of the study indicated, the results may not generalize beyond the specific parameters of the organization. The authors also concede that it may not simply be the individual's position within the organization that influences loneliness, and their interpretation of 'it's lonely at the top' may have been insufficient to capture the essence of what it means to be at the 'top'. For instance, the authors comment that loneliness at the top could be related to the isolation of decision-making at senior ranked positions, and the heavy weight of responsibility felt by those at higher levels of an organization. This factor is not always implicit in assessing the individual's hierarchical position within the organization. In essence, merely assessing job title and position within the hierarchy fails to capture the essence of what inherently makes the role potentially lonely. Given the methodological weaknesses of the research conducted to date, it is difficult to conclude whether leadership roles in organizations contribute to loneliness. Further research in this area would be interesting and may help answer the question of whether it is actually 'lonely at the top'.

A further study on loneliness at work, carried out by Chadsey-Rusch, DeStefano, O'Reilly, Gonzalez and Collet-Klingenberg (1992), empirically assessed loneliness amongst 51 workers with mental retardation employed by integrated and sheltered workshops. The overall results from the study suggest that loneliness and social dissatisfaction were not pervasive feelings for individuals with mild or moderate mental retardation. It could well be that the subtleties of social interaction would be less intense in a workplace shelter, thus creating a less constrained social environment.

However, their conclusions were limited by the fact that no comparative data were available on the loneliness of workers without mental retardation. It was apparent from their research however, that some individuals were experiencing significant loneliness at work and the researchers called for further research in this area.

A qualitative study carried out by Steinburg, Sullivan, and Montoya (1999) looked at the experience of loneliness and social isolation in the workplace for deaf adults. The authors hypothesized that because of social integration difficulties, deaf workers may experience poor vocational and psychological outcomes in the workplace. Fifteen deaf volunteers were interviewed for the study, which examined the participants' vocational experiences, social support, general perceptions of loneliness, and experiences with accommodations in their work setting. Their study, although not an extensive examination of the relationship between loneliness and work functioning, found that for some participants, communication barriers in the workplace did create social difficulties leading to loneliness, which negatively affected their work performance.

Several studies have been conducted looking at the occupational role of school principals who often express a sense of loneliness, isolation, and alienation. Such working conditions are thought to contribute to a diminished sense of meaningfulness, power, and job satisfaction (Dussault & Thibodeau, 1997). Researchers working in the area of school principal wellbeing argue that the conditions of the working environment reduce the possibility for interaction with colleagues and peers, and diminish the development of their informal networks (Dussault & Barnett, 1996). Barnett (1990) found that professional isolation could have a negative effect on principals who have to cope with it, and concluded that isolation could diminish the professional development of school administrators. Research by Allison (1997) indicates that in a sample of 643 elementary and secondary school principals, approximately half of the respondents reported feeling alone in their position and feeling dissatisfied with their jobs as a result of the 'loneliness of command'. In a study linking professional isolation with occupational stress, Dussault, Deaudelin, Royer and Loiselle (1999) found a strong and positive correlation between the two variables. Previous research by the present author (Cubitt[2] & Burt, 2002) on a sample of 293 primary school principals suggests that loneliness is a significant predictor of educator burnout.

---

[2]Maiden name

Qualitative doctoral research by Howard (2002) on the isolation of school principals in Georgia, USA found that the principalship was indeed isolating for the ten respondents interviewed. One of the respondents indicated 'It's very lonely ... there's nobody there with you to make the decision. There's nobody there to help you. You make the decision. You're held accountable ... you are ostracised because of your position' (p. 93). The findings from the research also suggest that the increased workload for principals impacted upon their feelings of loneliness. The principals described a paring down of their personal friends and reported spending less time in self-selected social activities with friends. Several of the principals described isolation from their peers and colleagues due to their ascension to the principalship or the lack of time to maintain their relationships. Some of the respondents characterized their relationships with their colleagues as 'territorial safeguarding' due to the increased accountability and competition in the education sector. The principals reported that such obstacles impeded the maintenance or even the establishment of satisfying interpersonal relationships with their colleagues (see also Chapter 5 in this book).

Other studies touching on loneliness in the workplace include research by Melamed, Szor and Bernstein (2001) who found a correlation between job satisfaction and a lack of loneliness amongst therapists working in an outpatient clinic. Research by Ukwuoma (1999) with Nigerian Catholic priests found that loneliness was a significant stressor in their daily working lives.

In summary, the research findings on loneliness in the workplace have thus far been inconsistent and have limited generalizability to the wider working population. While they offer noteworthy developments in how loneliness can manifest itself in the workplace, the empirical studies have generally been unfocused in their attention. However, what we can reap from previous research is the importance of conceptualizing the term 'workplace loneliness', the need to measure loneliness accurately and consistently across a range of occupational groups (see Wright, Burt & Strongman, 2006), and the need to assess the characteristics of the respondent's job and the features of their employing organization – not just their personal characteristics.

Loneliness, personality and the individual's environment

Despite the limited availability of empirical research on loneliness at work, a paradox appears to have emerged between the literature on loneliness and lay beliefs about work-based loneliness. Loneliness in the wider population is often researched in association with social incompetence or deficiencies in a person's character. It is often perceived as a selfish pursuit which is driven by interpersonal incompetence or social inhibition. Both in research settings and in the wider population, there appears to be a 'blame the victim' mentality for the development of loneliness. As such, personal factors tend to be overestimated as reasons for social difficulties, whilst only modest emphasis is given to environmental factors. However, if loneliness were peculiar to those who suffered from anxiety, poor self-image, ineffective interpersonal behaviours, and low self-esteem, then it does not explain why accomplished individuals in senior positions within organizations often report feelings of loneliness. In order to achieve seniority in a commercial environment, most employment decision-makers would agree that a certain level of social competence, self-assurance and interpersonal skills would be required. Therefore, it is possible that a well-adjusted, sociable character who achieves seniority and success might nevertheless feel lonely at work. It therefore seems reasonable to assume not all people are lonely simply because of their disposition. When the environment is not fulfilling social provisions adequately, a usually well-adjusted sociable character can develop the behaviours and thought processes typically attributable to lonely individuals (Ernst & Cacioppo, 1998). The current loneliness literature seems to have overlooked the common notion that highly successful, socially competent individuals can also experience bouts of loneliness.

In order to understand loneliness more accurately, one must not only consider the personality of the individual and the ways in which they operate in their social environment, but also the ways in which the social environment operates on the individual, either causing or perpetuating loneliness. Environments such as workplaces can, and do, exhibit characteristics that can lead to social and emotional isolation. Borrowing concepts from the poet Wordsworth (de Botton, 2002), who accused cities of fostering life-destroying emotions; organizations too can harbour unpleasantness, which erode the potential benefits of being part of a working community. In a fearful, untrusting or self-serving atmosphere, some organizations have the potential to foster an 'anxious' environment where meaningful social contact with other co-workers is not feasible. Such an environment would, to some extent, have a negative effect on even the most gregarious, sociable individuals. Characteristics of the working environment might therefore be considered 'loneliness-provoking factors' (de Jong-Gierveld, 1987) and may contribute to the development of loneliness at work. Such notions have not however been empirically examined.

Loneliness is the outcome of poor quality interpersonal relationships. As a general rule, fostering healthy social relationships is important for the effective functioning of an organization and is considered a necessary prerequisite for organizational health (Moore, 1996; Pfeifer & Veiga, 1999). In many cases, workplace relationships provide companionship for individuals who may not find it elsewhere. However, in some work environments the emphasis is often on individual achievement and competitiveness, volatility, and impersonal social relationships. Such alienating values can create interpersonal conflict and hinder the development of sincere relationships. Research by Rook (1988) indicates that interpersonal conflict within an individual's existing relationships can significantly contribute to feelings of loneliness. In earlier research, Rook (1984) indicated that the number of relationships elderly widowed women had involving conflict significantly predicted greater loneliness. Whilst this is not evidence for a cause and effect relationship (i.e. that conflict causes loneliness), it seems plausible that an elevated level of interpersonal conflict and/or political tension in the workplace may trigger loneliness by reducing the quality of interpersonal relationships, more so than perhaps workload or span of control issues. Rook (1984) also indicated that relationship development can be as problematic as relationship initiation when there is interpersonal conflict in the social environment.

Although work is largely a social institution, for some employees merely being in a social environment is not sufficient to conquer feelings of loneliness. Most relationships in the workplace are heavily influenced by organizational and job characteristics, such as hierarchical structure, individual competition, seniority, and intangible constructs such as the organization's community spirit or the emotional climate (see Chapter 4 in this book). In some extreme cases, organizations strongly discourage friendship at work for fear of improper behaviour or reduced productivity (Berman et al., 2002). Despite workplace policy however, it would be expected that a large proportion of employees anticipate some sort of natural socialization process, which leads to the development of social relationships at work.

In many respects, the climate of the organization can represent various indicators of interpersonal difficulties with workplace relationships. Ryan and Oestreich (1991) discuss fear in the workplace as an 'undiscussable' organizational problem. As such, the issues surrounding a negative emotional climate in a particular workplace are not often brought to light. This situation, together with the fact that loneliness is often considered a 'taboo' subject (Creagh, 1995), can make addressing poor emotional climates problematic. While it is often difficult to determine the initiating cause of the negative climate, managers and leaders often express ignorance (or perhaps wilful blindness) with regards to organizational morale problems, and the factors which may be causing the negativity. The key informants of organizational decisions and practices may therefore not have a good handle on the 'pulse' of employee problems (Jex & Crossley, 2005). However, pinpointing the cause of the negative climate can be difficult where deep-rooted organizational, personal, and behavioural issues exist. As such, the reasons for a negative emotional climate could vary considerably.

A lack of workplace cohesion may also contribute to feelings of loneliness. Seidenberg (1980) commented that working in an atmosphere of distrust and suspicion can have a brutalizing effect on one's character and sense of belonging within an organization. In many ways the workplace is replacing traditional social institutions, such as church and community groups, and as a result employees are becoming more aware of the quest for interpersonal fulfilment at work (Giacalone & Jurkiewicz, 2003). Consequently, the idea of the workplace being a social foundation for developing a sense of belonging is becoming increasingly relevant to organizational settings (Pfeffer, 2003).

This section has highlighted the importance of looking at the various ways the social environment can operate on the individual, either causing or perpetuating loneliness. This chapter argues that job and organizational characteristics, such as a negative emotional climate, lack of social cohesion, poor social support, and interpersonal conflict can contribute to loneliness. It is therefore important to look at the interaction of these variables with the individual's personal characteristics to determine how they contribute to loneliness. Despite the lack of research on this topic, looking at how organizational environments can affect loneliness is worthy of greater theoretical and empirical attention.

Practical implications: interventions for loneliness

Arguably, little can be done to change the nature of some occupational positions, and the potential isolation and loneliness that can accompany those positions (Cooper & Quick, 2003). However, given the problems poor quality social relationships at work can create, which may be symptomatic of a poor organizational climate, there are several interventions which could be implemented at both the individual and the organizational level.

Like occupational stress, loneliness interventions can be directly related to the core manifestation of the problem by providing individual assistance, or can be approached indirectly, such as attending to the nature of the individual's social network or the negative climate of the organization. It has been argued that work-related stress is most effectively managed by work-related sources of support, because the stress treatment occurs in the context of the stressful situation (Beehr, 1985). Therefore, attending to the work environment rather than remedying personal factors, may help to reduce feelings of loneliness at work. As such, organizational interventions may help to create a healthy work climate by attending to organizational values which instil positive social relations and emphasize a sense of belonging. In this respect, training can help orient organizational members, particularly senior management, toward the kinds of behaviours that will lead to a climate of trust, belonging and shared values. These behaviours could include, for example, encouraging employees to seek each other out for support. Such behaviours are contingent upon an overall structure and environment whereby organizational members are permitted to develop various social opportunities.

Organizations concerned with a consistently poor climate affecting individual welfare might consider creating (or improving) communication channels through which employees can confidentially voice their concerns without fear of retribution or ridicule. In terms of reducing fear and conflict in the work environment, rather than bury the predicament, Ryan and Oestreich (1991) propose interventions such as openly identifying acceptable and unacceptable work behaviours and actively coaching those who require behavioural change (see Chapters 10 and 11 in this book). Furthermore, managers can be encouraged to promote a climate of trust, openness and friendship among staff, and to model interactions which the organization seeks to promote (Rousseau, 1995). In reality however, employers cannot force employees not to be lonely. Because loneliness is an inherently personal experience (potentially exacerbated by the social environment), interventions may therefore be required at an individual level.

If we revisit the definition of work-related loneliness as 'the distress caused by the perceived lack of good quality interpersonal relationships between employees in a work environment', then interventions to alleviate loneliness should work by closing the gap between actual and desired interpersonal relationships. In this respect, the individual has to experience meaningful human contact and feel a sense of inclusion to ease the burden of loneliness. In very broad terms, loneliness interventions accomplish this by concentrating on evaluating the preferred level of interpersonal interaction for the individual (Peplau & Goldston, 1984). Therefore, the most appropriate intervention to alleviate an individual's loneliness is dependent upon the cause of the loneliness. For example, if a person is lonely at work because of a general negative outlook on life, cognitive therapy may be useful to mitigate feelings of loneliness (DeRubeis, Tang & Beck, 2001). On the other hand, if a person is feeling lonely because of limited social opportunities within their organization, or they dislike working alone, perhaps the best remedy would be to explore working as part of a team or joining a social group to gain a sense of belonging. However, such recommendations are potentially ill-fated if the underlying cause of the distress is not attended to. Overall, loneliness interventions have met with mixed or limited success (Ernst & Cacioppo, 1998). For instance, merely focusing on building social bonding and networks does not seem to facilitate an associated decrease in loneliness, in the short term at least. Because the development of meaningful interpersonal relationships tends to take time, interventions to remedy a deficient social network may not have an immediate effect on loneliness. With regards to workplace loneliness, individual treatments which help individuals understand their feelings of loneliness and encourage individuals to appreciate that both person and situation factors can contribute to loneliness may be useful.

Another intervention which may prove useful for work-related loneliness is journal writing or diary keeping. This approach, developed by Pennebaker (1997), aims to assist individuals who have experienced trauma, and requires participants to write about a personal traumatic event. There is evidence that such interventions do indeed reduce the level of self-reported symptoms and indicators of physical health (Pennebaker, 1997). In terms of the workplace, the act of personal writing may promote self-understanding regarding an individual's feeling of loneliness, and may help reframe the individual's distress over relationship deficiencies. It may also help provide insight for individuals who are socially anxious or feel defeated by their social relationships.

Other individual intervention strategies relating to the workplace could include the provision of peer support through coaching or mentoring programmes (Cooper & Quick, 2003). Such sources of social support may provide a work-based outlet for employees to speak freely about personal or work-related issues, and to help correct the perceived deficiency between actual and desired relationships at work. The underlying purpose behind these programmes should be to increase relationship-oriented behaviours so the beneficial consequences of social support can be achieved. The effectiveness of such interventions is, however, a matter of speculation. Empirically, the value of such interventions has yet to be evidenced.

Conclusion

Given the complex nature of interpersonal relationships, organizations, and loneliness, this chapter calls for increased attention to work-related loneliness so we may better understand the potential for people to feel lonely in organizational settings. In their conclusion Marangoni and Ickes (1989, p. 124) note that '... in addition to the variables documented to be individually and interactively influential in the experience of loneliness, researchers should focus greater attention on the domain where such variables would be most acutely felt: in the individual's ongoing, long-term, naturalistic patterns of relationship formation, elaboration and dissolution'. What better place to start than the workforce; an institution that consumes the majority of waking hours and absorbs most of our social opportunities?

References

Adamson, B. & Axmith, M. (2003). The CEO disconnect: Finding consistency between personal values and the demands of leadership. *Ivey Business Journal, May/June*, 1–6.

Allison, D. (1997). Assessing stress among public school principals in British Columbia. *Psychological Reports, 80*, 1103–1114.

Barnett, B. (1990). Peer assisted leadership: Expanding principals' knowledge through reflective practice. *Journal of Educational Administration, 28*(3), 67–76.

Beehr, T. (1985). The role of social support in coping with organizational stress. In T. Beehr and R. Bhagat (eds), *Human Stress and Cognition in Organizations: An Integrated Perspective* (pp. 375–398). New York: Wiley.

Bell, R. (1985). Conversational involvement and loneliness. *Communication Monographs, 52*, 218–235.

Bell, R. A., Roloff, M. E., Van Camp, K. & Karol, S. H. (1990). Is it lonely at the top? Career success and personal relationships. *Journal of Communication, 40*(1), 9–23.

Berman, E., West, J. & Richter, M. (2002). Workplace relations: Friendship patterns and consequences (according to managers). *Public Administration Review, 62*(2), 217–230.

Bragg, M. (1979). *A Comparative Study of Loneliness and Depression*. Unpublished doctoral dissertation. University of California, Los Angeles.

Burger, J. (1995). Individual differences in preference for solitude. *Journal of Research in Personality, 29*, 85–108.

Cacioppo, J. T. (2008). *Loneliness: Human Nature and the Need for Social Connection*. New York: Norton.

Cacioppo, J., Hawkley, L. & Bernston, G. (2003). The anatomy of loneliness. *Current Directions in Psychological Science, 12*, 71–74.

Caplan, R., Cobb, S., French, J., Van Harrison, R. & Pinneau, S. (1975). *Job Demands and Worker Health: Research Report*. University of Michigan: Institute for Social Research.

Chadsey-Rusch, J., DeStefano, L., O'Reilly, M., Gonzalez, P. & Collet-Klingenberg, L. (1992). Assessing the loneliness of workers with mental retardation. *Mental Retardation, 30*(2), 85–92.

Cooper, C. (1981). *The Stress Check*. Englewood Cliffs, CA: Prentice-Hall.

Cooper, C. & Quick, J. (2003). The stress and loneliness of success. *Counselling Psychology Quarterly, 16*(1), 1–7.

Creagh, T. (1995). *Loneliness: A Taboo Topic for New Zealand*. Orewa, NZ: Colcom Press.

Cubitt, S. & Burt, C. (2002). Leadership style, loneliness and occupational stress in New Zealand primary school principals. *New Zealand Journal of Educational Studies, 37*(2), 159–169.

De Botton, A. (2002). *The Art of Travel*. London: Hamish Hamilton.

De Jong-Gierveld, J. (1987). Developing and testing a model of loneliness. *Journal of Personality and Social Psychology, 53*, 119–128.

DeRubeis, R., Tang, T. & Beck, A. (2001). Cognitive Therapy. In K. Dobson (ed.), *Handbook of Cognitive-Behavioural Therapies*. New York: Guildford Press.

Dussault, M. & Barnett, B. (1996). Peer assisted leadership: Reducing educational managers' professional isolation. *Journal of Educational Administration, 34*(3), 5–14.

Dussault, M. & Thibodeau, S. (1997). Professional isolation and performance at work of school principals. *Journal of School Leadership, 7*, 521–536.

Dussault, M., Deaudelin, C., Royer, N. & Loiselle, J. (1999). Professional isolation and occupational stress in teachers. *Psychological Reports, 84*, 943–946.

Earle, W. B., Giuliano, T. & Archer, R. L. (1983). Lonely at the top: The effect of power on information flow in the dyad. *Personality and Social Psychology Bulletin, 9*(4), 629–637.

Ernst, J. & Cacioppo, J. (1998). Lonely hearts: Psychological perspectives on loneliness. *Applied & Preventative Psychology, 8*, 1–22.

Flanders, J. (1982). A general systems approach to loneliness. In L. Peplau & D. Perlman (eds), *Loneliness: A Sourcebook of Current Theory, Research and Therapy* (pp. 166–179). New York: John Wiley & Sons.

Gaev, D. (1976). *The Psychology of Loneliness*. Columbus: Adams.

Giacalone, R. & Jurkiewicz, C. (2003). Toward a science of workplace spirituality. In R. Giacalone & C. Jurkiewicz (eds), *Handbook of Workplace Spirituality and Organisational Performance*. Armonk, New York: M.E. Sharp.

Gotesky, R. (1965). Aloneness, loneliness, isolation, solitude. In J. Edie (ed.), *An Invitation to Phenomenology*. Chicago, IL: Quadrangle Books.

Gumpert, D. & Boyd, D. (1984). The loneliness of the small business owner. *Harvard Business Review, 62*(6), 33–38.

Hancock, B. (1986). *Loneliness: Symptoms and Social Concerns*. New York: University Press of America.

Hartog, J., Audy, J. & Cohen, Y. (1980). *The Anatomy of Loneliness*. New York: International Universities Press.

Horowitz, L., French, R. & Anderson, C. (1982). The prototype of a lonely person. In L. Peplau & D. Perlman (eds), *Loneliness: A Source Book of Current Theory, Research and Therapy* (pp. 351–378). New York: John Wiley & Sons.

Howard, M. (2002). *Perceptions of Isolation among Georgia High School Principals.* Unpublished doctoral dissertation. Georgia Southern University, Georgia.

Jex, S. & Crossley, C. (2005). Organizational consequences. In J. Barling, E. Kelloway & M. Frone (eds), *Handbook of Work Stress.* Thousand Oaks, CA: Sage Publications.

Joyce, A. (2004). Are friends good for business? *The Christchurch Press, July 17,* 11.

Killeen, C. (1998). Loneliness: An epidemic in modern society. *Journal of Advanced Nursing, 28,* 762–770.

Kirk, J. (2003). *It's Lonely at the (Executive) Top.* Retrieved from the World Wide Web on 24 July 2003 from www.workopolis.com/servlet/Content/torontostar/20030609/closed?section=TORSTAR.

Larson, R., Csikszentmihalyi, M. & Graef, R. (1982). Time alone in daily experience: Loneliness or renewal? In L. Peplau & D. Perlman (eds), *Loneliness: A Sourcebook of Current Theory, Research, and Therapy* (pp. 40–53). New York: John Wiley & Sons.

Marangoni, C. & Ickes, W. (1989). Loneliness: A theoretical review with implications for measurement. *Journal of Social & Personal Relationships, 6*(1), 93–128.

Melamed, Y., Szor, H. & Bernstein, E. (2001). The loneliness of the therapist in the public outpatient clinic. *Journal of Contemporary Psychotherapy, 31*(2), 103–112.

Mijuskovic, B. (1979). *Loneliness in Philosophy, Psychology, and Literature.* Assen: Van Gorcum.

Moore, T. (1996). Caring for the soul. *Executive Excellence, 13*(6), 14.

Murphy, P. & Kupshik, G. (1992). *Loneliness, Stress and Wellbeing: A Helper's Guide.* New York: Tavistock/Routledge.

Page, R. & Cole, G. (1991). Demographic predictors of self-reported loneliness in adults. *Psychological Reports, 68,* 939–945.

Pennebaker, J. (1997). *Opening Up: The Healing Power of Expressing Emotions.* New York: Jilford.

Peplau, L. & Goldston, S. (1984). *Preventing the Harmful Consequences of Severe and Persistent Loneliness.* Maryland: National Institute of Mental Health.

Peplau, L. (1985). Loneliness research: Basic concepts and findings. In I. Sarason & B. Sarason (eds), *Social Support: Theory, Research and Application* (pp. 270–286). Boston, MA: Martinus Nijhof.

Peplau, L. & Perlman, D. (1982). Perspectives on loneliness. In L. Peplau & D. Perlman (eds), *Loneliness: A Source Book of Current Theory, Research and Therapy.* New York: John Wiley & Sons.

Perlman, D. & Peplau, L. (1984). Loneliness research: A survey of empirical findings. In L. Peplau & S. Goldston (eds), *Preventing the Harmful Consequences of Severe and Persistent Loneliness.* Maryland: National Institute of Mental Health.

Pfeffer, J. (2003). Business and the spirit. In R. Giacalone & C. Jurkiewicz (eds), *Handbook of Workplace Spirituality and Organisational Performance.* Armonk, New York: M.E. Sharp.

Pfeifer, J. & Veiga, J. (1999). Putting people first for organization success. *Academy of Management Executive, 13*(2), 37–51.

Reinking, K. & Bell, R. (1991). Relationships among loneliness, communication competence, and career success in a state bureaucracy: A field study of the 'lonely at the top' maxim. *Communication Quarterly, 39*(4), 358–373.

Riesman, D. (1961). *The Lonely Crowd: A Study of the Changing American Character.* New Haven, CT: Yale University Press.

Rook, K. (1984). Promoting social bonding: Strategies for helping the lonely and social isolated. *American Psychologist, 39*(2), 1389–1407.

Rook, K. (1988). Toward a more differentiated view of loneliness. In S. Duck (ed). *Handbook of Personal Relationships: Theory, Research and Interventions.* New York: Wiley.

Rousseau, D. (1995). *Psychological Contracts in Organisations: Understanding Written and Unwritten Agreements.* Thousand Oaks, CA: Sage Publications.

Ryan, K. & Oestreich, D. (1991). *Driving Fear Out of the Organisation.* San Francisco: Jossey-Bass Publishers.

Seidenberg, R. (1980). The lonely marriage in corporate America. In J. Hartog, J. Audy & Y. Cohen (eds), *The Anatomy of Loneliness* (pp. 186–203). New York: International Universities Press.

Slater, P. (1976). *The Pursuit of Loneliness: American Culture at the Breaking Point.* Boston, MA: Beacon.

Steinburg, A., Sullivan, V. & Montoya, L. (1999). Loneliness and social isolation in the workforce for Deaf individuals during the transition years: A preliminary investigation. *Journal of Applied Rehabilitation Counselling, 30*(1), 22–30.

Ukwuoma, A. (1999). Sources of stress experienced by Nigerian Catholic priests. *Dissertation Abstracts International Section A: Humanities and Social Sciences, 60*(4-A), 1031.

Weiss, R. (1973). *Loneliness: The Experience of Emotional and Social Isolation.* Cambridge, MA: The MIT Press.

Wright, S., Burt, C. & Strongman, K. (2006). Loneliness in the workplace: Construct definition and scale development. *New Zealand Journal of Psychology, 35*(2), 59–68.

3

The Role of Newcomer – Insider Relationships During Organizational Socialization

Helena Cooper-Thomas

To be successful in a new organization, the newcomer employee needs to establish an adequate level of performance, develop cooperative relationships with colleagues, and fit into the overall culture of the organization (Cooper-Thomas & Anderson, 2006). This process of getting up to speed in a new role is referred to as organizational socialization. An optimal organizational socialization experience is critical for the wellbeing and performance of new employees and of their colleagues, and for continuing organizational productivity (Bauer, Bodner, Erdogan, Truxillo & Tucker, 2007; Saks, Uggerslev & Fassina, 2007).

Throughout organizational socialization research, the social aspects of the adjustment process have been confirmed as critical (Cooper-Thomas, Van Vianen & Anderson, 2004). Thus, the relationships that newcomers establish with colleagues – including supervisors, experienced peers, and other newcomers – enable newcomers to access role-related knowledge, social relationships and support, and to understand the culture and values of the organization, including acceptable ways of behaving (Louis, 1980; Reichers, 1987). Indeed, Ashforth, Sluss and Harrison (2007) argue that much socialization is localized or 'tribal' rather than organizational, since it occurs through group and interpersonal interactions (see also Anderson & Thomas, 1996). This chapter focuses on how organizational socialization is achieved through newcomer-insider relationships.

The chapter is divided into four sections. First, I review the various sources of socialization, with a particular emphasis on newcomer-insider relations. Second, I discuss briefly what is achieved when socialization into an organization is successful. Third, I present an interactive model of the process of organizational socialization that places a stronger emphasis on insiders relative to previous models. Finally, I suggest practical ways that newcomers, insiders, and organizations can improve the organizational socialization process, focusing specifically on how relationships can be developed and used to facilitate this.

1. Sources of organizational socialization

Historically, it was viewed as being the organization's responsibility and right, through supervisors and other colleagues, to mould the newcomer to fit the job (Brim & Wheeler, 1966; Feldman, 1976). Thus, socialization was from the organization and aimed at adjusting the presumed malleable newcomer to suit the organization's needs. Recently, there has been an increasing recognition and focus on the newcomers' role in shaping their own careers and hence taking a more active role in their organizational socialization (Ashford & Black, 1996; Feldman & Brett, 1983; Fisher, 1986; Wanberg & Kammeyer-Mueller, 2000). The common and critical factor in both approaches is the role of relationships between newcomers and their colleagues, that is, organizational insiders. Insiders include peers, supervisors, senior colleagues, buddies, mentors, and any other colleagues within the organization who may form part of the newcomer's network of contacts. Insiders are responsible for delivering formal organizational programmes, act as a resource for newcomer information seeking strategies, and may also self-initiate activities to socialize the newcomer (Louis, 1980; Reichers, 1987). I discuss these three sources of organizational socialization next, of the newcomer, insiders, and the organization (Klein, Fan & Preacher, 2006).

Socialization by the newcomer

Newcomer strategies. Newcomers have a variety of strategies at their disposal which they can use to overcome the uncertainty and stress of organizational entry. Cooper-Thomas, Anderson and Hughes (2009) categorize the range of newcomer strategies into three types: Opportunistic, self-determined, and shared (see Table 3.1 for the categories with examples). Newcomers using opportunistic strategies rely on colleagues and the work environment to provide learning opportunities, for example monitoring colleagues for information or attending organizational training events. Self-determined strategies are carried out to achieve socialization quasi-independently of colleagues, for example newcomers changing how they do their work or working longer hours. For shared strategies, newcomers rely directly on insider colleagues to engage jointly in specific activities that facilitate the newcomer's adjustment, for example direct enquiry and networking. The relationships that new-comers establish with insiders are critical to two of these three categories of newcomer strategies, that is, opportunistic and shared.

Table 3.1 The three categories of newcomer adjustment tactics with examples

Opportunistic	Self-determined	Shared
Attending: Training, demonstrations, induction events, meetings	**Minimizing:** Doing work that closely matches skills and experience to facilitate performance	**Asking:** Direct questioning to find out information
Following: Being guided by others' expectations	**Doing:** Learning by doing/experimenting	**Socializing:** Arranging or attending social events outside of work

Varied results have been found for the effects of specific newcomer strategies across studies. Looking solely at relationship building strategies, these positively predict social integration, task performance, job satisfaction and person-organization fit and negatively predict intent to turnover (but not actual turnover) (Ashford & Black, 1996; Kim, Cable & Kim, 2005; Wanberg & Kammeyer-Mueller, 2000).

Influences of newcomer strategy choice. Several authors have argued that newcomers' perceptions of social costs are a key influence on their choice of strategy (Ashford, 1986; Cooper-Thomas & Wilson, 2007; Miller & Jablin, 1991). Social costs refer to the risk of newcomers behaving in ways that may cause colleagues to form a negative impression of them. For example, repeatedly asking for feedback could be interpreted by insiders as revealing a newcomer's high anxiety or lack of knowledge, either of which could lead insiders to form a poor impression of the newcomer. This emphasis on social costs reveals the potential trade-off between becoming competent in the role (i.e., performance) and being accepted by new colleagues (i.e., social integration). Using strategies that enable effective performance but incur social costs may result in the newcomer being isolated, with implications for future wellbeing and performance (Nelson, Quick & Joplin, 1991). Yet poor performance itself may result in high social costs and turnover (Salamin & Hom, 2005).

There is some evidence for newcomers using strategies with lower social costs. New accountants used monitoring more than direct enquiry for most types of information, with the exception of technical information, for which they mostly used direct enquiry of colleagues (Morrison, 1993b; see also Morrison, 1993a). Thus, except when they needed specific, technical information, these newcomers opted for an opportunistic strategy that did not require input from insiders. Ashford and Black (1996) investigated a range of shared, proactive strategies, which potentially have higher social costs, for example, networking and relationship building. In line with the idea that higher perceived social costs inhibit strategy use, positive cognitive framing (lowest social costs) was used most, whereas negotiation of job changes (highest social costs) was the least used strategy. Other strategies, including information seeking and networking, were midway between these. These studies reveal the trade-off between role versus social competency, with newcomers limiting social costs except where unavoidable (see also Chan & Schmitt, 2000; Holder, 1996).

Newcomers' seeking of social support. As a subset of newcomer strategies, researchers have investigated newcomers' seeking and use of social support. There are three views as to when newcomers will seek and receive social support from colleagues (Fisher, 1985). One view is that newcomers have to show appropriate levels of performance potential and positive attitudes, which then lead to acceptance, and earn them such support. A second view is that social support is given to newcomers who show signs of needing it, such as those who have low levels of performance or satisfaction, or high levels of stress. A third view is that all newcomers need support to adjust to their jobs, regardless of any other factors, and that colleagues' respond to this perceived need. Fisher (1985) concluded that her research with nurse newcomers supported the third perspective, with social support having only main effects, being related to lower stress and intention to leave, and higher job satisfaction, organizational commitment, and self-rated performance. Further evidence for this perspective comes from Feldman and Brett (1983). They compared organizational newcomers with job changers, that is, those changing roles within an organization. They found that newcomers showed greater use of strategies that solicited aid and support from colleagues, such as seeking social support, getting task help, and soliciting information about performance appraisal, whereas job changers tended to use strategies that influenced their work environment, such as delegating responsibilities and changing work procedures. Thus, there seems to be an expectation that newcomers will seek and receive social support. Further, research has also shown that newcomers' use of general socializing and support seeking strategies are associated with greater job satisfaction (Ashford & Black, 1996; Gruman, Saks & Zweig, 2006; Wanberg & Kammeyer-Mueller, 2000). Overall then, the evidence suggests that newcomers seek and receive social support, and that this has positive effects on socialization. However, we note that as newcomers gradually lose their 'newcomer' status, social support may only be given either to those who deserve it or who need it, that is, the first two perspectives outlined above (Fisher, 1985). Moreover, needing social support will come to be viewed more negatively over time (i.e., higher social costs), with newcomers likely to be aware that they will increasingly need to prove their ability to work more independently (Nelson et al., 1991).

Newcomer personality. There are clear links between personality and strategy use, and between personality and outcomes, but no empirical research that confirms strategy use as mediating the relationship of personality with outcomes. Thus, extraversion and openness to experience are positive predictors of several proactive behaviours, including information seeking, feedback seeking and relationship building (Wanberg & Kammeyer-Mueller, 2000). Newcomers with proactive personalities show higher task mastery, role clarity, social integration, and political knowledge (Chan & Schmitt, 2000; Kammeyer-Mueller & Wanberg, 2003). Morrison (2002b) posits that individual personality factors may influence network formation, for example more proactive newcomers may build stronger and broader network ties. Different newcomer personality traits are likely to influence the extent to which the newcomer focuses on informational or friendship networks; for example, extravert newcomers may focus on social relationships and friendships more, to make work more enjoyable (Elsesser & Peplau, 2006), whereas those with a high need for achievement or power may focus more on instrumental ties (Morrison, 2002b). Despite the lack of empirical evidence, it is theoretically clear that newcomers who are more extraverted, open to experience, and proactive are more likely to seek information and develop relationships with colleagues (Morrison, 2002b), and that it is through these links that they can achieve better outcomes.

Socialization from insiders

Organizational insiders, that is, newcomers' more experienced colleagues, represent a second source of organizational socialization. These insiders may provide help, advice and support to newcomers, either because they are required to in their job (e.g., being assigned as a mentor) or through their own initiative. A range of organizational insiders may be involved in socializing newcomers, including supervisors, peers, mentors/sponsors, secretaries, support staff, and those Human Resources staff responsible for the recruitment, selection, and management of new employees. Indeed, researchers have noted that socialization begins long before organizational entry, with input from all those with information about the organization and with whom a potential newcomer interacts (Anderson & Ostroff, 1997; Nelson, 1991).

Co-workers. Research has consistently found that newcomers rate their co-workers as the most available resources during socialization and among the most helpful (Lee, 2008; Louis, Posner & Powell, 1983; Morrison, 1993b; Nelson & Quick, 1991). Newcomers' perceptions of co-worker helpfulness (either peers or senior co-workers, or both) have positive relationships with socialization learning, job satisfaction, organizational commitment, and negative relationships with intentions of leaving as well as – more surprisingly – performance (Lee, 2008; Louis et al., 1983; Nelson & Quick, 1991). This latter finding also fits with Morrison's (1993a) research: She found that newcomers who most frequently sought technical information from peers showed the lowest task mastery. Similar to Fisher's (1985) suggestions with regard to newcomer's access to social support (see heading 'newcomers seeking of social support' above), poorly performing newcomers may develop relationships with co-workers either because the newcomer is seeking advice to improve their performance, or because these colleagues perceive that the newcomer is struggling and therefore volunteer help. Regardless of the direction of causality, the fact that co-workers are closer both in role and hierarchy to the newcomer may make them both more accessible and more useful (Louis, 1990). Further, co-workers are lower risk sources of advice as they are less involved in formal organization processes such as performance appraisal and the distribution of associated rewards. Both of these are likely to facilitate relationships between newcomers and co-workers.

Similarly, research has shown that task interdependence and insider accessibility interact to predict newcomer proactivity, and that this relationship is more pronounced for low self-efficacy newcomers (Major & Kozlowski, 1997). That is, for newcomers who are less confident in their abilities, convenience factors relating to co-worker availability are even more strongly associated with newcomer proactivity. This is important given that newcomer proactivity is itself associated with more positive socialization outcomes (see above). Further, as the primary colleagues against whom newcomers will evaluate their fit, social integration with co-workers is important for newcomers to stay on in the organization (Schneider, 1987). Overall, there is consistent evidence of the importance of newcomer–co-worker relationships for organizational socialization.

Supervisors. After co-workers, supervisors are the most available resources for newcomers (Louis et al., 1983). Yet in spite of this, supervisor helpfulness has mostly weak relationships with socialization learning, job satisfaction, organizational commitment, intentions of leaving, actual leaving and psychological distress (Kammeyer-Mueller & Wanberg, 2003; Lee, 2008; Louis et al., 1983; Nelson & Quick, 1991; Ostroff & Kozlowski, 1992). Intriguingly, in spite of the relatively weak effects of supervisors as sources, other studies comparing different sources have found that supervisor behaviour is more important than newcomer behaviour in predicting adjustment (Bauer & Green, 1998), and more important than orientation programmes and co-workers (Anakwe & Greenhaus, 1999). This may be because the newcomer's supervisor is primarily responsible for guiding the newcomer and evaluating his/her performance, with the latter being an indicator of newcomer adjustment. Given this, newcomers may be more influenced by their supervisor's input relative to other sources, even if they do not consciously recognize this.

There have also been intriguing results for the relationship between supervisor helpfulness and newcomer performance. Nelson and Quick (1991) found that supervisor helpfulness was not associated with performance, whereas Ashford and Black's (1996) results showed that newcomers' attempts to build relationships with their boss were positively associated with job performance, and in Bauer and Green's (1998) research, they found that supervisor clarification of role-related information was strongly associated with newcomer performance efficacy. Overall, these results suggest that newcomers may receive greater positive benefits from their relationship with their supervisor when both parties are more proactive participants in the relationship.

Research has also investigated the influence of supervisor-newcomer role development processes during organizational socialization, specifically looking at leader-member exchange (LMX). Broadly viewed, LMX reflects the quality of the relationship between the newcomer and the supervisor. Importantly, LMX buffers the negative effects of newcomer unmet role expectations (role acceptance, conflict, and clarity) on outcomes of job satisfaction and intent to turnover (Major, Kozlowski, Chao

& Gardner, 1995). In summary, relationships between newcomers and their supervisors have an important role in newcomer adjustment, influencing newcomer performance and attitudes. Given that it is the supervisor who – arguably – has the most to gain or lose from the role performance and social integration of the newcomer in terms of the performance of his or her team overall, it seems sensible for the supervisor to make the most effort to facilitate newcomer learning and positive adjustment.

Mentors. Mentoring has been confirmed as predicting a range of outcomes for newcomers, particularly learning about the organization (Allen, McManus & Russell, 1999; Chao, Walz & Gardner, 1992; Ostroff & Kozlowski, 1993), perceived work-related stress (Allen et al., 1999), and person-organization fit (Chatman, 1991). Research on mentoring shows that protégés and mentors benefit from having input into the matching process, with this leading to greater mentorship satisfaction, mentorship quality, role modelling, and both career-related and socially supportive mentoring (Allen, Eby & Lentz, 2006). Input into matching is likely important because it allows both parties to choose a partner with whom they think they can establish a positive working relationship, for example due to shared characteristics.

The hierarchical distance of mentor and protégé is perceived differently by the two parties in terms of its influence on role modelling: specifically, protégés prefer to role model those more similar in rank whereas mentors think a greater rank distance enhances role modelling (Allen et al., 2006). This suggests that newcomers identify with those in more proximal, attainable senior roles (Kram & Isabella, 1985), and matches with evidence that knowledgeable peers can provide many of the same functions as mentors (Ostroff & Kozlowski, 1993). For newcomers, a range of insiders may provide quasi-mentoring outside of formal mentoring programmes; these relationships will become more critical as organizational hierarchies flatten (Allen et al., 1999).

Workgroups. The newcomer's immediate team or workgroup is an important source of socialization, especially given the increasing use of teamwork (Anderson & Thomas, 1996; Louis, 1990). Indeed, the workgroup is a key focus of employee attachment, with workgroup attachments (identification and commitment) typically stronger than organizational attachments (Riketta & Van Dick, 2005). Longitudinal research on teams has shown that initial team expectations of the newcomer positively influence both subsequent newcomer social exchanges within the team and subsequent team ratings of newcomer role performance (Chen & Klimoski, 2003). Research has found that newcomer's positive social exchanges with their team buffer some – but not all – of the negative relationships between unmet expectations with attitudes (Chen & Klimoski, 2003; Major et al., 1995).

Further, 'opportunity to interact' (a mixture of opportunity and proximity) positively predicts newcomer social integration and job satisfaction, and negatively predicts intent to turnover and actual turnover (Wanberg & Kammeyer-Mueller, 2000), while co-worker influence is associated with improved group integration and, in turn, higher levels of organizational commitment (Kammeyer-Mueller & Wanberg, 2003). A recent meta-analysis by Bauer and colleagues (2007) confirmed that newcomer social acceptance positively predicted outcomes of job performance, job satisfaction, organizational commitment, intent to stay and negatively predicted turnover. It seems possible, therefore, that there are two distinct paths of influence for the newcomer's team: one is through social exchanges which affect newcomer attitudes, and the second is through communication of work expectations which influence performance.

Insider networks. At the broadest level, newcomers' sources of informal and semi-formal influence may be investigated through looking at their networks of insider contacts. Morrison (2002a) linked the social network and organizational socialization literatures to investigate the relationship of various aspects of informational and social networks with five outcomes that reflect newcomer learning (organizational knowledge, task mastery, and role clarity) and assimilation (social integration and organizational commitment). Broadly, learning was more strongly associated with information network characteristics (having a larger, more dense network with greater range, strength, and status of contacts), whereas assimilation was more strongly associated with friendship network characteristics (having more, stronger contacts, with a greater range and status). Overall, this research shows that the configuration of newcomers' networks is important for their adjustment.

Newcomers need to develop appropriate organizational networks to support their adjustment. Morrison (2002b) suggests that organizational socialization tactics may influence the development of organizational networks, for example collective tactics – where newcomers experience a common orientation experience – may facilitate the development of friendship ties. Elsesser and Peplau's (2006) research shows that the most common ways of establishing work-based friendship networks are working with colleagues, having similar non-work-related interests, and physical proximity. Thus, a range of individual, interactive, organizational and organization environment factors influence the development of networks.

Socialization from the organization

Reflecting the early research focus on organizational actions, Van Maanen and Schein (1979) outlined six socialization tactics that organizations can use to shape newcomer outcomes. In subsequent research, Jones (1986) suggested that these six tactics could be divided into three categories, of social, context, and content (see Table 3.2). Social tactics refer to whether experienced insiders are available as resources for newcomers for learning from and modelling appropriate behaviours (*serial*) or not (*disjunctive*), and whether insiders and other organizational representatives make newcomers feel that their skills and abilities are valued (*investiture*) or not (*divestiture*). Context tactics refer to where socialization activities occur – either *collectively* with other newcomers or *individually*, and either in a *formal*, segregated setting away from insiders, or *informally* on-site. Content tactics refer to how socialization information is delivered, so either according to a *fixed* or *variable* schedule and with either a *sequential*, fixed series of steps in the process or *randomly*.

Table 3.2 Organizational socialization tactics

	Institutionalized	Individualized
social	serial	disjunctive
	investiture*	divestiture
context	collective	individual
	formal	informal
content	sequential	random
	fixed*	variable

Note: *Jones' (1986) differs from Van Maanen and Schein (1979) in reversing the placement of these tactics.

Of these, the two social tactics are most aligned with influencing relationships between newcomers and insiders. Serial tactics are more likely than disjunctive tactics to lead to supportive relationships between newcomers and insiders. In particular, supportive relationships are important such that newcomers feel able to ask questions and hence understand the underlying rationale for experienced insiders' actions. In turn, this enables newcomers to choose appropriate behaviours (as defined by the organization) for themselves. Further, when insiders show that they value newcomers' abilities (i.e., investiture tactic), newcomers are likely to perceive that they have at least some status with insiders. This may help newcomers feel confident in asking for information or advice, and facilitate the development of cooperative relationships. The two context tactics of collective and formal are likely to support the development of friendships between newcomers. Specifically, going through organizational socialization with other newcomers (i.e., collective tactic), who are dealing with similar issues, provides opportunities to share concerns and solutions, and hence develop social and instrumental support. However, where newcomers are subsequently competing for positions, collective socialization may encourage backstabbing and cheating, resulting in poor quality relationships between contesting newcomers.

Being segregated from most insiders (i.e., formal tactic) during this time may facilitate relationships between newcomers themselves, as these are the only collegial, same-level relationships available. A formal setting in which insiders fill an expert role as trainers or coaches is likely to put some distance between newcomers and these organizational insiders. This is likely to be seen most clearly when insiders' performance is evaluated based on enabling newcomers to achieve rigorous, standardized performance criteria, such as in military instruction or accountancy training.

Although there is no direct evidence for the effects of different tactics on the development of relationships between different groups of colleagues such as I propose above, there is now considerable data showing that the two social tactics (serial-disjunctive and investiture-divestiture), are the most influential for newcomer adjustment relative to the other tactics. Specifically, serial and investiture tactics predict a range of outcomes either more strongly or uniquely relative to the other four tactics. These outcomes include perceptions of person-organization fit, engagement, role ambiguity, role conflict, role orientation, job satisfaction, organizational commitment, intentions to quit, turnover and performance (Allen, 2006; Bauer et al., 2007; Cable & Parsons, 2001; Jones, 1986; Saks et al., 2007).

2.   Outcomes of organizational socialization

It is generally agreed that organizational socialization is most directly represented by newcomer learning (Saks & Ashforth, 1997). That is, the process of transitioning from newcomer to insider is achieved through developing relevant, local knowledge. Other desirable outcomes of organizational socialization, such as role performance, positive attitudes, fitting in and retention, occur more distally and are achieved via learning (Cooper-Thomas & Anderson, 2005). In addition to changes in the newcomer, there is also the potential for insiders to change as the result of the newcomer entering the organization.

Proximal outcomes: newcomer learning

The knowledge content that newcomers have to acquire can be most parsimoniously represented within three categories, comprising role, social, and organization information (Cooper-Thomas & Park, 2008). Role information includes understanding what the tasks of the role are, how to accomplish them, and what is considered good performance; social information refers to knowing who can provide help, and being included in social activities; organization knowledge comprises knowing the history, culture, and politics of the organization.

While some relevant information for role, social, and organizational knowledge can come from organizational documents (e.g., the role may be clearly depicted in the employment contract), much of the learning for each of these domains can only be attained with the cooperation of colleagues. For example, at the role level, the newcomer can only learn what his or her supervisor considers good performance either directly via feedback from that supervisor, or indirectly via information from other direct reports (i.e., the newcomer's peers). Newcomers can only know who, among their colleagues, is willing and able to provide help or advice by developing and testing social relationships at work. Last, some organizational knowledge is unwritten and can only be learnt via colleagues, either directly through being told or indirectly through having opportunities to observe colleagues and hence decipher this intangible side of the organization (Cooper-Thomas et al., 2009). As an example of this, Feldman (1977) found that newcomer employees at a hospital reported that they had to establish social relations with colleagues (being friendly and viewed as trustworthy) before these colleagues would share information that was critical to good job performance (see also Van Maanen, 1973). In summary, newcomer learning underpins organizational socialization, and that learning is partly dependent on the cooperation of colleagues, be they co-workers, supervisors, mentors, or part of the newcomer's workgroup or broader organizational network.

Distal outcomes: indicators of success

Newcomer learning alone is insufficient for successful socialization, and hence researchers have investigated a broader range of outcomes that occur subsequent to newcomer learning, and predicted by such learning. Thus, many researchers have used newcomer attitudes towards work and the organization to indicate organizational socialization success (Bauer et al., 2007; Saks et al., 2007). However, Cooper-Thomas and Anderson (2006) argue that these are insufficient as they do not reflect the totality of successful socialization. For example, job satisfaction is typically measured, but a newcomer may be perfectly content in their job and yet ostracized by peers and lousy at their job. Further, a focus on newcomer attitudes overlooks the perspectives of other stakeholders, such as the newcomer's supervisor.

Instead of newcomer attitudes, Cooper-Thomas and Anderson (2006) propose five indicators that represent success for all potential stakeholders. The first success indicator is role performance, which is critical for the newcomer to remain employed, and affects their own self-perceptions as well as having implications for the newcomer's supervisor, their workgroup and, ultimately, the organization (Chen & Klimoski, 2003; Watkins, 2003). The second success indicator is extra-role performance, which refers to those behaviours that help other colleagues and the organization achieve work-related goals (Lee & Allen, 2003; Podsakoff, Ahearne & MacKenzie, 1997), and also influence supervisors' perceptions of the newcomer (Johnson, 2001). Third is social cohesion, which refers to fitting in with colleagues and becoming part of the social fabric of the organization (Morrison, 1993a, b). Social ties and shared values and norms help the individual to develop a situational identity and commitment, and facilitate communication with colleagues and the smooth running of the organization (Ashforth, 2001; Schneider, 1987). The fourth outcome is internal stability, with low levels of newcomer absenteeism and turnover indicating that the newcomer is adjusting well, and that colleagues and other stakeholders (e.g., customers) are able to form stable relationships with the newcomer (Kammeyer-Mueller, Wanberg, Glomb & Ahlburg, 2005). The fifth and last level in the model is external representation, which is the broadest success indicator in terms of potentially affecting people both within and beyond the organization (e.g., insiders, clients). Newcomers are only likely to be given opportunities to represent their organization to external audiences if they are viewed as proficient in their role and knowledgeable about how the organization works (Louis, 1980).

Insider change

In addition to newcomer change through learning and success indicators, there is also the potential for the newcomer to influence colleagues

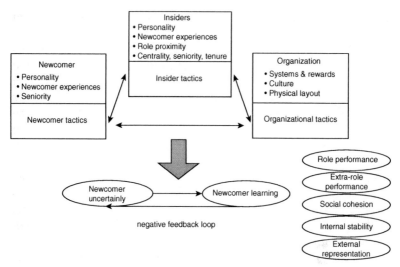

Figure 3.1 An interactive model of organizational socialization

(Anderson & Thomas, 1996). This may be seen particularly where the newcomer has unique talents that need to be integrated for the organization's benefit, for example specific technical expertise that colleagues need to learn and adopt. It also occurs when the newcomer is in a position of legitimate power over insiders, and hence subordinates may need to change their behaviours to fit their newcomer boss's requirements. Hence outcomes may also be assessed along various dimensions of insider change.

3. An interactive model of organizational socialization

Given the consistent evidence of the important role of insiders in organizational socialization, it is unsurprising that many models of newcomer socialization have included insiders (Ashforth et al., 2007a; Cooper-Thomas & Anderson, 2006; Louis, 1980; Reichers, 1987; Saks & Ashforth, 1997). However, in all cases, the role of insiders is only dealt with briefly and with little detail. To redress this, I present a model of organizational socialization that makes the role of insiders more explicit (see Figure 3.1). The central pathway at the bottom of the model, common to most process models of organizational socialization, is from newcomer uncertainty through to learning (e.g., Saks & Ashforth, 1997), and then to the five indicators of socialization success outlined above (Cooper-Thomas & Anderson, 2006). Above this pathway, the newcomer, insiders and the organization are represented in three separate but interacting boxes.

For the newcomer, the last decade of research in organizational socialization has established the influence of newcomer's personality on outcomes. Thus, newcomers who are more extraverted, open to experience, and proactive are likely to seek and use relationships with insiders and other relevant stakeholders to achieve their own socialization (Kammeyer-Mueller & Wanberg, 2003). Past work experiences are also likely to influence how the newcomer approaches socialization (Beyer & Hannah, 2002; Cooper-Thomas et al., 2009), and in particular what strategies they use, potentially having learnt both from their own mistakes and successes and also those of others. Last, there is evidence that newcomers entering at more senior levels are provided with fewer organization resources to facilitate their socialization (Ashford, Blatt & VandeWalle, 2003), hence depending more on their own resources. These three factors are indicated in Figure 3.1, and influence the tactics that newcomers use to effect their own socialization.

The central box, then, represents organizational insiders. While there is no empirical evidence to date on insider personality relating to their role in organizational socialization, it is likely that similar personality traits will influence them as have been confirmed for newcomers. Thus, insiders who are more extraverted, open to experience, and proactive are more likely to initiate relationships with newcomers, and offer help and advice. Further, those who have more experience of being a newcomer are likely to be more aware of newcomers' needs, motivating them to assist where possible. Louis (1990) notes that same level peers will have approximately similar perspectives to the newcomer on their particular functional and hierarchical part of the organization. Hence those in the same or related roles may provide appropriate technical information, and those in the same workgroup and/or with the same supervisor may provide social and appraisal information. Further, insiders who are more central and more senior are likely to have a 'truer' view of organizational reality (Van Maanen & Schein, 1979). Similarly, those who have been in the organization longer (i.e., greater tenure) will have had time to build up a more accurate view of organizational reality that will be more useful for newcomers. All of these factors will influence insiders in their use of strategies to socialize newcomers.

At the organization level, three factors are proposed as particularly influential: organizational systems, culture, and the physical layout. Where organizational systems are in place to support newcomer adjustment (e.g., mentoring, buddy programmes), and insiders are recognized appropriately for their efforts at achieving this (e.g., as part of performance appraisal), insiders are more likely to be involved in developing effective relationships with newcomers. In addition to formal organizational systems, the informal culture of the organization may serve to reinforce behaviours that establish and maintain relationships between insiders and newcomers (e.g., social events to welcome newcomers). Last, the physical layout of the work environment can help newcomers to develop relationships with insiders, and thus influence organizational socialization. Physical proximity is associated both with interaction frequency (Allen et al., 2006) and with the development of workplace friendships (Elsesser & Peplau, 2006). These various factors influence the extent to which insiders plan and participate in organizational socialization tactics that facilitate newcomer socialization. In particular, research shows the two social tactics (serial and investiture) have the strongest effects (Ashforth & Saks, 1996; Saks et al., 2007).

These three sources – the newcomer, insiders, and the organization – interact to influence newcomer learning and adjustment. To date, there has been limited investigation of the combined effects of strategies from these sources (Cooper-Thomas & Anderson, 2002; Kim et al., 2005; Mignerey, Rubin & Gorden, 1995; Saks & Ashforth, 1997b). In the one study that has investigated interactive effects, Kim et al. (2005) found that newcomer general socializing reinforced organizational institutionalized socialization tactics, but that relationship building with boss negated these tactics. This echoes early research by Van Maanen (1973) in the police force which showed that veteran police officers negated much of the formal content that rookie officers had learned during training. Since these initial findings suggest that interactions between newcomers and insiders are most influential in affecting newcomer outcomes, and can undermine formal sources, this is clearly an important area for further research.

4. Practical implications

The research I have presented above provides a consistent picture of the importance of newcomer–insider relationships during organizational socialization. Indeed, the significant degree to which newcomers depend on insiders highlights what several authors have called 'the liability of newness' (Krackhardt, 1996; Rollag, 2007). Thus, Krackhardt proposes that 'perhaps the most critical liability to the new manager is the lack of a clear understanding of how the current system of exchanges and relationships works in the organizational unit' (Krackhardt, 1996, p. 160). In line with this view, and with the interactive model of organizational socialization presented in Figure 3.1, I provide practical suggestions for newcomers, insiders and for those responsible for designing organizational socialization programmes.

Suggestions for newcomers

The increased rate at which employees are transitioning across organizations fits with the idea that people are increasingly managing their own careers (Arthur, 2008; Bureau of Labour Statistics, 2006; Macaulay, 2003). Success as a newcomer is dependent on building positive relationships with insiders, to provide access to advice, support, and information that is not available elsewhere. Indeed, research on newcomers' networks has shown the value of broader and stronger informational and friendship networks for learning and assimilation (Morrison, 2002b), and that number of interactions with insiders (network centrality) is positively related to faster adjustment (Rollag, 2007). I suggest that there are two considerations here which need to be balanced: one is for the newcomer to establish his or her own credibility, by proving the value that s/he can bring to the workgroup and supervisor/manager (Chen & Klimoski, 2003). However, this needs to be done without unduly questioning local norms or procedures, as this can alienate colleagues (Ashforth et al., 2007a). Building on this, a second consideration is to develop and maintain respectful relationships with a broad range of colleagues quickly (Morrison, 2002b), through joining in on meetings as appropriate, accepting invitations to at-work and after-work social gatherings, listening to advice, taking up offers of help or support, and maintaining links. A further option is to explicitly ask for a buddy and/or mentor as sources of advice and support, the former for local procedures and role-related questions, and the latter for organizational-wide issues and career advice.

Suggestions for insiders

Most insiders do not get explicitly rewarded for helping newcomers (although see the next section, 'suggestions for organizations'), so giving time and advice to newcomers is usually motivated either by kindness or self-interest, an example of the latter being where getting a newcomer up to speed helps the insider in an inter-dependent role. Insiders can provide all kinds of resources, ranging from technical advice through to social support. It is suggested that insiders explicitly discuss with newcomers what kinds of advice they can give, as well as how and when (e.g., regular scheduled meetings versus ad hoc, as needed). Consider also the research on mentors, which shows that most mentors report getting positive outcomes from providing mentoring, including both direct performance benefits (e.g., performance evaluations increased through developing others; enhanced promotion prospects due to developing replacement talent) and indirect ones (e.g., developing technical, resource, and power networks within the organization; informal recognition from colleagues) (Hunt & Michael, 1983).

It is also important to note the consistent research evidence showing that people tend to seek out and prefer others who are similar to them, that is, a preference for homophily (Ibarra, 1993). This raises a potential concern when newcomers enter the organization who are different to organizational norms in terms of sociodemographic variables including occupational background, work experience, sex, race, religion, and so on. Insiders are likely to prefer developing relationships with newcomers who they perceive as most similar to themselves (and hence whom they feel most comfortable with) (Allen et al., 2006) as well as higher performers (Chao, Walz & Gardner, 1992), and this may work well. Nonetheless, it is likely that those who are least similar to organizational insiders will be in most need of developing relationships to provide information, advice, and support (Jackson, Stone & Alvarez, 1993). Insiders should consider how they can support these newcomers in particular, recognizing that minority influence may stimulate their own performance.

Suggestions for organizations

Given the increasing rate of newcomers entering organizations, and the fact that most of these will be experienced workers taking up diverse roles (Bureau of Labour Statistics, 2006; Carr, Pearson, Vest & Boyar, 2006), it is efficient for organizations to facilitate newcomers in directing their own organizational socialization. Nonetheless, organizations should still play a critical role (Ashforth, Sluss & Saks, 2007b). There are two major areas which organizations should focus on. The first is to consider the social side of socialization, for example what social resources are put in place to help newcomers to establish useful work relationships. This includes the people who are made available (e.g., buddy, mentor), programmes (e.g., social events), and networks (e.g., contacts lists for different types of knowledge, skill or professional interest). These issues may be more critical at senior levels, where organizations more typically leave newcomers to figure it out for themselves (Ashford et al., 2003), providing more latitude and consequently less help. Chao (1988) raises the important issue that the organization should take care to select appropriate co-workers to socialize newcomers, to ensure that desirable attitudes, values, and behaviours are transmitted.

A second recommendation is to think about how organizational socialization is rewarded, that is both how insiders are rewarded for helping newcomers get up to speed, and how newcomers are rewarded for using appropriate strategies and helping themselves become proficient. For insiders, while verbal recognition is nice, more impact will come from effective HR/ HCM policies that provide valued rewards to insiders for helping newcomers. For newcomers, discussions around both suitable and inappropriate adjustment behaviours can reduce the cost and implications of errors, and increase newcomers' confidence to more vigorously pursue their own adjustment. Watkins (2003) suggests that it takes about six months for a manager to reach the breakeven point and provide more than they have cost to the organization, and Rollag (2004, 2007) provides the 30% rule, with a newcomer becoming an insider once they have reached the 30% tenure point. If organizations can help newcomers become effective more rapidly, it will benefit the newcomer (e.g., self-confidence), the workgroup (e.g., ease of communication, better performance), and the wider organization (e.g., higher performance, lower turnover).

Beyond this, research shows that providing information, support, and a structured and planned socialization process is associated with better outcomes (Bauer et al., 2007; Saks et al., 2007). Thus, ensuring that newcomers receive realistic information during recruitment enables them to start to develop an accurate picture of their future work (Wanous & Colella, 1989). The arrival of newcomers should be anticipated and, in addition to making sure an appropriate workspace is available, colleagues should be briefed on the newcomer's abilities and needs, and any necessary training should be scheduled. Last, newcomers need to know if they are on track and, if not, early corrective action is needed. The organization can ensure a regular series of low-key performance feedback sessions in the early weeks and months, from supervisors and senior colleagues, to maximize newcomers' performance contributions. This has benefits to all parties, and in particular will reduce the stress of uncertainty for the newcomer.

5. Summary

In this chapter, I have considered three sources through which newcomers achieve organizational socialization: the newcomer him- or herself, various insiders, and formal organizational influences, in particular the socialization tactics used. I then discussed the outcomes that organizational socialization aims to achieve through these sources, focusing on proximal learning outcomes, as well as more distal indicators of success for the newcomer, and also insider adjustment. Following this, I presented an interactive model of organizational socialization which depicts the inter-relationships between these various sources, and factors that determine the relative efforts – and hence influence – of each. Last, I provided practical recommendations relating to these sources, with a focus especially on relational aspects of newcomer adjustment.

From this review, it is clear that relationships between newcomers and insiders are critical for effective socialization. Insiders provide the conduit for organizational attempts to influence the newcomer as well as newcomer proactive efforts at becoming socialized, not forgetting that insiders may also pursue their own agendas regarding the socialization of newcomers. As organizations are faced with a greater flux of employees of various types (e.g., range of contracts, socio-demographic diversity) and into a variety of roles (e.g., various levels, different departments), it seems likely – and even advisable – for organizations to increasingly rely on flexible, informal socialization delivered primarily through relationships between insiders and newcomers. This is not to condone a laissez-faire approach, particularly since planned socialization programmes are significantly more successful relative to unplanned programmes (Ashforth, Saks & Lee, 1997). Thus, all parties need to plan for more flexible, accessible, local and relevant organizational socialization delivered through, and dependent on, effective newcomer-insider relationships.

References

Allen, T. D., Eby, L. T. & Lentz, E. (2006). Mentorship behaviors and mentorship quality associated with formal mentoring programs: Closing the gap between research and practice. *Journal of Applied Psychology, 91*(3), 567–578.

Allen, T. D., McManus, S. E. & Russell, J. E. A. (1999). Newcomer socialization and stress: Formal peer relationships as a source of support. *Journal of Vocational Behavior, 54*(3), 453–470.

Anakwe, U. P. & Greenhaus, J. H. (1999). Effective socialization of employees: Socialization content perspective. *Journal of Managerial Issues, 11*(3), 315–329.

Anderson, N. & Ostroff, C. (1997). Selection as socialization. In N. Anderson & P. Herriot (eds), *International Handbook of Selection and Assessment* (pp. 413–440). Chichester: Wiley.

Anderson, N. & Thomas, H. D. C. (1996). Workgroup socialization. In M. A. West (ed.), *Handbook of Workgroups* (pp. 423–450). Chichester: Wiley.

Arthur, M. B. (2008). Examining contemporary careers: A call for interdisciplinary inquiry. *Human Relations, 61*(2), 163–186.

Ashford, S. J. (1986). Feedback-seeking in individual adaptation: A resource perspective. *Academy of Management Journal, 29*(3), 465–487.

Ashford, S. J. & Black, J. S. (1996). Proactivity during organizational entry: The role of desire for control. *Journal of Applied Psychology, 81*(2), 199–214.

Ashford, S. J., Blatt, R. & VandeWalle, D. (2003). Reflections on the looking glass: A review of research on feedback-seeking behavior in organizations. *Journal of Management, 29*(6), 773–799.

Ashforth, B. E. (2001). *Role Transitions in Organizational Life: An Identity-based Perspective.* Mahwah, NJ: Erlbaum.

Ashforth, B. E. & Saks, A. M. (1996). Socialization tactics: Longitudinal effects on newcomer adjustment. *Academy of Management Journal, 39*(1), 149–178.

Ashforth, B. E., Saks, A. M. & Lee, R. T. (1997). On the dimensionality of Jones' (1986) measures of organizational socialization tactics. *International Journal of Selection and Assessment, 5*(4), 200–214.

Ashforth, B. E., Sluss, D. M. & Harrison, S. H. (2007a). Socialization in organizational contexts. In G. P. Hodgkinson & J. K. Ford (eds), *International Review of Industrial and Organizational Psychology* (Vol. 22, pp. 1–70). New York: Wiley.

Ashforth, B. E., Sluss, D. M. & Saks, A. M. (2007b). Socialization tactics, proactive behavior, and newcomer learning: Integrating socialization models. *Journal of Vocational Behavior, 70*(3), 447–462.

Bauer, T. N., Bodner, T., Erdogan, B., Truxillo, D. M. & Tucker, J. S. (2007). Newcomer adjustment during organizational socialization: A meta-analytic review of antecedents, outcomes, and methods. *Journal of Applied Psychology, 92*(3), 707–721.

Bauer, T. N. & Green, S. G. (1998). Testing the combined effects of newcomer information seeking and manager behavior on socialization. *Journal of Applied Psychology, 83*(1), 72–83.

Beyer, J. M. & Hannah, D. R. (2002). Building on the past: Enacting established personal identities in a new work setting. *Organization Science, 13*(6), 636–652.

Brim, O. G., Jr & Wheeler, S. (1966). *Socialization After Childhood: Two Essays.* New York: Wiley.

Cable, D. M. & Parsons, C. K. (2001). Socialization tactics and person-organization fit. *Personnel Psychology, 54*(1), 1–23.

Carr, J. C., Pearson, A. W., Vest, M. J. & Boyar, S. L. (2006). Prior occupational experience, anticipatory socialization, and employee retention. *Journal of Management, 32*(3), 343–359.

Chan, D. & Schmitt, N. (2000). Interindividual differences in intraindividual changes in proactivity during organizational entry: A latent growth modeling approach to understanding newcomer adaptation. *Journal of Applied Psychology, 85*(2), 190–210.

Chao, G. T. (1988). The socialization process: Building newcomer commitment. In M. London & E. Mone (eds), *Career Growth and Human Resource Strategies* (pp. 31–47). Westport, CT: Quorum.

Chao, G. T., Walz, P. M. & Gardner, P. D. (1992). Formal and informal mentor-ships: A comparison on mentoring functions and contrast with nonmentored counterparts. *Personnel Psychology, 45*(3), 619–636.

Chen, G. & Klimos ki, R. J. (2003). The impact of expectations on newcomer performance in teams as mediated by work characteristics, social exchanges, and empowerment. *Academy of Management Journal, 46*(5), 591–607.

Cooper-Thomas, H. D. & Anderson, N. (2002). Newcomer adjustment: The relationship between organizational socialization tactics, information acquisition and attitudes. *Journal of Occupational & Organizational Psychology, 75*(4), 423–437.

Cooper-Thomas, H. D. & Anderson, N. (2005). Organizational socialization: A field study into socialization success and rate. *International Journal of Selection and Assessment, 13*(2), 116–128.

Cooper-Thomas, H. D. & Anderson, N. (2006). Organizational socialization: A new theoretical model and recommendations for future research and HRM practices in organizations. *Journal of Managerial Psychology, 21*(5), 492–516.

Cooper-Thomas, H. D., Anderson, N. & Hughes, M. L. (2009). *Investigating Newcomer Adjustment Strategies: HR and Newcomer Perspectives.* Manuscript submitted for publication.

Cooper-Thomas, H. D. & Park, J. H. (2008, April). *Measuring Organizational Socialization: A Psychometric Comparison of Four Measures.* Paper presented at the Society for Industrial and Organisational Psychology Annual Conference, San Francisco, CA.

Cooper-Thomas, H. D., Van Vianen, A. & Anderson, N. (2004). Changes in person-organization fit: The impact of socialization tactics on perceived and actual P-O fit. *European Journal of Work and Organizational Psychology, 13*(1), 52–78.

Cooper-Thomas, H. D. & Wilson, M. G. (2007, August). *Newcomer Adjustment Strategies: A Cost-Benefit Model.* Paper presented at the Academy of Management Conference, Philadelphia, PA.

Elsesser, K. & Peplau, L. A. (2006). The glass partition: Obstacles to cross-sex friendships at work. *Human Relations, 59*(8), 1077–1100.

Feldman, D. C. (1976). A contingency theory of socialization. *Administrative Science Quarterly, 21*, 433–452.

Feldman, D. C. (1977). The role of initiation activities in socialization. *Human Relations, 30*(11), 977–990.

Feldman, D. C. & Brett, J. M. (1983). Coping with new jobs: A comparative study of new hires and job changers. *Academy of Management Journal, 26*(2), 258–272.

Fisher, C. D. (1985). Social support and adjustment to work: A longitudinal study. *Journal of Management, 11*(3), 39–53.

Fisher, C. D. (1986). Organizational socialization: An integrative review. In, K. Roland & G. Ferris (eds) *Research in Personnel and Human Resources Management*, (Vol. 4, pp. 101–145). Greenwich, CT: JAI.

Gruman, J. A., Saks, A. M. & Zweig, D. I. (2006). Organizational socialization tactics and newcomer proactive behaviors: An integrative study. *Journal of Vocational Behavior, 69*(1), 90–104.

Holder, T. (1996). Women in nontraditional occupations: Information-seeking during organizational entry. *Journal of Business Communication, 33*(1), 9–26.

Hunt, D. M. & Michael, C. (1983). Mentorship: A career training and development tool. *Academy of Management Review, 8*(3), 475–485.

Jackson, S. E., Stone, V. K. & Alvarez, E. B. (1993). Socialization amidst diversity: The impact of demographics on work team oldtimers and newcomers. In L. L. Cummings & B. M. Staw (eds), *Research in Organizational Behavior* (Vol. 15, pp. 45–109). Greenwich, CT: Erlbaum.

Johnson, J. W. (2001). The relative importance of task and contextual performance dimensions to supervisor judgments of overall performance. *Journal of Applied Psychology, 86*, 984–996.

Jones, G. R. (1986). Socialization tactics, self-efficacy, and newcomers' adjustments to organizations. *Academy of Management Journal, 29*(2), 262–279.

Kammeyer-Mueller, J. D. & Wanberg, C. R. (2003). Unwrapping the organizational entry process: Disentangling multiple antecedents and their pathways to adjustment. *Journal of Applied Psychology, 88*(5), 779–794.

Kammeyer-Mueller, J. D., Wanberg, C. R., Glomb, T. M. & Ahlburg, D. (2005). Turnover processes in a temporal context: It's about time. *Journal of Applied Psychology, 90*(4), 644–658.

Kim, T. Y., Cable, D. M. & Kim, S. P. (2005). Socialization tactics, employee proactivity, and person-organization fit. *Journal of Applied Psychology, 90*(2), 232–241.

Klein, H. J., Fan, J. & Preacher, K. J. (2006). The effects of early socialization experiences on content mastery and outcomes: A mediational approach. *Journal of Vocational Behavior, 68*, 96–115.

Krackhardt, D. (1996). Social networks and the liability of newness for managers. In C. L. Cooper & D. M. Rousseau (eds), *Trends in Organizational Behavior* (Vol. 3, pp. 159–173). Chichester, UK: Wiley.

Kram, K. E. & Isabella, L. A. (1985). Mentoring alternatives: The role of peer relationships in career development. *Academy of Management Journal, 28*(1), 110–132.

Lee, H. (2008). *Stress and Social Support During Organisational Socialisation.* Unpublished master's thesis, University of Auckland, Auckland, New Zealand.

Louis, M. R. (1980). Surprise and sense making: What newcomers experience in entering unfamiliar organizational settings. *Administrative Science Quarterly, 25*(2), 226–251.

Louis, M. R. (1990). Acculturation in the workplace: Newcomers as lay ethnographers. In B. Schneider (ed.), *Organizational Climate and Culture* (pp. 85–129). San Francisco, MA: Jossey-Bass.

Louis, M. R., Posner, B. Z. & Powell, G. N. (1983). The availability and helpfulness of socialization practices. *Personnel Psychology, 36*(4), 857–866.

Macaulay, D. (2003). *Job Mobility and Job Tenure in the UK.* Retrieved 4 April 2008, from http://www.statistics.gov.uk/articles/labour_market_trends/job-mobility_nov03.pdf

Major, D. A. & Kozlowski, S. W. J. (1997). Newcomer information seeking: Individual and contextual influences. *International Journal of Selection and Assessment, 5*(1), 16–28.

Major, D. A., Kozlowski, S. W. J., Chao, G. T. & Gardner, P. D. (1995). A longitudinal investigation of newcomer expectations, early socialization outcomes, and the moderating effects of role development factors. *Journal of Applied Psychology, 80*(3), 418–431.

Mignerey, J. T., Rubin, R. B. & Gorden, W. I. (1995). Organizational entry: An investigation of newcomer communication behavior and uncertainty. *Communication Research, 22*(1), 54–85.

Miller, V. D. & Jablin, F. M. (1991). Information seeking during organizational entry – influences, tactics, and a model of the process. *Academy of Management Review, 16*(1), 92–120.

Morrison, E. W. (1993a). Longitudinal-study of the effects of information seeking on newcomer socialization. *Journal of Applied Psychology, 78*(2), 173–183.

Morrison, E. W. (1993b). Newcomer information-seeking – exploring types, modes, sources, and outcomes. *Academy of Management Journal, 36*(3), 557–589.

Morrison, E. W. (2002a). Information seeking within organizations. *Human Communication Research, 28*(2), 229–242.

Morrison, E. W. (2002b). Newcomers' relationships: The role of social network ties during socialization. *Academy of Management Journal, 45*(6), 1149–1160.

Nelson, D. L. & Quick, J. C. (1991). Social support and newcomer adjustment in organizations: Attachment theory at work? *Journal of Organizational Behavior, 12*(6), 543–554.

Nelson, D. L., Quick, J. C. & Joplin, J. R. (1991). Psychological contracting and newcomer socialization: An attachment theory foundation. *Journal of Social Behavior & Personality, 6*(7), 55–72.

Ostroff, C. & Kozlowski, S. W. (1992). Organizational socialization as a learning process: The role of information acquisition. *Personnel Psychology, 45*(4), 849–874.

Ostroff, C. & Kozlowski, S. W. (1993). The role of mentoring in the information gathering processes of newcomers during early organizational socialization. *Journal of Vocational Behavior, 42*, 170–183.

Podsakoff, P. M., Ahearne, M. & MacKenzie, S. B. (1997). Organizational citizenship behavior and the quantity and quality of workgroup performance. *Journal of Applied Psychology, 82*(2), 262–270.

Reichers, A. (1987). An interactionist perspective on newcomer socialization rates. *Academy of Management Review, 12*(2), 276–287.

Riketta, M. & Van Dick, R. (2005). Foci of attachment in organizations: A meta-analytic comparison of the strength and correlates of workgroup versus organizational identification and commitment. *Journal of Vocational Behavior, 67*, 490–510.

Rollag, K. (2004). The impact of relative tenure on newcomer socialization dynamics. *Journal of Organizational Behavior, 25*(7), 853–872.

Rollag, K. (2007). Defining the term 'new' in new employee research. *Journal of Occupational & Organizational Psychology, 80*, 63–75.

Saks, A. M. & Ashforth, B. E. (1997a). Organizational socialization: Making sense of the past and present as a prologue for the future. *Journal of Vocational Behavior, 51*(2), 234–279.

Saks, A. M. & Ashforth, B. E. (1997b). Socialization tactics and newcomer information acquisition. *International Journal of Selection and Assessment, 5*(1), 48–61.

Saks, A. M., Uggerslev, K. L. & Fassina, N. E. (2007). Socialization tactics and newcomer adjustment: A meta-analytic review and test of a model. *Journal of Vocational Behavior, 70*(3), 413–446.

Salamin, A. & Hom, P. W. (2005). In search of the elusive u-shaped performance-turnover relationship: Are high performing Swiss bankers more liable to quit? *Journal of Applied Psychology, 90*(6), 1204–1216.

Schneider, B. (1987). The people make the place. *Personnel Psychology, 40*(3), 437–453.

Statistics, B. o. L. (2006). Retrieved 25 February 2008, from http://www.bls.gov/news.release/pdf/nlsoy.pdf

Van Maanen, J. (1973). Observations on the making of policemen. *Human Organizations, 32*, 407–418.

Van Maanen, J. & Schein, E. H. (1979). Toward a theory of organizational socialization. In B. M. Staw (ed.), *Research in Organizational Behavior* (Vol. 1, pp. 209–264). Greenwich, CT: JAI Press.

Wanberg, C. R. & Kammeyer-Mueller, J. D. (2000). Predictors and outcomes of proactivity in the socialization process. *Journal of Applied Psychology, 85*(3), 373–385.

Wanous, J. P. & Colella, A. (1989). Organizational entry research: Current status and further directions. In K. Rowland & G. Ferris (eds), *Research in Personnel and Human Resource Management*. Greenwich, CT: JAI Press.

4
Organizational Climate, Organizational Culture and Workplace Relationships

Terry Nolan and Wendelin Küpers

Introduction

This chapter examines the interplay between three interdependent concepts – climate, culture and interpersonal relationships. We present organizations as life-worlds in which climate and culture have a reciprocally influencing relationship which, in turn, impacts upon workplace peer relationships.

To help contextualize the chapter we begin by posing a variety of questions that highlight possible organizational scenarios. We invite you to spend some moments reflecting upon these questions before continuing.

- How would working in a 'silence climate' (Milliken, Morrison & Hewlin, 2003), where employees choose to withhold their opinions and concerns about organizational problems compare with a climate of honesty where all are ready to hear and face the truth (Collins, 2001)?
- How would a climate of stability, safety and trust compare with one of uncertainty, insecurity, and distrust?
- What is the difference between climates of optimism and hope and those of pessimism and gloom?
- Can climates of stress and cynicism be transformed into climates of effective energy and humour or irony?
- How does a climate for diversity affect organizational and work-related attitudes and perceptions (Hicks-Clark & Iles, 2000)?
- How would work in climates of motivation (Pareek, 1989) compare to work in climates of demotivation (Wunderer & Küpers, 2003)?

At the macro organizational level:

- Why do constant change initiatives trigger some organizations to thrive, while others to fail?
- How do functional or structural limitations such as cost-cutting practices, social transformations and increasing job insecurity affect relationships between employees?
- How does the style of leadership affect the organizational climate, and subsequently, employee relationships?

Organizational climates can work to facilitate or impair work relationships. Thus, the climate of an organization is one of the key influencing forces which affects the individual employee's perceptions, feelings and actions, as well as their interpersonal relationships. To explore this relational nexus, the chapter focuses on the influencing dynamics and interplay *between* an organizational climate and the quality of peer work relationships.

Understanding organizational climate and culture

Despite a great deal of research focusing on organizational climate and culture, there remains some ambiguity with respect to how these concepts are connected and their impact on peer work relationships. The concept of organizational climate became popular in the industrial and organizational literature particularly in the 1960s and 1970s (Jones & James, 1979; Litwin & Stringer, 1968) and has remained a controversial issue.

For example, organizational climate has been defined as a 'set of characteristics that describe an organization and that (a) distinguish one organization from another (b) are relatively enduring over a period of time and (c) influence the behaviour of people in the organization' (Forehand & Von Haller, 1964, p. 363).

Organizational climate has been found to have a close, albeit ambiguous, relationship with organizational culture to the extent that the terms are sometimes used synonymously or indiscriminately. However, the various literatures on these concepts do distinguish between them. Both the climate and the culture of an organization are key forces which influence employees' perceptions of, and relationship towards, each other. Moreover, both climate and culture are, in turn, partially created by the quality of peer relationships. In other words, how people relate to each other influences the climate and culture of an organization.

Climate and culture research appears to be addressing common phenomena: organizational culture concerns the basic shared assumptions, values and practices (including all those formal and informal rules, norms and customs), and organizational climate refers to the way the organization is perceived by employees (Schein, 1985). Climate can be characterized as a perceived manifestation or representation which is rooted in, or part of, the organization's culture (Schein, 1985), or a subset of organizational culture with an applicable set of workable dimensions (Denison, 1996; Stringer, 2001; Turnipseed, 1988). Consequently, climate does not exist independently of culture. According to Burke (1994) climate is experienced and created in the workgroup and changes to climate are more achievable than changes in culture, as climate is associated with the 'transactional level of human behaviour – the everyday interactions and exchanges' (p. 127).

Objective, subjective and integral understandings of organizational climate

A major concern for researchers has been to clarify whether climate should be conceived of as the objective (physical or structural) features *of* the organization or the subjective (perceptual and personal) reactions and responses *to* the organization. Thus, on one hand, the focus has been on objective, measurable organizational features of climate as determinants of attitudes and behaviour and, on the other hand, upon subjective interpretations of climate i.e., as a situated and shared place. We examine these two conceptions in detail below.

The objective view of climate

The objective view of climate focuses on organizational artefacts which present visual or sensually perceptible indicators as to the emotional climate and the quality of life in an organization (Dandridge, Mitroff & Joyce, 1980). For example, the architectural design of the reception or the internal design of the office influences the feelings of employees and customers and thus the emotional climate (Ornstein, 1986; Takahashi, 1995). Architecture, layout, décor and music can be purposely designed to create a particular atmosphere in line with the organization's primary and overt goals. Thus in George Orwell's 1984 we observe the stark and forbidding architectural form of the 'Ministry of Truth' building, designed to instil fear and obedience across society (Orwell, 1949). In contrast, the dome and main chamber of Germany's *Reichstag* with its internal spiralling public staircase demonstrates in both form and function the shared ownership and transparency of a modern democracy. Likewise paintings or symbolic objects or aesthetic symbols serve as emotional cues and exert an influence on emotions and a corresponding climate (Seago, 1996; Wasserman, Rafaeli & Kluger, 2000). Music is believed by many to improve mood during work (Oldham, Cummings, Mischel, Schmidtke & Zhou, 1995). The clothing employees wear acts to symbolize social identities and power, whilst simultaneously serving the communication of values (Pratt & Rafaeli, 1997). The symbolic effects of the physical setting on climate may be potent as they are subtle and pervasive, with the work environment shaping interaction and evoking inferences and expectations (Ashforth, 1985).

The nature of objectively conceived, purposeful design achieves a simple cause and effect relationship between artefacts and members' attitudes and behaviour. At an abstract, but no less important level, the organizational structure with its levels of hierarchies and functions is also a form of objective design; but in this case it is the owners or managers who are its architects. The bureaucratic organizational structure was designed for efficiency through control and division of labour, a concept that has a role within organizations that require standardized outputs such as government departments. Yet how often are aspects of the bureaucratic structure to be seen in organizations that deal with complex outputs and where creativity and spontaneity are acclaimed and required from its workers? An outcome from this mixing of forms is confusion among the workforce as they ask themselves what the organization stands for and how its members are expected to relate to each other. This confusion represents the subjective nature of climate whereby individuals attempt to make sense of what they perceive.

The subjective view of climate

Organizational climate consists of empirically accessible elements such as perceptual, behavioural and attitudinal characteristics (Moran & Volkwein, 1992) and communication practices (Poole, 1985). Accordingly the study of climate has seen a shift in direction from focusing on organizational characteristics to emphasizing individual's perception and sense-making (Schneider & Rentsch, 1988). In reflecting this subjective interpretation, Schneider and Reichers (1993) define climate as 'the influence of work contexts on employee behaviour and attitudes, which are grounded in perceptions' whereas Reichers and Schneider (1990) represented climate as the 'shared perceptions of organisational policies, practices, and procedures, both formal and informal' (p. 22). Jones and James (1979) suggested that the term 'psychological climate' be used to emphasize the aggregated cognitive interpretations of an organizational work-force which arise from experience in the organization and provide a representation of the meaning inherent in the organizational features, events and processes (Kozlowski & Farr, 1988) and, "on a day-to-day basis" (Schneider, Gunnarson & Niles Jolly, 1994).

The combination of symbolic interactions and role behaviours (Petti-grew, 1990; Schneider, 1990; Schneider & Reichers, 1983) renders a clim-ate relatively stable whilst open to change, as well as being collectively influential (Woodman & King, 1978). Furthermore an organizational climate provides guidance for interpreting members' intentions (Falcione, Sussmann & Herden, 1987; Küpers & Weibler, 2008). Climate should not be thought of as a homogeneous organizational entity. Sub climates will form – representing differing perceptions among diverse individuals, groups, departments or other forms of business units (Powell & Butterfield, 1978).

We now turn our attention to two *types* of organizational climate: emotional and ethical. We then detail the final element in the triad – the enactment of workplace relationships.

Emotional and ethical climates

Two important conceptions of organizational climate, the emotional and the ethical, are now explored to demonstrate the complex influence of atmospheric and climate-related dimensions on peer relationships and vice-versa. As we will see, emotional and ethical climates are both of par-ticular significance in terms of their effect on the quality of relationships in organizations.

Emotional climate

As outlined earlier, organizational climate influences the relationship between people, structures and situations in various ways. An organ-ization's emotional climate is perhaps most reflective of the members' feelings and attitudes, both in relation to each other and towards the organization itself. This 'emotional ecology' is created in organizations so that care, human connection and compassion can be enabled or disabled (Frost, Dutton, Worline & Wilson, 2000).

From a phenomenological perspective, the atmosphere is described as a sensual and emotional life-world (Küpers & Weibler, 2008). Accordingly, it makes a difference whether the atmosphere of an organization is filled with anger, dread, anxiety or even despair, or with joy, exuberance, excite-ment and hope. When walking around in an organization one often senses a 'feeling in the air' that provides a flavour of the place. Similarly, specific feelings like shame, embarrassment or fear will impact relationships very differently than feelings of pride and friendliness.

The emotional climate is relatively unstable and subject to change to the extent that even one individual's behaviour can have a major influence. In their study into the effects of negative relations on workplace atmosphere (Felps, Mitchell & Byington, 2006) when a coworker, described as 'particularly caustic' and 'always making fun of other people' was away ill for several days, the atmosphere of the office changed dramatically. People started helping each other, playing classical music on their radios and going out for drinks after work. But when this person returned to the office, things returned to the unpleasant way they were. Prior to the illness this employee was not considered as being very influential in the office and it was only on his return to work that his profound and negative impact was understood. He truly was the 'bad apple' that spoiled the barrel. Companies need to move quickly to deal with such problems because the negativity of just one individual is pervasive and destructive and can spread quickly, due to emotional contagion (Hatfield, Cacioppo & Rapson, 1992). The study by Felps et al. (2006) identified three ways in which group members may react to a negative member. The first step is to express concern and to ask the person to change his or her behaviour. If this proves unsuccessful, the individual may be removed from the environment. These strategies require team members to have sufficient power, as a lack of power leads people to become frustrated and distracted. A third strategy, defensiveness, results from team members' lack of power. Common coping mechanisms include denial, social withdrawal, anger, anxiety and fear. Felps et al. explain that, as trust weakens and the positive climate wanes, members disengage themselves physically and psychologically from the team. The study concluded that negative behaviour has a greater impact than positive behaviour. The contagious effect of one 'bad apple' means that unethical or deviant behaviours need to be nipped in the bud at the group-level before they exert a significant influence on the rest of the workforce (Frost & Robinson, 1999; Robinson & O'Leary-Kelly, 1998). This preventative role can be undertaken by an appointed "toxic handler" who deals with staff members' frustration and anger (Frost & Robinson, 1999).

Emotions may serve as a medium for expressing and identifying the nature of a climate such as 'productive', 'satisfying' or 'de-motivating' (Jones & James, 1979; Pettigrew, 1990). Importantly the emotional climate is constructed as a dynamic process between the involved parties, depending on their responses to each other. Tendencies to perceive a specific climate are strengthened or weakened by organizational context variables such as warmth, level of support and tolerance of conflict (Litwin & Stringer, 1968). Mano and Gabriel (2006) describe a climate that discourages friendly or even romantic attachments as 'cold'. By contrast, a 'hot' climate provides more hospitable surroundings for the burgeoning of romance among organizational members and will involve ongoing narrative practices such as rumour and gossip. Between both types of climates, they proposed a 'temperate' climate, which allows for pockets or margins in which romantic attachments may prosper.

Climate can be likened to the organization's mood; positive moods can lead to unrealistic optimism or self-contented attitudes whereas negative moods can contribute to a more realistic perception or analytical attitudes (Alloy & Abramson, 1982; Schwarz & Bohner, 1996). Positive or negative moods may have wider behavioural influences (Isen & Baron, 1991) such as absenteeism (George, 1989), job-(dis)satisfaction (Connolly & Viswesvaran, 2000), 'pro-social' occupational citizenship behaviour (Williams & Shiaw, 1999) and cooperative group processes (George, 1991; George & Brief, 1992). Further influences affect levels of creativity (Lofy, 1998) and performance and productivity (Wright & Staw, 1999). As such, a positive climate creates "a specific atmosphere and organizational dynamic... contributing to the generation of innovative ideas, the readiness for change and is imperative for facilitating learning processes in organizations" (Tran, 1998, p. 101).

Furthermore, emotions can also be manipulated to serve vested interests or to maintain power relations, and in doing so may maintain stifling or unhelpful ideologies (Cameron, Mulligan & Wheatley, 2004). In other words, emotions can be powerful agents of social control (Lewis & Zare, 1999) and coercion in political action within omnipresent organizational micro-hierarchies. As a kind of productive power, emotions and their management can thus become a key micro-political instrument, used either to energize or de-energize (Downing, 1997). Negative affectivity (Watson, Clark & Tellegen, 1988) and dysfunctional emotional expressions and behaviours can result in poor work performance and disturbed relations with colleagues.

In more extreme situations, negative emotional states can lead to oppositional practices (Collinson, 1994) and organizational retaliatory or anti-citizenship behaviours. These dysfunctional, anti-social (Folger & Cropanzano, 1998) and recalcitrant behaviours include sabotage, absenteeism, disobedience and decreased productivity (Ackroyd & Thompson, 1999). Climates where mobbing, bullying, incivility and distrust, stifled innovation and reduced creativity are present, rendering the organization passive and debilitated, undermining the best intentions and change initiatives, as well as incurring significant costs (Ostell, 1996). Organizations create an emotional ecology where care and human connection are enabled or disabled. Emotional ecology can facilitate or retard compassionate action (Frost et al., 2000). Many factors influence either a supportive or alienating emotional climate. Some of these factors include an environment characterized by high versus low levels of trust; optimism versus cynicism and fear; acceptance versus threat and judgment; cooperation and mutual problem solving versus coercion and destructive competition; authenticity versus deception and hidden agenda; empathy and warmth versus cold detachment; valuing and respecting versus humiliating others; democracy versus authoritarianism; appreciation of diversity and divergent views versus intolerance; encouragement for experimentation versus blame for failure; engendering versus stifling creativity and innovation; motivating versus de-motivating; and empowering versus disempowering. The emotional climate triggers self-reinforcing behaviour cycles, with stark differences between behaviour patterns engendered in supportive versus alienating emotional climates. In supportive emotional climates reinforced behaviours include: ethical conduct and practice; open communication; cooperative team building; willing sharing of knowledge and resources; authentic/emotionally honest patterns of behaving and relating to others; care and concern for others; a focus on action and goal achievement, active experimentation and exploring creative solutions; assertive communication and constructive negotiation. In contrast, negative emotional climates engender active politicking – manipulative, deceitful and intimidating patterns of behaviour and unethical practices. Individual effort is focused on enhancing personal position and influence in a fiercely competitive environment, rather than on achieving organizational performance goals. Inevitably this process of personal aggrandizement involves undermining and destroying the perceived competition, assigning blame and discrediting others whilst concealing one's own agenda and mistakes. In the resultant 'survival-of-the-fittest' battleground, sabotage, retaliation, aggressive, abusive and threatening behaviour patterns, intimidating and deceptive practices are rife. To survive in this hostile climate, people engage in a variety of self-protective behaviours. Trust vanishes and fear reigns supreme.

Emotions do not always lead to obvious outcomes. For example, disproportionately displayed pride about an achievement might elicit envy in other colleagues (Lazarus & Cohen-Charash, 2001), or too much joy may actually distract people and hinder task completion (Morrison & Nolan, 2007; Parrot & Spackman, 2000). Furthermore the emotional involvement that comes with close bonding by a warm social climate of employees-as-family members (Céleste & Lee, 2007); one which invokes "pre-industrial romantic images of kinship bonding and shared struggles against adversity" (Casey, 1999, p. 162), can also generate ambivalent effects, for example, either intense commitment or alienation (Casey, 1999) and may be misused by manipulating employees' attachment to organizations (Illes & Ritchie, 1999).

Ethical climate

The ethical climate of an organization may be considered as a shared set of values and an understanding about what constitutes correct behaviour and how ethical issues will be handled. Formally defined, ethical behaviour is that which is morally accepted as 'good' and 'right' as opposed to 'bad' or 'wrong' in a particular setting. The ethical climate sets the tone for decision-making and also for behaviour at all levels and in various organizational circumstances. Recent corporate scandals and frauds such as Enron, WorldCom and Tyco, among many others, showed the dangers of unethical business practices which also have extensive impacts on peer relationships.

A broad scope of factors has been found to influence the ethical climate in an organization (Neubert, 1999). These include personal self-interest and morality, group behaviours to profit-orientation, rewarding practices, social responsibility, rules, laws and professional codes (Sims, 1992) and also the operational environment and event history (Baucus & Near, 1991). According to Victor and Cullen (1988) an ethical climate is based upon three categories of moral judgement: *egoistic*, *benevolent* and *principled*. While egoism strives for the maximising of one's own interest, benevolence aims for maximising the interests of as many people as possible and a principled orientation refers to the adherence to universal standards and beliefs (Victor & Cullen, 1988). The following different ethical climates have been identified:

(1) *Professional*. Workers follow the rules and guidelines set out by their professional order, or the laws set out by the government. They look outside the organization for cues concerning how to behave ethically.
(2) *Caring*. In a caring climate, employees within the organization are genuinely interested in the welfare of others, both within and outside their organizations. The actions of a group demonstrating this

climate would show a concern for all those affected by their decisions.

(3) *Rules.* In the rules climate, employees are expected to strictly follow the rules of their department or organization.

(4) *Instrumental.* In the instrumental climate, members of an organization look out for their own self-interests, often at the expense of others.

(5) *Efficiency.* In this climate, the right way to do things within the organization is the most efficient.

(6) *Independence.* In the independence climate, employees are strongly guided by their own sense of right and wrong.

For Victor and Cullen (1987), a given type of climate may be more prone to particular ethical behaviour potentials or problems. For example, employees in a caring climate, who feel that their organization is concerned with their welfare, will probably be less likely to experience or engage in unethical behaviour (Despande, 1996). By contrast, individuals working in an instrumental climate were more likely to engage in far-reaching deviant workplace behaviour (Appelbaum & Lay, 2005) and unethical behaviour in general (Wimbush, Shepard & Markham, 1997) e.g., lying, spreading rumours, gossiping, withholding effort or anti-social types of behaviour, including sexual harassment, verbal abuse, blaming, stealing from or endangering co-workers and also competing or showing favouritism. Such behaviour is, not surprisingly, likely to have a significant negative influence on relationships with co-workers, and supervisors (Despande, 1996).

Sims (1992) also proposes a *principled* climate; one where an organization describes its goals in terms of abstract principles independent of situational outcomes. For example, a 'bottom-line mentality' emphasizes the principle of financial success, possibly at the expense of other values. By this it is 'promoting short-term solutions that are financially sound, despite the fact that they cause problems for others within the organization or the organization as a whole' (Sims, 1992, p. 92), interpreting ethics as an obstacle to profit. In a 'rules' climate, employees are expected to strictly follow the rules of their department or organization. Rules can be both internally or externally set and sanctioned (Victor and Cullen, 1987). These climates can be further differentiated at individual and local levels. In an egoistic-individual ethical climate, people protect their own interests above other considerations. Correspondingly in an egoistic-local ethical climate, people are expected to do anything to further the company's interest. In a benevolent-individual ethical climate, people look out for each other's good, while in a benevolent-local ethical climate the major consideration is what is best for everyone in the organization. In the principled-individual ethical climate people expect to be given the independence to follow their one personal and moral belief whereas in a principled-local ethical climate it is important to follow strictly the company's rules and procedures.

Enacting workplace relationships

Relationships are governed by the covert cognitive and affective responses and overt behavioural events that occur when people interact (Adams & Blieszner, 1994; Blieszner & Adams, 1992). Experiences of emotional climates trigger self-reinforcing behaviour cycles, with stark differences between behaviour patterns engendered in supportive and alienating climates. These multiple factors are categorized in Table 4.1 in terms of cognitive, affective and behavioural domains to demonstrate the dynamic between perception of climate and human activity in the workplace. *Cognitive* processes reflect the internal thoughts of each partner (about herself, her partner, the friendship etc). These include interpretations of behaviour, assessments of the stability of the relationship, and evaluations of the attractiveness, value, character and similarity to oneself of the other person. *Affective* processes are the emotional reactions to others; these may be positive (affection, trust, loyalty, commitment, joy) or negative (anger, hostility, jealousy). *Behavioural* processes are the action components of relationships and include communication/disclosure, displays of affection, resource exchange, cooperation and the sharing of activities. Negative behaviours can include concealment, manipulation, conflict and competition (Adams & Blieszner, 1994; Blieszner & Adams, 1992).

The two columns in Table 4.1 represent the positive and negative sides of human relational activities caused by and causative of, emotional and ethical workplace climates.

Table 4.1 and the chapter so far support a clear link between workplace climate and employee behaviour. Our discussion demonstrates that a climate which is perceived to be supportive will engender open and honest behaviours, whilst a climate perceived to be negative will encourage closed, protective behaviours with the possibility of unethical practices. Logically, therefore, the symbiotic nature of behaviour and climate means that endless iterations will occur to reinforce a prevailing climate unless and until an intervention occurs to disrupt this process.

Table 4.1   Cognitive, affective and behavioural outcomes of supportive compared to negative organizational climates

Supportive Climate *perceived as being...*	Negative Climate *perceived as being...*
Democratic	Authoritarian
Cohesive	Individualist

Cognitive Processes

High levels of trust	Low levels of trust, cynicism hidden agendas
Optimism	Pessimism
Acceptance of others	Threatening, judgmental
Appreciation of diversity and divergent views	Intolerance

Affective Processes

Serenity	Fear
Cooperation and mutual problem solving	Coercion and destructive competition
Empathy and warmth, care and concern for others	Cold detachment
Pride	Humiliation, embarrassment
Empowered	Disempowered
Motivating	De-motivating
Relaxed	Stressed
Commitment	Alienation

Behavioural Factors

Experimentation, creativity and innovation	Blame, risk-averse, concealing mistakes
Valuing and respecting others	Humiliating people, undermining, destroying perceived competitors
Authenticity/emotionally honest patterns of behaving and relating to others	Deception and active politicking
Assertive communication	Assigning blame and discrediting others
Constructive negotiation	
Focus on action and goal achievement	Self-protective behaviours
Ethical conduct and practice	Unethical practices – stealing, sabotage, retaliation, aggressive, abusive and threatening behaviour patterns
Willingness to share knowledge and resources	'Knowledge is power' and 'survival-of-the-fittest' mentality

Creating an organizational climate that promotes commitment, enthusiasm, morale, loyalty and attachment requires managers (and organizations) to simultaneously motivate workers while, above all, *decreasing barriers to motivation* (Küpers & Statler, 2008; Wunderer & Küpers, 2003), which may be present in some styles of management (Zeffane, 1994) and organizational conditions. Therefore it is important to identify those domains of an organizational climate that could de-motivate workers and thus produce negative attitudes and effects.

The climate of an organization can be cultivated by developing an integral organizational and leadership practice (Küpers & Edwards, 2008). As a diagnostic tool an understanding of an organizational climate can help in identifying those domains that require alteration or modification to advance the correspondence (fit) between needs and particularities of employees and groups, and the requirements of the organization.

Implications of emotional climate on relationships

Developing emotional intelligence at the group level is one factor that can support an effective emotional climate (Druskat & Wolff, 2001). More importantly, a change in leadership styles or administrative policies is likely to have a large impact upon the state of the emotional climate (De Rivera, 1992) as misalignments between leadership style and climate can be problematic for organizational performance (Haakonsson, Burton, Obel & Lauridsen, 2008).

Interventions that strengthen an organization's ethical climate may help manage ethical behaviour within organizations (Bartels, Harrick, Martell & Strickland, 1988). Furthermore, different systems and reward structures can assist in fostering an ethical climate i.e., promoting good behaviour and ethical values like honesty integrity, fidelity, fairness, caring, respect and accountability at all levels within the organization.

Sims (1992) provides a comprehensive set of recommendations on ethical practices for organizations. For example, internal regulation may involve the use of codes of corporate ethics, and the availability of appeals processes. As many situations have no simple solution (Cooke & Slack, 1991) it is important to provide for diversity and dissent. Grievance or complaint mechanisms or other internal review procedures should be established to tolerate whistle-blowing and the voicing of ethical concerns (Harrington, 1991). Graham (1986) called this provision "principled organizational dissent": the effort by individuals in the organization to protest the status quo because of their objection to some practice or policy on ethical grounds. Principled organizational dissent does not seek to punish dissenting voices and is an important concept linking organizational culture to ethical behaviour. Drake (1988) suggests the introduction of ethics training programmes for all employees to explain the underlying ethical and legal principles and present practical aspects of carrying out procedural guidelines.

As previously stated, an organization's emotional climate is perhaps most reflective of the members' feelings and attitudes, both in relation to each other and towards the organization itself. These feelings and attitudes are manifest in patterns of behaviour, which can be either positively or negatively oriented towards performance. Thus when high levels of trust exist in the workplace, communication is likely to be informal, supportive and imbued with a sense of fun. Ideas and information are likely to be shared more openly as the level of perceived risk reduces. Guidance and mentoring will increase levels of self-esteem and capability. Collaboration, team working and genuine friendship are more likely to occur naturally within such an environment (Morrison & Nolan, 2007).

Implications for the management of relationships

The literature largely advocates management *action* in fashioning an organizational climate to maximize performance and capability. However, our contention is for managers to adopt an indirect approach towards organizational climate by proposing a type of management *inaction*. The starting point for this approach is for managers to consider the organization as being *alive*, i.e. consisting of people engaged in purposeful activities that are directed towards multiple goals (Senge, 1997). This notion of a living system is in contrast to the view that business organizations exist only as economic entities in which control is exercised through formal procedures and instructions for guiding the rational activities of its members. The informal structures, by contrast, are 'fluid and fluctuating networks of communication' (Capra, 2003, p. 96) – a typology that has been greatly enhanced by the emergence of 'virtual organizations' linked by information and communication technologies. By adopting the broader view; that organizations are a combination of economic and social systems, is to give credence to the individual, human, emotional and creative characteristics and capacities that are endemic within.

Merely recognizing the interaction between the economic and social functions of the organization does not go far enough. As Capra (2003) points out, a living system is organized as a network and will contain smaller networks within its boundary. It is within these networks that people operate and create meaning for themselves and for their work.

Interpersonal relationships are embedded in social networks that exist within formal boundaries; informally and ethereally (i.e. online) thus making them difficult to identify (Wenger, 1998). It is at this network – and sub-network – level that managers should engage, for it is here that climate and relationships co-exist and co-create themselves. By considering an organization as a network of vivid (emotional and ethical) lifeworlds, we suggest that attempts at directly managing climate may prove to be futile, and that an indirect approach is more appropriate; a theme we develop below.

Sustaining relationships – Cultivating a 'wise' atmosphere

Managing a climate indirectly requires the creation of a 'wisdom atmosphere' (Meacham, 1990) or 'culture of wisdom' (Jones, 2005, p. 370) as a means of promoting an emotionally sensitive and ethical climate where positive relationships can develop. The notion of a 'wise climate' is founded on the basis that emotions are constructed in the social context (Frijda & Mesquita, 1994) of an organization. Indeed, as Babad and Wallbott (1986) noted, by concentrating many people within a bounded context, organizations magnify the impact of emotions on behaviour. In practical terms, members are supported in their interpersonal relationships such that they '...may safely discover and reveal the limitations of, and doubts regarding, what they know...' (Meacham, 1990, p. 209). This means that members may share with confidence their limited knowledge without being exposed to the scepticism of others.

Wise climates should be incorporated into both the formal and informal organizational systems if they are to facilitate ethical and wise conduct (Treviño, Butterfield & McCabe, 1988; Victor & Cullen, 1988). A wisdom orientation has far-reaching consequences for a more integral organizational development (Küpers & Statler, 2008), but also for leadership education, development and learning (Statler, 2005). The implications for managers is that they should behave towards their workers in ways that have a positive effect on emotions such as helpfulness, friendliness, supportiveness, giving recognition, courtesy and warmth (McNamee & Gergen, 1999). Further attitudes and skills which should be fostered include optimism, self-regulation and conflict management (Härtel, Gough & Härtel, 2008).

Conclusion and afterword

This chapter has treated organizational climate as a comprehensive and integral concept; as a *relational and atmospheric event*, which influences and is being influenced by, peer work relationships. Consequently the discussion has been handled in an integrated fashion so as to reinforce the immediate and simultaneous nature of this nexus. As we have seen, climates are connected to perceptions. Individual and social perceptions are transferred via affective attitude formation into modes of behaviour; principally directed towards other workers. The nature of relationships therefore sets the mood of a climate within the organization. Climate exists as a perceived state of the organizational life-world and is therefore constantly vulnerable to perturbations and remains in a constant state of flux. Human relationships, indeed human life itself, are embedded within atmospheres. As human beings we are at home, dwelling within organizations as life-worlds, forming a part of the larger environmental ecology. The integral nature this relationship extends even to the phenomenon of global climate change. Tremendous and far-reaching repercussions may result from our harmful treatment of the environment – the atmosphere – in which we are embedded. Thus by reflecting on the role of atmospheres and by cultivating wise emotional and ethical organizational climates a more sustainable way of living can be had. Therefore it is important to recognize the inseparable link between the micro-climate of peer relationships in organizations and in society at large (Küpers, 2005). This integral understanding may lead to more proactive strategies for corporate social responsibility and corporate citizenship as part of sustainable business strategy and civic organizational practice.

References

Ackroyd, S. & Thompson, P. (1999). *Organisational Misbehaviour: Sage.*

Adams, R. G. & Blieszner, R. (1994). An integrative conceptual framework for friendship research. *Journal of Social and Personal Relationships, 11*, 163–184.

Alloy, L. B. & Abramson, L. T. (1982). Learned helplessness, depression, and the illusion of control. *Journal of Personality and Social Psychology, 42*, 1114–1126.

Appelbaum, S. H., Deguire, K. J. & Lay, M. (2005). The relationship of ethical climate to deviant workplace behaviour. *Corporate Governance, 5*(4), 43–56.

Ashforth, B. E. (1985). Climate formation: issues and extensions. *Academy of Management Review, 10*(4), 837–847.

Babad, E. Y. & Wallbott, H. G. (1986). The effects of social factors on emotional reactions. In K. R. Scherer, H. G. Wallbott & A. B. Summerfield (eds), Experiencing emotion: A cross cultural study. Cambridge: Cambridge University Press.

Bartels, K. K., Harrick, E., Martell, K. & Strickland, D. (1988). The relationship between ethical climate and ethical problems within human resource management. *Journal of Business Ethics, 17*(7), 799–804.

Baucus, M. S. & Near, J. P. (1991). Can illegal corporate behaviour be predicted? An event history analysis. *Academy of Management Journal, 34*(10), 9–36.

Blieszner, R. & Adams, R. (1992). *Adult Friendship*. Newbury Park, CA: Sage.

Burke, W. (1994). *Organization Development: A Process of Learning and Changing*. Reading, Mass.: Addison-Wesley.

Cameron, J., Mulligan, M. & Wheatley, V. (2004). Building a place-responsive society through inclusive local projects and networks. *Local Environment, 9,* 147–161.

Capra, F. (2003). *The Hidden Connections*. London: Flamingo.

Casey, C. (1999). Come, join our family: Discipline and integration in corporate organisational culture. *Human Relations, 52,* 155–178.

Céleste, M. & Lee, R. T. (2007). We are family: Congruity between organisational and family functioning constructs. *Human Relations, 60*(12), 1873–1888.

Collins, J. (2001). *Good to Great*. London: Random House.

Collinson, D. (1994). Naming men as men: Implications for work organization and management. *Gender, Work, and Organisation, 1*(1), 2.

Connolly, J. J. & Viswesvaran, C. (2000). The role of affectivity in job satisfaction: A meta-analysis. *Personality & Individual Differences, 29,* 265–281.

Cooke, S. & Slack, N. (1991). *Making Management Decisions*. London: Prentice-Hall.

Dandridge, T. C., Mitroff, I. & Joyce, W. F. (1980). Organisational symbolism: A topic to expand organizational analysis. *Academy of Management Review, 5*(1), 77–82.

De Rivera, J. (1992). Emotional climate: Social structure and emotional dynamics. In K. T. Strongman (ed.), *International Review of Studies on Emotion* (Vol. 2, pp. 197–218). New York: John Wiley & Sons.

Denison, D. R. (1996). What is the difference between organisational culture and organizational climate? A native's point of view on a decade of paradigm wars. *The Academy of Management Review, 21*(3), 619–654.

Despande, S. P. (1996). Ethical climate and the link between success and ethical behaviour: An empirical investigation of a non-profit organisation. *Journal of Business Ethics, 15,* 315–320.

Downing, S. J. (1997). Learning the plot: Emotional momentum in search of dramatic logic. *Management Learning, 28,* 1.

Drake, D. (1988). *Problems of Conduct: An Introductory Survey of Ethics*: Questia. Online.

Druskat, V. U. & Wolff, S. B. (2001). Group emotional competence and its influence on group effectiveness. In C. C. a. D. Goleman (ed.), *The Emotionally Intelligent Workplace* (pp. 132–155). San Francisco: Jossey-Bass.

Falcione, R. L. Sussmann, L. & Herden, R. P. (1987). Communication climate in organizations. In F. M. Jablin, L. L. Putman, R. K. H. & P. L. W. (eds), *Handbook of Organisational* Communication (pp. 195–227). London.

Felps, W., Mitchell, T. R. & Byington, E. (2006). *How, When, and Why Bad Apples Spoil the Barrel: Negative Group Members and Dysfunctional Groups Research in Organisational Behaviour, 27.*

Folger, R. G. & Cropanzano, R. (1998). *Organisational Justice and Human Resource Management*. Thousand Oaks, California: Sage Publications.

Forehand, G. A. & Von Haller, G. (1964). Environmental variations in studies of organisational behaviour. *Psychological Bulletin, 62,* 362–381.

Frijda, N. H. & Mesquita, B. (1994). The social roles and functions of emotions. In S. K. H. R. Markus (ed.), *Emotion and Culture: Empirical Studies of*

Mutual Influence (pp. 51–87). Washington, DC: American Psychological Association.

Frost, P. & Robinson, S. (1999). The toxic handler: Organisational hero – and casualty. *Harvard Business Review, 77*(4), 96–106.

Frost, P. J., Dutton, J. E., Worline, M. C. & Wilson, A. (2000). Narratives of compassion in organisations. In S. Fineman (ed.), *Emotion in Organisations 2nd ed* (pp. 22–45). London: Thousand Oaks, Sage.

George, J. M. (1989). Mood and absence. *Journal of Applied Psychology, 74*(Summer), 317–324.

George, J. M. (1991). State or trait: effects of positive mood on prosocial behaviours at work. *Journal of Applied Psychology, 76*(Summer), 299–307.

George, J. M. & Brief, A. P. (1992). Feeling good-doing good: A conceptual analysis of the mood at work-organisational spontaneity relationship. *Psychological Bulletin, 112*, 310–329.

Graham, J. W. (1986). Principal organizational dissent: A theoretical essay. *Research in Organisational Behavior, 8*, 1–52.

Haakonsson, D., Burton, R. M., Obel, B. & Lauridsen, J. (2008). How failure to align organisational climate and leadership style affects performance. *Management Decision, 46*(3), 406–432.

Harrington, H. J. (1991). *Business Process Improvement the Breakthrough Strategy for Total Quality, Productivity, and Competitiveness: The Breakthrough Strategy for Total Quality, Productivity, and Competitiveness.* New York: McGraw-Hill Professional.

Härtel, C. E. J., Gough, H. & Härtel, G. F. (2008). Work-group emotional climate, emotion management skills, and service attitudes and performance. *Asia Pacific Journal of Human Resources, 46*(1), 21–37.

Hatfield, E., Cacioppo, J. T. & Rapson, R. L. (1992). *Emotional Contagion.* Cambridge: Cambridge University Press.

Hicks-Clark, D. & Iles, P. (2000). Climate for diversity and its effect on career and organisational attitudes and perceptions. *Personnel Revue, 29*, 324–345.

Illes, L. M. & Ritchie, J. B. (1999). Change metaphor: Grappling with the two-headed organizational behemoth. *Journal of Management Inquiry, 8*, 91–100.

Isen, A. M. & Baron, R. A. (1991). Positive affect as a factor in organisational behaviour. *Research in Organisational Behaviour, 13*, 1–53.

Jones, A. & James, L. (1979). Psychological climate: Dimensions of and relationships of individual and aggregated work perception. *Organisation Behaviour and Human Performance, 23*, 201–250.

Jones, A. C. (2005). Wisdom paradigms for the enhancement of ethical and profitable business practices. *Journal of Business Ethics, 5* 57, 363–375.

Kozlowski, S. W. J. & Farr, J. L. (1988). An integrative model of updating and performance. *Human Performance, 1*, 5–29.

Küpers, W. (2005). Phenomenology and integral phenopheno-practice practice of embodied well-be(com)ing in organisations. *Culture and Organisation, 11*(3), 221–231.

Küpers, W. & Edwards, M. (2008). Integrating plurality – towards an integral perspective on leadership and organisation. In C. Wankel (ed.), *Handbook of 21st Century Management* (pp. 311–322). London: Sage.

Küpers, W. & Statler, M. (2008). Practically wise leadership: Toward an integral understanding. *Culture and Organisation,* forthcoming.

Küpers, W. & Weibler, J. (2008). Emotions in organisation – An integral perspective. *International Journal of Emotion and Work, 3*(1).

Lazarus, R. S. & Cohen-Charash, Y. (2001). Discrete emotions in organisational life. In R. L. Payne and C. L. Cooper (eds), *Emotions at Work: Theory, Research and Applications for Management*. Chichester: John Wiley.

Lewis, G. W. & Zare, N. C. (1999). *Workplace Hostility: Myth and Reality, xvi,* 171. Philadelphia, PA, US: Accelerated Development, Inc.

Litwin, G. & Stringer, R. (1968). *Motivation and Organizational Climate.* Boston: Harvard University Press.

Lofy, M. M. (1998). The impact on creativity in organisations. *Empowerment in Organisations, 6*(1), 5–12.

Mano, R. & Gabriel, Y. (2006). Workplace romances in hot and cold organisational climates. *Human Relations, 59*(7).

McNamee, S. & Gergen, K. J. (1999). *Relational Responsibility: Resources for Sustainable Dialogue.* Thousand Oaks: Sage.

Meacham, J. A. (1990). The loss of wisdom. In R. J. Sternberg (ed.), *Wisdom, Its Nature, Origins, and Development* (Vol. 181–212). Cambridge: Cambridge University Press.

Milliken, F. Morrison, E. & Hewlin, P. (2003). An exploratory study of employee silence: Issues that employees don't communicate upward and why. *Journal of Management Studies, 40*(6), 1453–1476.

Moran, E. T. & Volkwein, J. F. (1992). The cultural approach to the formation of organisational climate. *Human Relations, 45*(1), 19–47.

Morrison, R. L. & Nolan, T. (2007). Too much of a good thing? Difficulties with workplace friendships. *University of Auckland Business Review, 9*(2), 33–42.

Neubert, M. J. (1999). Too much of a good thing or the more the merrier? *Small Group Research, 30*(5), 635–647.

Oldham, G. R., Cummings, A., Mischel, L. J., Schmidtke, J. M. & Zhou, J. (1995). Listen while you work? Quasi-experimental relations between personal-stereo headset use and employee work responses. *Journal of Applied Psychology, 80*(5), 547–564.

Ornstein, S. (1986). Organisational symbols: A study of their meanings and influences on perceived psychological climate. *Organisational Behaviour and Human Decision Processes, 38,* 207–229.

Orwell, G. (1949). *Nineteen Eighty-Four.* London: Secker and Warburg.

Ostell, A. (1996). Managing dysfunction emotions in organisation. *Journal of Management Studies, 33*(4), 525–557.

Pareek, U. (1989). Motivational Analysis of Organisations – Climate (MAO-C). In J. W. Pfeifer (ed.), *The 1989 Annual: Developing Human Resources* (pp. 161–180). San Diego: California: University Associates.

Parrot, W. G. & Spackman, M. P. (2000). Emotion and memory. In M. Lewis & J. M. Haviland-Jones (eds), *Handbook of Emotions* (2nd ed., pp. 476–490). New York, NY: The Guilford Press.

Pettigrew, A. (1990). Organisational climate and cultures: Two constructs in search of a role. In B. Schneider (ed.), *Organisational Climate and Culture* (pp. 413–433). San Francisco, CA: Jossey-Bass.

Poole, M. S. (1985). Communication and organisational climates: Review, critique, and a new perspective. In McPhee & P. K. Tompkins (eds), *Organisational*

Communication: Traditional Themes and New Directions (Vol. 79–108). London: Sage.

Powell, G. N. & Butterfield, D. A. (1978). The case for subsystem climates in organisations. *Academy of Management Review, 3*, 151–157.

Pratt, M. G. & Rafaeli, A. (1997). Organisational dress as a symbol of multi-layered social identities. *Academy of Management Journal, 40*, 862–898.

Reichers, A. E. & Schneider, B. (1990). Climate and culture: An evolution of constructs. In B. Schneider (ed.), *Organisational Climate and Culture* (pp. 5–39). San Francisco: Jossey-Bass.

Robinson, S. & O'Leary-Kelly, A. (1998). Monkey see, monkey do: The influence of work groups on the antisocial behaviour of employees. *Academy of Management Journal, 658–672*.

Schein, E. H. (1985). *Organisational Culture and Leadership: A Dynamic View.* San Francisco: Jossey-Bass.

Schneider, B. (1990). *Organisational Climate and Culture.* San Francisco: Jossey-Bass.

Schneider, B., Gunnarson, S. K. & Niles Jolly, K. (1994). Creating the climate and culture of success. *Organisational Dynamics, 23*(1), 17–29.

Schneider, B. & Reichers, A. (1993). On the etimology of climates. *Personal Psychology, 28*, 447–479.

Schneider, B. & Reichers, A. E. (1983). On the etiology of climates. *Personnel Psychology, 36*(1), 19–39.

Schneider, B. & Rentsch, J. (1988). Managing climates and cultures: A futures perspective. In J. Hage (ed.), *The Futures of Organisations* (pp. 181–200). Lexington, MA: Lexington Books.

Schwarz, N. & Bohner, G. (1996). Feelings and their motivational implications. Moods and the action sequence. In P. M. Gollwitzer & J. A. Bargh (eds), *The Psychology of Action. Linking Cognition and Motivation to Behaviour* (pp. 119–145). New York.

Seago, J. A. (1996). *Work Group Culture, Workplace Stress, and Hostility: Correlations with Absenteeism and Turnover in Hospital Nurses.* Seago, Jean Ann: U California, San Francisco, US.

Senge, P. M. (1997). *The Living Company.* In A. De Geus (ed.). Boston: Harvard Business School Press.

Sims, R. (1992). The challenge of ethical behaviour in organisations. *Journal of Business Ethics, 11*, 505–513.

Statler, M. (2005). Practical wisdom and serious play: Reflections on management understanding. In H. Schrat (ed.), *Sophisticated Survival Techniques/Strategies in Art and Economy* (pp. 399–412). Berlin: Kulturverlag Kadmos.

Stringer, R. (2001). *Leadership and Organisational Climate.* London: Prentice Hall.

Takahashi, S. (1995). Aesthetic properties of pictorial perceptions. *Psychological Review, 102*(4), 671–683.

Tran, V. (1998). *The Role of the Emotional Climate in Learning Organisations.* Paper presented at the ECLO (European Consortium for the Learning Organisation).

Treviño, L. K., Butterfield, K. & McCabe, D. (1988). The ethical context in organisations: Influences on employee attitudes and behaviours. *Business Ethics Quarterly, 8*, 447–476.

Turnipseed, D. (1988). An integrated, interactive model of organisational climate, culture, and effectiveness. *Leadership and Organisation Development Journal, 9,* 17–21.

Victor, B. & Cullen, J. B. (1987). A theory and measure of ethical climate in organisations. In W. C. a. P. Frederick, L. (ed.), *Research in Corporate Social Performance and Policy* (Vol. 9, pp. 51–71). Greenwich, CT: JAI Press Inc.

Victor, B. & Cullen, J. B. (1988). The organisational bases of ethical work climates. *Administrative Science Quarterly, 33*(1), 101–125.

Wasserman, V., Rafaeli, A. & Kluger, A. N. (2000). Aesthetic symbols as emotional cues. In S. Fineman (ed.), *Emotion in Organisations* (pp. 140–166). London: Sage.

Watson, D., Clark, L. A. & Tellegen, A. (1988). Development and validation of brief measures of positive and negative affect: The PANAS scales. *Journal of Personality and Social Psychology, 54*(6), 1063–1070.

Wenger, E. (1998). *Communities of Practice.* Cambridge: Cambridge University Press.

Williams, S. J. & Shiaw, W. T. (1999). Mood and organisational citizenship behaviour: The effects of positive affect on employee organisational citizenship behaviour intentions. *Journal of Psychology, 133*(6), 656–668.

Wimbush, J. C., Shepard, J. M. & Markham, S. E. (1997). An empirical examination of the relationship between ethical climate and ethical behaviour from multiple levels of analysis. *Journal of Business Ethics, 16*(16), 1705–1716.

Woodman, R. W. & King, D. C. (1978). Organisational climate science or folklore? *Academy of Management Review, 3*(4), 816–826.

Wright, T. A. & Staw, B. M. (1999). Affect and favorable work outcomes: Two longitudinal tests of the happy-productive worker thesis. *Journal of Organisational Behaviour, 20,* 1–23.

Wunderer, R. & Küpers, W. (2003). *Demotivation Remotivation.* Neuwied: Luchterhand-Kluwer-Wolters.

Zeffane, R. (1994). Patterns of organisational commitment and perceived management style: A comparison of public and private sector employees. *Human Relations, 47,* 977–1010.

5
Developing, Maintaining and Disengaging from Workplace Friendships

Patricia M. Sias and Erin Gallagher

An 'organizational chart' is a document that illustrates the formal reporting lines among different employees and units in an organization. The chart's lines represent formal relationships that typically bear little resemblance to how the organization actually functions. Instead, organizing occurs primarily in the context of *informal* relationships that are invisible in the organizational chart, but exist in the chart's 'white spaces' (Eisenberg & Goodall, 2004). Among the most ubiquitous and powerful of these informal relationships are workplace friendships.

This chapter addresses workplace friendship. Our specific task is to discuss the dynamics of such relationships, focusing on why and how workplace friendships develop, deteriorate, and maintain stability. Given the central role workplace friendships play in organizational processes, these topics have many scholarly and practical implications which we address in the following sections. We approached this task with some trepidation, however, because while existing research provides us with knowledge regarding workplace friendship development and deterioration, workplace friendship maintenance has not been studied and we therefore, know little about such processes. Accordingly, our chapter provides both a glance at the past and a glimpse into the future. Our glance at the past provides a summary of existing research in friendship development and deterioration at work. Our glimpse into the future sets forth a set of propositions that speculate about the factors that might motivate an employee to maintain, rather than disengage from, a workplace friendship and factors that influence the types of tactics an employee will choose in attempting to maintain a workplace friendship.

We turn first to discussion of the characteristics that distinguish workplace friendships from other types of workplace relationships. We then discuss existing research in the areas of friendship development and deterioration. We next address the lack of research on workplace friendship maintenance in the latter part of the chapter and set forth a set of propositions designed as a starting point for future studies of workplace friendship maintenance processes. Finally, we highlight the ways practitioners might use the knowledge generated by such research to benefit employees and the organizations in which they work.

Defining workplace friendship

Friendship is considered by many to be 'a core aspect' of life (Fehr, 1996, p. 1). Nearly everyone has friends in a variety of settings, and the workplace is no exception. Friendships readily develop in a variety of workplace settings and across all levels of the workplace environment (Marks, 1994). In fact, the common occupational interests and experiences co-workers share make the workplace a somewhat natural 'incubator' for personal relationships that extend beyond the professional boundary.

Although workplace friendships share similarities with other types of workplace relationships, they are also characterized by important differences. Workplace friendships are distinct in two primary ways. First, *'friendships are essentially voluntary.* People make and unmake friendships of their own choosing and according to their own standards; outside sources cannot impose friendship on two persons' (Rawlins, 1992, p. 11, emphasis added). Most people do not have the opportunity to choose their co-workers. However, we do choose which of our co-workers we befriend (Sias & Cahill, 1998). Second, *'friendship is a personal relationship* that is privately negotiated between particular individuals. One views a friend as a unique individual' (Rawlins, 1992, p. 11; emphasis added). Compared to other workplace relationships, friendships focus more on the individual and less on his or her organizational role. Communication between friends tends to cover a greater variety of topics and is characterized by greater intimacy than communication between co-workers who are not friends, providing workplace friendships with a *personalistic focus* (Sias & Cahill, 1998).

Benefits of workplace friendship

Employees and organizations reap a variety of benefits from workplace friendships. For the individual, workplace friendships are important sources of social support. Friends support one another by sharing feelings, information, and activities on a continual basis (Sias & Bartoo, 2007). Such support is crucial for helping employees deal with a central component of organizational life – uncertainty. Organizations are characterized by nearly constant uncertainty about one's tasks, abilities, and social relationships (Sias & Wyers, 2001; Teboul, 1994), making uncertainty '…a natural and pervasive aspect of any employee's working life' (Sias, 2005, p. 376). A primary assumption of uncertainty reduction theory is that people are motivated to reduce uncertainty with the goal of increased predictability and control in their lives (Berger & Calabrese, 1975). Social support is very important in helping employees cope with and manage uncertainty. Support from friends helps reduce anxiety and stress regarding an uncertain environment and provides individuals with a greater sense of control (Albrecht & Adelman, 1987). Developing friendships is, therefore, important for all employees, including both veteran employees and new hires who seek social support from others as they negotiate their role in the organization (Nelson & Quick, 1991; see also Chapter 3 in this book). As Albrecht and Adelman (1987) state, 'Support from friends is profoundly linked to our sense of belonging and social integration' (p. 105).

Social support and workplace friendships are associated with job satisfaction and may reduce job stress and anxiety and even discourage employee turnover (Kwesiga & Bell, 2004; Nelson & Quick, 1991), which benefits both the individual and the organization. Kruger, Bernstein and Botman (1995), for example, examined friendship and burnout in teams of employees at a residential facility for troubled youth. The results indicated that friendships among team members were associated with higher levels of personal satisfaction and lower levels of emotional exhaustion. Similarly, trust and emotional support can decrease employee burnout and turnover rates (Kahn, 2001). Kahn (2001) discussed support in the context of 'holding environments' in which employees need help dealing with high levels of anxiety. As Kahn (2001) explains, '… adults who experience strong emotions often need settings in which to safely express and interpret their experiences, that is, to temporarily regress to intentionally nurturing environments' (Kahn, 2001, p. 236). Friends can provide that 'safe' environment and the support and understanding needed to assist someone who is 'floundering in anxiety' which they are unable to handle on their own.

Friendship networks also serve as modes of information sharing and systems for decision-making (Lincoln & Miller, 1979). Rawlins (1992) suggested that friends in the workplace are a necessary element of successful participation and career-building and that there are 'clear advantages for those who cultivate friendly relations with numerous professional associates' (p. 166). Friends are important sources of information and can provide each other with backup. The sharing of information can provide employees with 'technical knowledge and perspective on the organization that better enable them to get their work done' (Kram & Isabella, 1985, p. 117). Similarly, as friendships develop over time, communication encompasses a great variety of topics and types of information (Sias & Cahill, 1998). Sias (2005) found that employees who had friendships with supervisors were considerably better informed than those who did not consider themselves to be friends with their supervisor.

Friendship *networks* also have important benefits for both the individual and the organization. Brass and Burkhardt (1993) found that 'People in central network positions have greater access to, and potential control over, relevant resources such as information' (p. 444). Informal networks can also provide access to mentors, job leads, and other business contacts (Hood & Koberg, 1994). For the organization, friendship networks can help promote organizational change (McGrath & Krackhardt, 2003). Specifically, friendship fosters trust, which is an important element of organizational change because it influences how employees perceive change as well as how they identify with aspects of the organization. The authors explain,

> As one's individual friendship ties are spread more widely throughout the organization, one identifies more with the larger organizational entity and is more willing to engage in cooperative and altruistic behaviors necessary to make the change work for the organization (McGrath & Krackhardt, 2003, p. 326).

As the above indicates, workplace friendships are important entities that provide great benefits to both employees and organizations. They are also voluntary relationships. Thus, how and why employees develop friendships with co-workers is an important issue. In the following section, we discuss the factors and communication processes that contribute to workplace friendship development.

Workplace friendship development

Employees generally have little choice regarding their co-workers. Individuals do, however, choose which of their co-workers to befriend (Sias & Cahill, 1998). This choice is influenced by a variety of factors. In particular, workplace friendship development is motivated by both *personal* and *contextual* factors (Sias & Cahill, 1998). Personal factors are associated with the individuals involved in the relationship. For example, similarity is one of the most important factors that facilitate friendship develop-ment. *Demographic similarity* such as age, gender and ethnicity contribute to friendship development (e.g., Graves & Elsass, 2005; Sias, Smith & Avdeyeva, 2003). Coworkers are often similar in terms of the jobs they perform and hierarchical level within the workplace. However, actual similarity is not always enough to spark the development of a friendship between coworkers. Rather, *perceived similarity* of interests, attitudes and values is more important to the friendship development process (Sias & Cahill, 1998). In addition, Sias and Cahill (1998) also found that *personality* contributed to friendship development. Friends report being attracted to one another's particular personality traits (e.g. being friendly or having a great sense of humour).

Contextual factors stem from the situation surrounding the develop-ment of the friendship. In the workplace, *physical proximity* and frequent exposure to particular individuals facilitate friendship development (Fehr, 1996; Sias & Cahill, 1998). In addition, the extent to which coworkers *share tasks* and work interdependently contributes to the likelihood that a friendship will develop between them. *Work-related problems,* such as dealing with a difficult or unfair supervisor, can bring coworkers closer together and, therefore, contribute to friendship development (Sias & Cahill, 1998). Finally, contextual factors beyond the workplace also con-tribute to friendship development. For example, Sias and Cahill (1998) found that *extra organizational socializing* and *life events* were important to workplace friendship development. Extra-organizational socializing refers to time spent together outside the workplace, such as going out to lunch or for drinks after work. Life events refer to major occurrences in one's personal life, such as divorce or illness.

Like all interpersonal relationships, workplace friendships are consti-tuted in the interaction of the relationship partners (Sias & Cahill, 1998; Sigman, 1995). Thus, communication changes as coworkers develop a friendship. Sias and Cahill (1998) and Sias et al. (2003) found that as coworkers become friends, their conversations become more frequent, increasingly focused on nonwork and personal topics, less cautious, and more intimate.

Workplace friendships tend to experience three primary transitions as they grow closer: co-workers-to-friend, friend-to-close friend, and close friend-to-almost best friend (Sias & Cahill, 1998; Sias, Heath, Perry, Silva & Fix, 2004). It is important to note that not all relationships experience all three transitions. Some never evolve to the very close friend stage, for example. In addition, relationships do not necessarily develop in a linear fashion; rather many experience deterioration from one level to another (as discussed later in this chapter) or move quickly from coworker to close friend, for example. Regardless of a relationship's particular trajectory, however, research indicates that developmental factors, and the communication that accompanies this development, function differently across transitions (Sias & Cahill, 1998; Sias et al., 2004). Table 5.1 summarizes the developmental factors and communication changes associated with these transitions.

Table 5.1 Workplace friendship development

Transition 1 *Acquaintance to Friend*	Transition 2 *Friend to Close Friend*	Transition 3 *Close Friend to 'Almost' Best Friend*
	Developmental Factors	
Physical proximity	Life events	Work-related problems
Shared tasks	Extra-organizational	Life events
Similarity	socializing	Extra-organizational
Personality	Work-related problems	socializing
	Communication Processes	
Increased frequency	Increased intimacy	Increased discussion of work-related problems
Increased discussion of non-work topics	Increased discussion of work-related problems	Increased intimacy
Decreased caution	Decreased caution Increased discussion of non-work topics	Decreased caution

The transition from *co-worker-to-friend* is motivated primarily by contextual factors such as proximity, shared tasks, and extra-organizational socializing (Sias & Cahill, 1998). The individual factors that contribute to this initial stage of friendship development centre on perceived similarity. Essentially, when co-workers work together on projects they are in close proximity with one another and they may begin to develop a friendship that goes beyond simple work acquaintance. In addition, individuals who perceive they are similar to one another and enjoy one another's personality are likely to initiate a friendship. Communication at this stage of friendship development remains primarily on a surface level rather than intimate topics. However, conversations become increasingly focused on non-work and personal topics, and somewhat less cautious.

The second transition, from *friend-to-close friend* tends to be propelled by contextual factors such as important life events and socializing outside the workplace, as well as problems in the workplace setting (Sias & Cahill, 1998). Personal factors become less important at this level. Communication embodies increased discussion of non-work related topics, decreased caution, and increased intimacy. At this stage, co-workers also feel comfortable discussing work-related problems with one another.

Similar to the second transition, the final transition, from *close friend-to-almost best friend* tends to be associated with contextual factors such as extra-organizational socializing, life events, and work-related problems (Sias & Cahill, 1998). Communication at this stage becomes increasingly less cautious and more intimate, with friends feeling comfortable talking about virtually anything with one another (Sias & Cahill, 1998).

In sum, as Table 5.1 illustrates, as workplace friendships develop, they become increasingly less constrained by the workplace boundary and increasingly span the work/personal spheres.

Gender and workplace friendship development

Although friends provide each other with social support and information, not every employee has access to informal friendship networks. Specifically, female and ethnic/racial minorities often do not have access to the same social support systems as majority employees (Hood & Koberg, 1994; Ibarra, 1993; Ibarra, 1995; Kwesiga & Bell, 2004; Nelson & Quick, 1991). As previously mentioned, individuals are generally drawn to other people who they perceive to be similar to themselves (Sias & Cahill, 1998). However, women and ethnic/racial minority employees tend to be under-represented in organizations, and in particular at management levels, which means that minority employees have fewer people to potentially target for friendship (Ibarra, 1995; McMillan-Capehart, 2005).

Women and ethnic/racial minority employees often face barriers to making connections with potential mentors and other social networks. Hood and Koberg (1994) stated, 'Although they need effective networks containing both men and women, women are generally omitted from informal groups composed of men' (p. 165). Similarly, 'Exclusion from social networks explains the failure of minority managers to advance more rapidly in their careers and organizations' (Ibarra, 1995, p. 673). Others argue that the failure to make personal connections is one of the primary reasons that women and minority employees do not advance to upper management positions as frequently as majority employees (e.g., Kwesiga & Bell, 2004; McMillan-Capehart, 2005). Failure to make connections to social support systems within the organization has also been cited as a reason for higher levels of turnover among women and minority newcomers (McMillan-Capehart, 2005; Ragins, Cotton & Miller, 2000).

Essentially, women and minorities (in particular) have fewer 'similar others' to choose from as they develop friendships in the workplace. Because perceived similarity is one of the most important factors in transitioning from acquaintance-to-friend (Sias & Cahill, 1998), this can have a detrimental effect on an employee's ability to develop and maintain workplace friendships. Consequently, women and minority employees may not enjoy the same benefits as their peers who do have friends in the workplace. This can make them more susceptible to stress, burnout, and turnover, all of which have a detrimental effect on the organization as well as the individual.

Challenges to workplace friendship

Once developed, workplace friendships do not necessarily remain stable. Instead, these important relationships face a number of challenges that threaten the friendship's survival. Among these challenges are dialectic tensions that naturally result from the blending of friendship and work, and a number of personal and contextual factors.

Dialectical Tensions

Bridge and Baxter (1992) were the first to acknowledge workplace friendships as 'blended relationships.' Workplace friendships blend two different types of relationships – the co-worker relationship and the friend relationship. Like any interpersonal relationship, each carries unique expectations and at times these expectations conflict with one another, creating tensions that strain the relationship. *Dialectical* tensions emerge when relationship partners experience dilemmas created by contradictory or conflicting role expectations. Bridge and Baxter (1992) identified five such tensions individuals tend to experience in workplace friendships. Contradictions between organizational norms of objective and impartial treatment of employees and friendship norms of favoritism and unconditional support create the *impartiality and favoritism* tension. Friends expect one another to be honest and openly share information with one another, yet organizations, and the co-worker role, carry expectations of confidentiality and caution about information-sharing. This contradiction creates the *openness and closedness* dialectical tension. The *autonomy and connection* tension refers to the contradiction between the benefits of contact for friends and the possibility that daily contact among co-workers may provide little autonomy for the relationship partners, 'jeopardizing their friendship through excessive connection' (Bridge & Baxter, 1992, p. 204). Friends expect mutual affirmation and acceptance from one another, yet their organizational roles often require critical evaluation of employees. This contradiction creates *the judgment and acceptance* tension. Finally, workplace friends experience the *equality-inequality* dialectical tension when they face a contradiction between friendship expectations of equality and workplace expectations of unequal status. These dialectical tensions challenge workplace friendships and threaten the ongoing maintenance of those relationships.

Contextual and personal factors

In addition to the dialectical tensions described above, Sias et al. (2004) identified five factors or events that can challenge and often lead to the deterioration of workplace friendships. Many of these involve the dialectical tensions identified by Bridge and Baxter (1992), while others are unique from such situations. One of the most common causes of deterioration is *conflicting expectations*. Consistent with the notion of a dialectical tension, conflicting expectations refer to situations in which the workplace friends have different expectations for how each should behave (e.g., an employee might expect his/her friend to provide unconditional support of the employee's proposal in a meeting, but the friend might assume s/he should provide a more objective, less supportive critique in such a meeting). Workplace friendships can also deteriorate due to a *problem personality*, or situations in which one of the relationship partners finds an aspect of the other's personality to be annoying or no longer tolerable. Often problems in an individual's personal life can distract him/her from the job and impact others in the workplace. Such *distracting life events* can also lead to the deterioration of workplace friendships. Sias et al. (2004) also found *betrayal* to be a common cause of relational deterioration. Finally, workplace friends found their relationship deteriorated when one of the partners was *promoted* to a position of formal authority over the other. Individuals in these situations often experienced the impartiality-favoritism and equality-inequality dialectical tensions.

Gender composition of the friendship

Cross-sex friendships between female and male coworkers can also be problematic (Sias, Smith & Avdeyeva, 2003). Cross-sex friendships are complicated by what Fehr (1996) refers to as the 'sexual challenge.' When a man and a woman are friends, there is often an implicit assumption by both the partners and observers of the relationship that the relationship has the potential to develop into a romance. The sexual challenge is particularly difficult in the workplace context because rumors about the nature of the relationship can potentially affect an individual's reputation and career (Sias et al., 2003).

Research indicates that the sexual challenge can limit growth in cross-sex workplace friendships (Sias et al., 2003). Recall that Sias and Cahill (1998) found that contextual factors relating to the workplace environment tend to decrease in importance as same-sex friendships develop over time (Sias & Cahill, 1998). For example, same-sex friends increase the degree of self-disclosure in conversation and increase the amount of time spent in extra-organizational socializing. A study of cross-sex workplace friendship indicates, however, that the workplace context appears to maintain its importance as *cross-sex* friends become closer. As Sias et al. (2003) noted, 'Individuals in cross-sex friendships try to maintain the boundary between work and personal spheres by keeping the relationship defined as a 'workplace' friendship' (p. 336). Maintaining a focus on contextual factors such as shared tasks keeps the relationship 'safe' because it is less likely that other employees will perceive the relationship partners as 'more than friends' (Sias et al., 2003). These findings suggest that cross-sex workplace friendships do not develop in the same way as same-sex friendships. Cross-sex friends may resist a friendship that begins to move from *friend to close friend* or *close friend to almost best friend* because the relationship must move out of the 'safe-zone' and may be interpreted in a variety of ways by other co-workers. Same-sex friends, however, do not experience this particular challenge to workplace friendship development.[1] Regardless of sex composition, all workplace friends may face challenges to their relationship at one time or another. In the following section we address the various ways in which individuals may respond to these challenges.

Responding to relationship challenges

When faced with the challenges detailed above, employees can respond in one of two general ways. They can either disengage from the friendship or they can act to resist the challenges and maintain the relationship. To date, no research has addressed factors that might lead an employee to choose disengagement or resistance. In essence, the question has to do with the extent to which an employee is motivated to maintain the friendship. If s/he has little motivation to maintain the relationship, s/he will likely disengage from the friendship. In contrast, employees who

---

[1] It is important to note that this study did not address the ways such dynamics may function among coworkers who are openly homosexual. Future research should examine the extent to which platonic same-sex friendships among gay employees may also be subject to the 'sexual challenge'.

are motivated to keep the friendship alive will be more willing to put forth the effort needed to do so. In this section, we use social exchange theory to discuss factors that are likely to impact motivation to maintain the relationship.

Motivation to maintain a workplace friendship

As noted above, scholars have not addressed the concept of employee motivation to maintain a workplace friendship. Interpersonal scholars, however, have long relied on social exchange theory (Blau, 1964; Thibault & Kelley, 1952) in their studies of relationship maintenance in non-work relationships.

Social exchange theory is based on a few fundamental assumptions. First, the theory assumes that human behavior is based upon a system of exchange. Thus, for example, individuals disclose information to others when they believe they will receive information in return (e.g., Altman & Taylor, 1973). Second, the exchange involves incurring costs for some sort of benefit. For example, self-disclosure represents a cost to the discloser in that it provides a potential risk to the discloser's image. Yet the act of disclosing has the potential to reap benefits in the form of information provided by the other person. Third, relationships operate on the basis of social exchange and individuals consider the costs and benefits they incur from their relationships as they negotiate those relationships. In particular, and most relevant to this chapter, the theory predicts that when the costs of maintaining a relationship outweigh the benefits incurred from that relationship, an individual will choose to end the relationship. In contrast, when the benefits derived from the relationship outweigh the costs, an individual will be motivated to expend the effort necessary to maintain the relationship (Blau, 1964; Thibault & Kelley, 1952).

As noted earlier, workplace friendships provide employees with many benefits including access to valuable information, instrumental support, and emotional support. Costs are incurred, however in developing and maintaining a friendship. As voluntary relationships, employees are required to spend time and energy beyond that required to do their jobs when participating in a workplace friendship. In addition, just as an employee reaps the benefits described above, s/he is also required to provide those benefits to his/her relationship partners. Thus, costs also include *providing* information and support. When the costs outweigh the benefits, an individual may decide to disengage from the relationship. This disengagement process is discussed in the following section.

Disengaging from a workplace friendship

Just as individuals choose which of their coworkers to befriend, they may also choose to disengage from a friendship if it becomes too costly or the challenges to the relationship are too difficult to manage. Disengaging from a friendship is a strategic process that may be carried out in several different ways.

As previously discussed, Sias et al. (2004) identified factors or events that can lead to the deterioration of workplace friendships. Their study also identified the communication strategies employees use to disengage from a workplace friendship. With little exception, the participants in the study relied on indirect communication strategies, one of which was *avoidance of non-work topics* in conversation (Sias et al., 2004). Friendships are unique because they have a personalistic focus (Rawlins, 1992). Sias and Cahill (1998) similarly noted that workplace friends tend to focus more on each other as individuals and less on their respective roles within the organization. Consequently, avoiding conversation topics that are unrelated to work detracts from the personalistic focus and emphasizes role specific goals instead (Sias et al., 2004). Limiting the conversation to work or role related topics transforms the relationship into one in which the individuals are simply co-workers rather than co-workers who are also friends. Therefore, 'workplace friendship deterioration can be accomplished by making nonwork topics "taboo"' (Sias et al., 2004, p. 335).

Employees also disengage from friendships by using *nonverbal distancing strategies* (Sias et al., 2004). These strategies emphasize that what we say is not always as important as how we say it. In other words, tone of voice can be an effective tool when distancing oneself from a friendship. As Sias et al. (2004) explain, 'Respondents who were the targets of such cues reported that these tactics were very effective; through "snappy" and "condescending" vocal tones, the initiators of friendship deterioration made their feelings about the partner clear, effectively ending the friendship' (p. 336).

Although less common, some employees accomplish friendship deterioration by using *cost-rendering* strategies (Sias et al., 2004). These strategies communicate a 'desire to decrease the closeness of the friendship by making the friendship too costly' (Sias et al., 2004, p. 336). However, these tactics were uncommon, which was probably due to the fact that peer coworkers must be able to continue working together after they have ended a friendship. Similarly, because they are required to spend time together in the workplace, ex-friends cannot typically avoid each other altogether. Consequently, many employees simply *avoided socializing outside the workplace*. Sias et al. (2004) indicated that 'the relationship becomes workplace specific when the individuals no longer spend time with one another beyond that mandated by their formal organizational roles' (pp. 336–337).

In a subsequent study, Sias and Perry (2004) used the narratives from Sias et al. (2004) study to conduct a quantitative analysis that described how individuals disengage from workplace relationships. Similar to what is discussed above, the results indicate that individuals are most likely to use a *depersonalization* strategy in which they steer clear of communication topics that are personal in nature and avoid extra-organizational socializing. This allows the relationship to return to one that emphasizes the members' roles within the organization. Sias and Perry (2004) also found that employees use *cost rendering* and direct *state-of-the-relationship talk;* however these tactics were much less common than the *depersonalization* strategy.

To summarize, individuals are likely to use indirect communication strategies to disengage from a workplace friendship. Specifically, they may choose to avoid conversation topics of a personal nature and even use nonverbal communication to strategically distance themselves from their relational partner. In rare instances individuals may use direct methods of conversation to disengage from the friendship. However, despite the disengagement strategies we have discussed, individuals usually choose to maintain their workplace friendship, rather than disengage.

Maintaining workplace friendships

Not all workplace friendships succumb to challenges. Instead, many survive these threats and are maintained for a long period of time. In this section, we discuss workplace friendship maintenance. Because no research has directly addressed this topic, we know very little about how employees maintain their workplace friendships. Prior research does provide some direction for speculation regarding these issues. In particular, we discuss types of workplace relationship maintenance tactics and how those tactics might be impacted by the status of the situation and the level of task interdependence shared by the friends. In addition, we use politeness theory (Brown & Levinson, 1987) to speculate about how individuals choose various relationship maintenance strategies.

The status of the situation

Lee and Jablin (1995) identified three primary types of situations that compel individuals to attempt relationship maintenance. *Escalating situa-*

tions refer to situations in which one relationship partner feels the relationship is moving toward a closer level with which the employee is uncomfortable. *Deteriorating situations* are those in which one relationship partner feels the relationship is degenerating to a level with which s/he is not comfortable. *Routine situations* are those in which employees are *not* concerned with their relationships growing too close or too distant, but nonetheless feel the need for relationship maintenance. Here we address only the escalating and deteriorating situations. This is due to space limitations of the chapter and also due to our intention to focus on strategic relationship maintenance behaviour. Strategic behaviour refers to 'behavior that is consciously and intentionally enacted to meet a particular goal' (Stafford, Dainton & Haas, 2000, p. 307). Although routine relationship maintenance behaviour can be enacted in an intentional and conscious manner (e.g., Lee & Jablin, 1995), scholars note that routine behaviors tend to be 'those that people perform that foster relational maintenance more in the manner of a "by-product"'(Stafford et al., 2000, p. 307).

Relationship maintenance tactics

Lee and Jablin (1995) and Lee (1998) identified several tactics employees use to maintain their workplace relationships. Although their studies focused on supervisor-subordinate relationships that were not necessarily friendships, the tactics they identified are also applicable to workplace friendships at any level. For example, one can imagine an employee feeling uncomfortable when their peer co-worker/friend attempts to increase the closeness of the friendship by sharing intimate information, or feeling concerned about the relationship when their friend begins to withdraw by, perhaps, declining invitations to lunch. And, given the important role workplace friendships play for employees, one can imagine ongoing attention to maintaining such relationships.

Avoidance of interaction refers to intentional attempts to avoid physical and communicative contact with the relationship partner (e.g., sitting away from him/her at a meeting, avoiding meetings the partner is expected to attend, not responding when the partner initiates a conversation). *Indirect conversational refocus* refers to tactics by which an employee deliberately but indirectly focuses or changes the topic of a conversation to work-related issues and away from personal topics. *Direct conversational refocus* refers to deliberately focusing or changing the topic of a conversation explicitly and directly (e.g., saying 'none of your business' when the partner brings up a personal topic, or specifically stating s/he does not want to discuss personal issues). *Openness* refers to direct and explicit statements of concern regarding the direction the relationship is taking and one's desire to maintain it at its current level. *Creating closeness* refers to tactics by which the individual intentionally tries to empha-size the personal, rather than professional relationship (e.g., asking the partner about his/her personal life, initiating informal convers-ations). *Deception/distortion* includes the intentional withholding or mis-representation of information, particularly bad news or information the partner might perceive of as negative. *Circumspectiveness* refers to generally exercising caution in how one communicates with the rela-tionship partner (e.g., avoiding saying things that might embarrass the other person, caution in criticizing the relationship partner). Finally, people engage in *self-promotion* when they emphasize their successes on the job or how hard they work.

According to Lee and Jablin (1995), employees do not use these tactics in every situation but rather show preferences for tactics depending on the status of the situation. Specifically, employees experiencing an esca-lating situation tend to rely on avoidance of interaction, indirect con-versational refocus, and direct conversational refocus to prevent the relationship from moving to a closer level. These tactics are effective in that they maintain a boundary between the work and personal spheres. Such tactics are also likely to be used frequently in maintaining workplace friendships. Recall that a defining characteristic of friendship is a per-sonalistic focus which involves interacting with the partner as a whole person, rather than just a role occupant. An employee can effectively manage or maintain the extent of that personalistic focus by minimizing the extent to which s/he discusses personal topics with the relationship partner.

In contrast, employees experiencing deteriorating situations tend to rely on openness, creating closeness, deception/distortion, circum-spectiveness, and self-promotion to prevent the relationship from degen-erating to lower levels of closeness. Again, given friendship's personalistic focus, tactics such as openness and creating closeness would be parti-cularly effective in attempts to prevent relational deterioration because they function to maintain the relationship's focus on partners' personal lives. Deception, circumspectiveness and self-promotion would also function to prevent an employee's co-worker from obtaining negative information that could potentially damage the relationship and further propel it toward deterioration.

Strategic maintenance tactic choice, however, is likely more com-plex than the above paragraphs suggest. A variety of factors may impact the likelihood of an employee choosing openness, creating closeness, or deception when attempting to prevent relationship deterioration. In the following section, we rely on politeness theory (Brown & Levinson, 1987) and the concept of task interdependence to develop a set of propositions regarding such strategic choices.

Politeness and task interdependence

Politeness theory (Brown & Levinson, 1987) provides some guidance for speculation regarding why employees may choose particular tactics to maintain a workplace friendship. Politeness theory centres on Goffman's (1967) concept of *face,* or an individual's public self-image. Goffman (1967) conceptualized face as a fluid, rather than stable, phenomenon that is constituted, and must be continually attended to, in interaction (Sias et al., 2003). According to politeness theory, individuals consider both their own face and their conversation partner's face when choosing communication strategies that they hope will enable them to achieve their message goals such as relationship maintenance (Brown & Levinson, 1987). Messages that consider the other's feelings and desires reflect a concern for face. In contrast, messages that show little concern for the conversation partner's feeling or that express dislike or disapproval reflect threats to face.

Scholars have not examined the extent to which workplace relationship maintenance tactics are perceived to be face-threatening. Consideration of the characteristics of each tactic, however, suggests that they vary somewhat in their concern for the face of both relationship partners. *Direct conversational refocus,* for example, is potentially more face-threatening to the hearer than *indirect conversational refocus* because of the explicit and direct manner in which the speaker expresses his/her desire to close off discussion of personal topics which could be interpreted by the co-worker as expression of dislike or disrespect. *Openness* could be similarly interpreted in escalating situations because the co-worker may interpret speaker's statements of concern regarding increased closeness as a statement of dislike or disrespect. Openness could also threaten the face of the speaker in deteriorating situations in that the co-worker may respond negatively to the speaker's expressed desire to maintain a close relationship. *Avoidance of interaction* could also be considered a face-threatening act in that the explicit avoidance of contact indicates dislike for the coworker.

In contrast, *indirect conversational refocus* appears to be less face-threatening in that such messages convey a concern for the other's feelings and tactful, subtle ways of managing the amount of personal conversation in which the co-workers engage. Similarly, *circumspectiveness* represents tactful, indirect, and subtle attempts to manage interaction, indicating a concern for the feelings of the relationship partner. *Deception/ distortion,* while dishonest, represents little face threat to the co-worker in that the withholding of negative information is not explicitly insulting or hurtful. Finally, *self-promotion* provides commentary not on the relationship itself, nor on the relationship partner, but on the speaker. Thus, this strategy provides no threat to the hearer's face and likely little threat to the speaker due to its positive nature. Consistent with these arguments, we forward the following proposition:

Proposition 1: Direct conversational refocus, openness and avoidance of interaction are perceived by employees as more face-threatening than indirect conversational refocus, circumspectiveness, deception/ distortion, and self-promotion.

At a broad level, employees are likely to generally avoid face-threatening strategies when attempting to maintain a workplace friendship due to the potential negative consequences of such messages. Along these lines, Carson and Cupach (2000) found that face-threatening communication has a number of negative consequences. Their study focused on how managers address employee performance errors in their discussions with those employees. In particular, the study assessed four primary types of 'reproach' messages: *polite, bald on record, aggravating,* and *very aggravating.* Polite reproaches included those in which the supervisor tried to 'soften' the reproach by 'showing respect, being courteous and positive, acting "kindly," correcting the employee and asking for compliance in a pleading manner, and using a very nice tone' (Carson & Cupach, 2000, p. 225). 'Bald on record' reproaches were direct and straightforward, focusing on information sharing, using a mild tone, and a 'pleasant demeanor' (Carson & Cupach, 2000, p. 225). In contrast, the 'aggravating' and 'very aggravating' reproaches were, to varying extents, more negative, stern, condescending, accusatory, aggressive and sarcastic. Participants rated 'very aggravating' reproaches as the most face-threatening, followed, in order, by 'aggravating,' 'bald on record' and 'polite' reproaches. Of particular relevance to this chapter, results of their study indicated that the more 'face-threatening' a reproach was perceived to be by the employee, the less satisfied that employee was with the outcome of the conversation, the less competent the employee perceived the supervisor to be as a communicator, and the more angry the employee was after the incident, indicating that face-threatening communication has important negative repercussions in the workplace.

Although employees are likely to be generally concerned about politeness and face-saving in their communication, situational factors may impact the extent of such concerns and, in turn, their choice of communication strategies. Scholars for many years have acknowledged organizations as social systems. Borrowing concepts and terminology from biological systems theory (Bertalanffy, 1962), organizational scholars conceptualized the organization as a social system, emphasizing the holistic nature of such systems and, in particular, emphasizing the interdependent nature of system components such as departments, groups, and individuals (Katz & Kahn, 1966). The interdependent nature of organizational systems means that what happens in one part of the system impacts the other system components. Acknowledging organizations as interdependent systems helps scholars and practitioners consider not only the parts of a system, but how those parts are connected (Wheatley, 2001).

One form of connection derives from tasks. In any organization, employees perform a variety of tasks that are in some way linked to one another. For example, at a broad level, engineers and designers in an auto manufacturing company design new automobile models that are then built by employees in the company's manufacturing plants. At a more micro level, manufacturing employees in such a company perform tasks that are highly interdependent on one another as a car moves down the assembly line for production. The more an employee's ability to complete tasks depends on another employee's ability to complete tasks, the more interdependent their tasks. It is likely that co-workers who are highly interdependent will be concerned about maintaining effective relationships with one another so that they may minimize any potential threat to task completion. On the other hand, co-workers with little task interdependence may be less concerned about such potential threats. Thus, as shown in Figure 5.1, we suggest that employees who perceive high levels of task interdependence with their workplace friends will be more likely to choose the less potentially face-threatening maintenance tactics than those who perceive lower levels of task interdependence. Specifically, we set forth the following propositions:

Proposition 2a: Individuals with high levels of task interdependence with their coworker/friend will be more likely to use indirect conversational refocus and avoidance of interaction than will individuals with low levels of task interdependence to prevent their workplace friendship from escalating.

Proposition 2b: Individuals with low levels of task interdependence with their coworker/friend will be more likely to use direct conversational refocus and openness than will individuals with high levels of task interdependence to prevent their workplace friendships from escalating.

Proposition 3a: Individuals with high levels of task interdependence with the coworker/friend will be more likely to use circumspectiveness, self-promotion and deception/distortion than will individuals with low levels of task interdependence to prevent their workplace friendship from deteriorating.

Proposition 3b: Individuals with low levels of task interdependence with their co-worker/friend will be more likely to use openness and creating closeness than will individuals with high levels of task interdependence to prevent their workplace friendship from deteriorating.

In sum, existing research identifies a variety of personal and contextual factors that propel the development of co-worker relationships

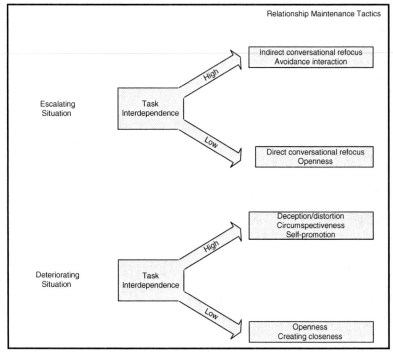

Figure 5.1 Relationship maintenance tactic choice

into workplace friendships. Research also demonstrates that communication is central to such relationship development. Organizational scholars have also revealed the reasons such relationships deteriorate and the communication strategies individuals use to transform a workplace friendship back to a 'just co-worker' relationship. As noted above, when a workplace friendship is challenged and its survival is threatened, employees may choose to terminate the friendship, or they may decide to try to maintain the relationship. No research has directly examined how such choices are made or how employees actively work to maintain a workplace friendship. Accordingly, we speculate regarding such processes and offer a brief set of propositions that might guide research in this area. Our discussion of workplace friendship development, deterioration, and maintenance has a variety of important implications which we discuss below.

Implications and conclusion

Workplace friendships are clearly important relationships. Their distinct characteristics blend the professional and personal spheres. They are both rewarding and challenging. Organizations and employees reap great benefits from workplace friendship, yet must deal with a variety of challenges that threaten the functionality and the very survival of such relationships. Because of their importance, how and why individuals develop and maintain workplace friendships is an important issue for both scholars and practitioners.

Research on workplace friendship development suggests several ways practitioners may encourage a more equitable and rewarding workplace. As noted earlier, informal friendship networks are significant information distribution systems via which employees share important, often proprietary information that can help their job performance and career progression (Ibarra, 1995; Sias, 2005). Individuals marginalized from these informal networks are at a substantial disadvantage. Understanding the factors that encourage the development of these relationships provides some direction for providing more equitable access to informal networks. Essentially, workplace friendship development requires opportunities for interaction and managers should make efforts toward providing such opportunities for all employees. For example, physical proximity is central to the initiation of a friendship because of the opportunities for interaction proximity provides (Sias & Cahill, 1998). Ensuring that typically marginalized employees (e.g., women or minority employees) enjoy proximity to members central to the informal network can encourage inclusion of those often excluded employees. In addition, many friendships develop from co-workers working together on a project. Managers concerned that certain employees are isolated from the social network might assign those employees to a joint project with employees who are active in the network to encourage their inclusion.

Workplace friendship deterioration has the potential for serious damage to the work environment, impacting employee attitudes and performance (Sias et al., 2004; Sias & Perry, 2004). Understanding the communicative nature of relationships provides suggestions for effective management of such relational deterioration. Specifically, research demonstrates that communication regarding personal topics constructs the personalistic focus necessary for a friendship (Sias et al., 2004). Removing that personalistic focus is key to transforming a friendship back to a 'just co-worker' relationship. Practitioners who become aware of problems between co-worker/friends might benefit from decreasing opportunities for interaction between the relationship partners when possible to assist the individuals in the transition. Thus, managers might consider having the employees work in different physical locations and reducing the extent to which they work together on projects or tasks.

Employees don't always want their workplace friendship to grow closer or to deteriorate, however. Instead, they work to maintain their relationships at a stable level. Scholars have yet to study friendship maintenance in a workplace context and we hope this chapter provides a useful starting point for research in this area. Workplace friendships play a central role in organizational processes. Thus, their stability impacts the stability of the organization itself. Consequently, understanding why and how employees maintain these relationships is of importance for both scholars and practitioners.

Toward that end, we rely on existing theory and research in interpersonal relationships and supervisor-subordinate relationships to provide preliminary speculation regarding the factors that might motivate an employee to maintain, rather than transform, a workplace friendship and factors that might impact the processes associated with such relational maintenance. We stress that our propositions are preliminary and appropriate for exploratory studies. The relationship maintenance strategies we incorporate, for example, were derived from studies of supervisor-subordinate relationships that were not necessarily friendships. It is possible there are other strategies that are uniquely suited to the maintenance of workplace friendships. We encourage organizational scholars to direct their research efforts toward understanding the workplace friendship maintenance processes.

References

Albrecht, T. L. & Adelman, M. B. (1987). *Communicating Social Support*. Newbury Park, CA: Sage.

Altman, I. & Taylor, D. A. (1973). *Social Penetration: The Development of Interpersonal Relationships*. New York: Holt, Rinehart & Winston.

Berger, C. R. & Calabrese, R. J. (1975). Some explorations in initial interaction and beyond: Toward a developmental theory of interpersonal communication. *Human Communication Research, 1*, 99–112.

Bertalanffy, L. von (1962). General systems theory. *General Systems, 7*, 1–12.

Blau, P. (1964). *Exchange and Power in Social Life*. New York: John Wiley.

Brass, D. J. & Burkhardt, M. A. (1993). Potential power and power use: An investigation of structure and behavior. *Academy of Management Journal, 36*, 441–471.

Bridge, K. & Baxter, L. A. (1992). Blended relationships: Friends as work associates. *Western Journal of Communication, 56*, 200–225.

Brown, P. & Levinson, S. (1987). *Politeness: Some Universals in Language Use*. Cambridge, England: Cambridge University Press.

Carson, C. L. & Cupach, W. R. (2000). Facing corrections in the workplace: The influence of perceived face threat on the consequences of managerial reproaches. *Journal of Applied Communication Research, 28*, 215–234.

Eisenberg, E. M. & Goodall, H. L. Jr. (2004). *Organizational Communication: Balancing Creativity and Constraint* (4th ed). Boston: Bedford/St. Martin's Press.

Fehr, B. (1996). *Friendship Processes*. Thousand Oaks, CA: Sage.

Goffman, E. (1967). *Interaction Ritual*. Garden City, NY: Doubleday.

Graves, L. M. & Elsass, P. M. (2005). Sex and sex dissimilarity effects in ongoing teams: Some surprising findings. *Human Relations, 58*, 191–221.

Hood, J. N. & Koberg, C. S. (1994). Patterns of differential assimilation and acculturation for women in business organizations. *Human Relations, 47*, 159–182.

Ibarra, H. (1993). Personal networks of women and minorities in management: A conceptual framework. *The Academy of Management Review, 18*, 56–88.

Ibarra, H. (1995). Race, opportunity, and diversity of social circles in managerial networks. *Academy of Management Journal, 38*, 673–704.

Kahn, W. A. (2001). Holding environments at work. *The Journal of Applied Behavioral Science, 37*, 260–279.

Katz, D. & Kahn, R. (1966). *The Social Psychology of Organizations*. New York: John Wiley & Sons.

Kram, K. E. & Isabella, L. A. (1985). Mentoring alternatives: The role of peer relationships in career development. *Academy of Management Journal, 28*, 110–132.

Kruger, L. J., Bernstein, G. & Botman, H. (1995). The relationship between team friendships and burnout among residential counselors. *The Journal of Social Psychology, 135*, 191.

Kwesiga, E. & Bell, M. P. (2004). Back to organizational socialization: Building a case for the advancement of women in organizations. *Equal Opportunities International, 23*, 3–20.

Lee, J. (1998). Maintenance communication in superior-subordinate relationships: An exploratory investigation of group social context and the 'Pelz Effect'. *Southern Communication Journal, 63*, 144–159.

Lee, J. & Jablin, F. M. (1995). Maintenance communication in superior-subordinate work relationships. *Human Communication Research, 22*, 220–257.

Lincoln, J. R. & Miller, J. (1979). Work and friendship ties in organizations: A comparative analysis of relational networks. *Administrative Science Quarterly, 24*, 181–199.

Marks, S. R. (1994). Intimacy in the public realm: The Case of co-workers. *Social Forces, 72*, 843–858.

McGrath, C. & Krackhardt, D. (2003). Network conditions for organizational change. *The Journal of Applied Behavioral Science, 39*, 324–336.

McMillan-Capehart, A. (2005). A configurational framework for diversity: Socialization and culture. *Personnel Review, 34*, 488–503.

Nelson, D. L. & Quick, J. C. (1991). Social support and newcomer adjustment in organizations: Attachment theory at work? *Journal of Organizational Behavior, 12*, 543–554.

Ragins, B. R., Cotton, J. L. & Miller, J. S. (2000). Marginal mentoring: The effects of type of mentor, quality of relationship and program design on work and career attitudes. *Academy of Management Journal, 43*, 1177–1194.

Rawlins, W. K. (1992). *Friendship Matters: Communication, Dialectics, and the Life Course*. New York: Aldine de Gruyter.

Sias, P. M. (2005). Workplace relationship quality and employee information experiences. *Communication Studies, 56*, 375–395.

Sias, P. M. & Bartoo, H. (2007). Friendship, social support, and health. In L. L'Abate, D. D. Embrey & M. S. Baggett (eds). *Handbook of Low-Cost Interventions to Promote Physical and Mental Health: Theory, Research, and Practice* (pp. 455–472). New York: Springer.

Sias, P. M. & Cahill, D. J. (1998). From coworkers to friends: The development of peer friendships in the workplace. *Western Journal of Communication, 62*, 273–299.

Sias, P. M., Heath, R. G., Perry, T., Silva, D. & Fix, B. (2004). Narratives of workplace friendship deterioration. *Journal of Social and Personal Relationships, 21*, 321–340.

Sias, P. M. & Perry, T. (2004) Disengaging from workplace relationships: A research note. *Human Communication Research, 30*, 589–602.

Sias, P.M., Smith, G., & Avdeyeva, T. (2003). Sex and sex-composition differences and similarities in peer workplace friendship development. *Communication Studies, 54*, 322–340.

Sias, P. M. & Wyers, T. D. (2001). Employee uncertainty and information-seeking in newly-formed expansion organizations. *Management Communication Quarterly, 14*, 549–573.

Sigman, S. J. (1995). Order and continuity in human relationships: A social communication approach to defining 'relationship'. In W. Leeds-Hurwitz (ed.), *Social Approaches to Communication* (pp. 188–200). New York: Guilford Press.

Stafford, L., Dainton, M. & Haas, S. (2000). Measuring routine and strategic relational maintenance: Scale revision, sex versus gender roles, and the prediction of relational characteristics. *Communication Monographs, 67*, 306–323.

Teboul, J. C. B. (1994). Facing and coping with uncertainty during organizational encounter. *Management Communication Quarterly, 8*, 190–224.

Thibault, J. W. & Kelley, H. H. (1952). *The Social Psychology of Groups*. New York: John Wiley & Sons.

Wheatley, M. (2001). *Leadership and the New Science: Discovering Order in a Chaotic World*. San Francisco: Jossey Bass.

6
Cooperative Behaviours in Organizations

Karin Sanders

By 1938 effective organisations were characterized as systems in which individuals cooperated with each other to reach organizational ends (Barnard, 1938). In those days cooperative behaviours were studied under the heading of solidarity within organizations, and were focused on solidarity between employees in conflict with management or in the enforcement of workgroup norms (Roethlisberger & Dickson, 1939; Seashore, 1954; Blau, 1955, 1964; Homans, 1961). *Cooperative behaviours* became a focus of research when organizations started to structure employees into teams or groups, such as management teams, project groups or self-managed teams (Cohen & Bailey, 1997; Goodman, 1986).

One of the most important characteristics of these teams is that the responsibility for attaining production goals is transferred from management to the employees (Cooper & Lewis, 1999), with the result being that employees from different backgrounds enjoy a considerable amount of autonomy, and can perform more challenging tasks. The flip side of this autonomy is that employees have to work together and behave cooperatively to keep the organization running (Appelbaum & Batt, 1994; Handy, 1995; Wickens, 1995; Maier, 1999; Probert, 1999; Singh & Vinnicombe, 2000). Research has shown that cooperative behaviour is related to organizational outcomes. For example, cooperative behaviour is negatively related to employees' resistance to organizational changes (Torenvlied & Velner, 1998), and to short-term absenteeism (Sanders & Hoekstra, 1998; Sanders, 2004).

More recently, cooperative employee behaviours have been conceptualized under different headings, such as 'willingness to cooperate' (Barnard, 1938), 'organisational loyalty' (Hirschman, 1970; Hage, 1980), 'organisational commitment' (Mowday, Steers & Porter, 1982), 'solidarity' (Hechter, 1987) 'solidarity behaviours' (Koster, 2005), 'contextual performance'

(Borman & Motowidlo, 1993) and extra role behaviours such as 'organisational citizenship behaviour (OCB)', 'pro-social organisational behaviour', 'whistle blowing', and 'principled organisational dissent' (Morrison & Phelps, 1999; Van Dyne, Cummings & McLean Parks, 1995). All of these concepts refer to effort and creativity beyond the formal contract of employment (Organ, 1997).[1] Examples of cooperative behaviour are knowledge sharing, helping a colleague, "breaking in" new colleagues, working overtime, and submitting information needed to keep the organization running. Cooperative behaviour refers to the choices individuals make between individual interests and collective ones (Hechter, 1987; Aquino, 1998; Miller, 1992).

One can argue that there is always a tension between individual and collective interests, simply because cooperative behaviour is more costly for individuals (e.g. in terms of time, than non-cooperative behaviour). At the same time everyone in the group is better off if everyone cooperates (see also Sanders, Van Emmerik & Raub, 2005). In other words, by being cooperative to other employees an individual's core tasks may be affected; tasks which have to be completed afterwards possibly cutting into leisure time. The employee, therefore, may have an incentive to refrain from cooperative behaviours and stick to formally assigned tasks.

In the past two decades cooperative behaviour has been the focus of a great deal of research, mostly in terms of Organisational Citizenship Behaviour (OCB; Podsakoff, MacKenzie, Paine & Bachrach, 2000; Motowidlo, Borman & Schmit, 1997; Motowidlo & Van Scotter, 1994; Organ,

---

[1]Although it is well-known that cooperative behaviours are important for the organization, these outcomes share the problem that they cannot be tackled by means of labour agreements. While contracts are a standard way of protecting parties against opportunistic behaviour and other risks for the organization, the uses of contracts as a safeguard for problems between employees and supervisors are limited (Macaulay, 1963). Explicit contracting to lessen problems concerning cooperative behaviours are associated with transaction costs (Williamson, 1975, 1996), such as the costs of attempting to anticipate all conceivable contingencies that might arise in the course of the relationship, the bargaining and decision costs associated with reaching an agreement on how to deal with these contingencies, the costs of writing a sufficiently clear and unambiguous contract that can be externally enforced and the costs of external enforcement itself (Hart, 1987). Moreover, cooperative behaviours are difficult to measure and verify, especially for third parties, such as a judge. In other words, contractual enforcement of cooperative behaviour is difficult and costly, if not impossible. Therefore, transactions often rely on implicit contracts (Azariadis, 1987), i.e., contracts that are partially unwritten, tacit and not formally binding (see also Macneil, 1980).

1990, 1997; Organ & Lingl, 1995; MacKenzie, Podsakoff & Fetter, 1991). These studies generally focus on individual characteristics of the employees and aim to answer questions about if and why some employees behave more cooperatively than others. The limitation of these studies, however, is that they neglect the reciprocal nature of cooperative behaviour. Cooperative behaviour should not be examined as an individual characteristic of employees, but as a characteristic of the interpersonal relationship which includes the behaviour of others. Therefore the assumption is made here that cooperative behaviour involves at least two people, is directed to specific others, and is affected by the behaviours of others.

This chapter follows the relational perspective of cooperative behaviours, and argues that cooperative behaviours should not be examined as a characteristic of employees, but as a result of the relationships employees have with others inside the organization (see next section). The relevant question is what influences these different relationships. Some authors argue that social context, such as the *social embeddedness of relationships* is an important predictor of relationship outcomes (Hodson 1999; Raub, 1997; Raub & Weesie, 1990, 2000). In general, the extent to which a relationship is embedded can be described in terms of three kinds of embeddedness within organisations: temporal embeddedness, network embeddedness and institutional embeddedness (Raub, 1997; Raub & Weesie, 1990, 2000). Temporal embeddedness refers to the duration and expected future length of employment relationships.[2] Network embeddedness refers to the network of social relationships between employees, for example friendships or status hierarchies. Institutional embeddedness refers to the rules of an organization, such as career progression, and performance systems.[3] Paying attention to three forms of social embeddedness of relationships not only offers the possibility of explaining the emergence of friends, but can also explain the emergence of enemies. In the following sections these three kinds of embeddedness are discussed and are related to cooperative behaviours. Results of empirical research are added in the different sections. The chapter ends with a short summary.

---

[2]These three kinds of embeddedness may be related to each other. For instance, tenure or career systems are part of the institutional context, but will also influence the temporal embeddedness of employees' behaviours. Also, the social networks of employees within an organization may influence temporal embeddedness by shaping employees' intention to stay or leave (and vice versa).
[3]Although most formal and informal rules are included within institutional context in this section we only focus on the formal rules.

Cooperative behaviour within organisations[4]

As mentioned in the introduction, probably the most frequently studied form of cooperative employee behaviour is Organisational Citizenship Behaviour (OCB; Organ, 1997).[5] For a review and a sketch of the historical development of this research which originated in the early eighties (Bateman & Organ, 1983; Smith, Organ & Near, 1983, see Podsakoff et al., 2000). OCB focuses on employee behaviour that has an overall positive effect on the functioning of the organization and cannot be enforced by the employment contract. Although OCB has proven itself a fruitful concept for research, there are some problems (LePine, Erez & Johnson, 2002; Motowidlo, 2000; Pond, Nacoste, Mohr & Rodriguez, 1997; Van Dyne, Graham & Dienesch, 1994).

Most of the issues have to do with OCB as a concept (for example, what the dimensions of OCB are) and the theoretical foundation of OCB (see for an overview Koster & Sanders, 2006a). The first problem is concerned with what kinds of behaviour should be classified as OCB. For instance, many articles pose the question whether it is possible to distinguish in-role from extra-role behaviour: does OCB consist of types of behaviour that are beyond the job description or does it also include contractually required behaviour? The dimensionality of the OCB construct is also a recurring problem in the literature. Here, the question is how many dimensions of OCB can be distinguished. A third and final problem is the lack of a clear theoretical approach to OCB in the literature.

Most of the problems related to OCB research can be dealt with using a relational approach to cooperative behaviour within organisations (see Koster 2005; Koster & Sanders, 2006a). In a relational approach, cooperative behaviour is explicitly defined as behaviour involving at least two people, a point that has not been fully developed in OCB literature. Since the relationships between colleagues and supervisors are qualitatively different relationships, they should be distinguished (Smith,

---

[4]This section is based on Koster and Sanders (2006a), Sanders and Van Emmerik (2004), and Sanders et al. (2005).

[5]In a recent review of this field, OCB was defined as: 'Individual behaviour that is discretionary, not directly or explicitly recognized by the formal reward system and that in aggregate promotes the effective functioning of the organization. By discretionary, we mean that the behaviour is not an enforceable requirement of the role or job description, that is, the clearly specifiable terms of the person's employment contract with the organization; the behaviour is rather a matter of personal choice, such that the omission is not generally understood as punishable' (Organ, 1988, p. 4).

Carroll & Ashford, 1995). The distinction between OCB-I and OCB-O (Williams & Anderson, 1991) is a step in the direction of specifying to whom the behaviour is directed. OCB-I may be defined as cooperative behaviour to colleagues and OCB-O may be defined as cooperative behaviour to the supervisor. However this conceptualisation ignores whether the other person cooperates or not.

Based on the norm of reciprocity (Gouldner, 1960), social exchange theorists (Blau, 1964; Homans, 1961) focus on cooperation in social relationships where the cooperative behaviours of an individual will be repaid in kind. That is, where employees will reciprocate cooperative behaviours received from both their colleagues and their supervisor. However if it is acknowledged that cooperation involves more than one person, the minimal unit of analysis should be the dyad and the behaviour of both sides has to be known. Some recent attempts that suggest linking OCB to social exchange theory (Podsakoff et al., 2000) take a step in that direction since social exchange theory explicitly models the exchange between two individuals (Blau, 1964; Homans, 1961).

To test the theoretical ideas and measure differences between cooperative behaviour and OCB, Koster and Sanders (2006a; see also Koster, 2005) compared two basic OCB dimensions (generalized compliance and altruism) with cooperative behaviour to colleagues and cooperative behaviour to the supervisor. Generalized compliance captures several different behaviours, of which cooperative behaviour toward the supervisor may be one. Altruism has to do with behaviour towards colleagues, such as helping someone out. The data set consisted of 674 employees from nine organizations and the different dimensions were compared by means of a Multiple Group Method Analysis (Guttman, 1952; Hendriks & Kiers, 1999). Data were collected on cooperative behaviour towards colleagues and to the supervisor, and on generalized compliance and altruism. In addition, data were collected concerning the perceived cooperative behaviour *received* both from colleagues and from the supervisor. The analyses show that the OCB and cooperative behaviour dimensions measure different forms of behaviour. The cooperative behaviours measured turned out to have a higher reliability than did the two OCB dimensions. Furthermore, the results indicated that cooperative behaviour toward the colleagues and to the supervisor is related to the perceived behaviour of the other person(s) (i.e. reciprocity), while this is not the case for OCB. These findings confirm the reciprocal nature of cooperative behaviour and show that it is important to take the behaviour of other participants into account.

Research also shows that cooperative behaviour in one relationship, for instance a relationship between colleagues, does not automatically imply cooperative behaviour in other relationships such as the employee–supervisor relationship. In addition these two forms of cooperative behaviour are not even necessarily positively related to each other. For example, research on short-term absenteeism shows that cooperative behaviour between employees does not always mean that employees show cooperative behaviour toward the supervisor (Sanders & Hoekstra, 1998; Sanders, 2004; Sanders & Schyns, 2006a; Sanders, Seminara & Koster, 2006). Employees within a team may know that their colleagues are calling in sick when they are not unwell, and may cover for them. In this situation, employees are behaving cooperatively towards their team members but not towards the supervisor. Thus the group's goals may detract from organisational goals by reducing individual efforts, which negatively influences organisational productivity. Such a norm can be consolidated through informal mutual control, as the goals and interests of employees and employers become increasingly divergent (Flache, 1996). The consequences of this are that team members become friends, while individual employees and their supervisor become enemies.

This section discussed the reciprocal nature of cooperative behaviour and how it relates to OCB. It also explored the idea that cooperative behaviour in one relationship does not always imply cooperative behaviour in another relationship. An employee can have a cooperative relationship with colleague A, but not with colleague B or with the supervisor. The following sections discuss temporal, network and institutional embeddedness.

Temporal embeddedness[6]

Temporal embeddedness of relationships captures both the history and the (expected) future of relationships. If a relationship has a long history, individuals in relationships have had more opportunities to gain information about each other's reliability and previous behaviours, and to learn from the experience (Raub & Weesie, 1990, 2000). A common future allows both the promise of future rewards and the threat of negative sanctions. In the following paragraphs the effects of past experiences as a learning mechanism, and expectations about future interactions as a control mechanism, will be elaborated.

---

[6]This section is based on Koster and Sanders (2006a, 2006b), and Koster, Hodson, Stokman and Sanders (2007).

Learning about another person's behaviour may affect the level of cooperation that an employee shows towards that person. The reasoning behind this expectation is that cooperative behaviour requires a certain level of trust between individuals (Raub & Weesie, 2000; Sanders et al., 2005). Trust problems between employees have two characteristics (Coleman, 1990). First, each party gains when trust is placed and honoured. Second, an employee takes a risk when placing trust in other employees because the colleague can take advantage of the situation and abuse the trust (Raub & Weesie, 2000). When a colleague asks another employee for a favour, a trust problem arises because the employee does not know for sure if the colleague will return the favour later. It is quite possible that the colleague may behave opportunistically by accepting the help without returning it. Given this trust problem, the likelihood that an employee will assist a colleague may be very low.

If the employee has more information about the trustworthiness of their colleague, it can be expected that the employee will be more willing to place trust. Estimating the other's trustworthiness is easier when there have been previous interactions between the employees in which information is gathered about the behaviour and intentions of the other employee. As time passes and there are more interactions between them, the employee will know whether it is reasonable to expect that their colleague will show cooperative behaviour (Rholes, Newman & Ruble, 1990; Hinds, Carley, Krackhardt & Wholey, 2000). If the employee has shown cooperative behaviour toward a colleague in the past but does not show cooperative behaviour on a later occasion, the employee knows that the colleague acted opportunistically and is perhaps not a reliable person. Thus the level of cooperative behaviour between employees depends on the exchanges that have taken place between them over the course of their relationship.

Another result of a shared history is the accumulation of relation-specific investments (Raub & Weesie, 2000). Relation-specific investments can be described as investments that make the relationship more valuable for both partners. Within an organization, an example can be found in good productive relationships among employees, and between employees and supervisors. These valuable assets will be lost if an employee decides to accept a job offer from another organization. Mutual relation-specific investments reduce opportunistic behaviours and stabilize the relationship (Williamson, 1975, 1996).

A shared future promotes cooperative behaviours through conditional cooperation (Axelrod, 1984). When it is likely that there will be interactions between them in the future, an employee can try to exercise control over the behaviour of a colleague through the provision of rewards for cooperative behaviour and punishments for non-cooperative behaviour. As a result, it becomes rewarding for the colleague to show cooperative behaviour. If there is a future between colleagues, a series of cooperative moves between the employees can occur, since a good move by one employee can be rewarded by the other and a bad move can be punished with a negative sanction (Axelrod, 1984).

It can be expected that past experience will influence the effect of a shared future (Raub, 1997; Batenburg, Raub & Snijders, 2002). When there have been no interactions between them in the past, employees cannot predict each other's behaviour. If they have interacted in the past, cooperative behaviour may have developed. People tend to expect that other's future interactions will be similar to those in the past (Rholes et al., 1990). When someone has behaved cooperatively toward a fellow employee, the cooperative behaviour of that colleague will be likely to increase because there is good reason to trust the colleague. If the employees do not expect to interact in the future, or when there is a lack of cooperation between them, these incentives are much lower.

Empirical studies show mixed evidence for the expected effect of temporal embeddedness on the cooperative behaviour of employees. For instance, in a study of seventeen organisations, Sanders and Van Emmerik (2004) found no effect on cooperative behaviour of type of labour contract or number of years an employee expected to stay within the organization. Koster and Sanders (2006b) on the other hand found in two studies – a survey (736 respondents in ten organisations) and a vignette study (1040 vignettes, 260 respondents) empirical evidence for the learning hypothesis (shadow of the past). The control hypothesis (shadow of the future) could also be confirmed from the survey data. Negative experiences were shown to decrease willingness to help the other person and positive experiences increased willingness. Choosing to help and cooperate with a colleague is therefore highly dependent on the behaviour that colleague has demonstrated in the past.

Temporal embeddedness becomes especially an issue when focusing on employment status (temporary versus permanent) of employees. In order to satisfy the demands of a rapidly changing environment and increasingly competitive markets, the number of non-standard employment relationships has increased rapidly, and the use of temporary employment has found its way into virtually every organization (Piore, 2002; Blyton & Morris, 1992). It is assumed that temporary workers have a short-term relationship with their colleagues and that permanent workers have a long-term relationship with their colleagues. However, this assumption about the employment relationship may not hold in all instances, since both temporary and permanent workers can have relationships with colleagues that have a limited time-horizon. For instance, permanent workers may be moving to a different part of the organization or may even be considering leaving the organization. This aspect of the relationship cannot be accounted for when the distinction between temporary and permanent employment contracts is made.

In line with this theoretical reasoning, Koster and Sanders (2006b) and Sanders and Van Emmerik (2004) show that permanent and temporary workers do not differ in their cooperative behaviour towards colleagues and cooperative behaviour does not result from the length of the relationship. Instead cooperative behaviour of both permanent and temporary workers depends on their past and future interactions with colleagues. Furthermore, Koster, Sanders and Van Emmerik (2003) reported in a survey study (262 PhD students from a Dutch university) a curvilinear relationship between the temporary contract and cooperative behaviour. The analyses show that PhD students demonstrated less cooperative behaviour in the first and last year of the project than in the intervening years. This result confirms the notion that cooperative behaviour needs time to grow. The decline of cooperative behaviour at the end of the contract is consistent with the expectation that cooperative behaviour is affected by considerations pertaining to future interactions.

In this section we examined the effects of a relationship's *temporal embeddedness* on cooperative behaviour towards fellow employees and supervisors. It was shown that there is empirical evidence for the effects of the shadow of the past (past experience of cooperativeness), by means of a learning mechanism and shadow of the future (expected future cooperativeness), by means of a control mechanism. Both learning and control mechanisms can also be found in the explanation of the impact of *network embeddedness* and *institutional embeddedness* on cooperative behaviour. This will be shown in the next sections.

Network embeddedness[7]

Network embeddedness relates to the effect the number and quality of an employee's relationships has on the behaviour of that individual. In addition, the term relates to aspects of the structure of the networks these relationships constitute (Granovetter, 1985). Two individuals in a

---

[7]This section is based on Koster et al. (2003).

relationship may also have relationships with third parties at work. This means that a relationship between two people, for instance two team members, is not isolated and independent, but is embedded in the relationships within that network. Networks provide information and serve as a means for the direct and indirect rewarding of cooperative behaviour and direct and indirect sanctioning of non cooperative behaviour.

Network embeddedness can be either formal or informal. Formal networks are impersonal and explicit, whereas informal network are personal and implicit. In order to understand cooperative behaviour, both formal and informal networks should be taken into account. Formal networks of employees refer to organizational positions designated by organizations. In addition to these formal networks, informal network structures may also be – and usually are – present within an organization. Informal networks consisting of personal relations also shape the behaviour of employees. Using the informal network, activities both within and outside the organization can be organized. For instance, non-work activities might include having lunch with team members, going for a drink together after work and visiting each other at home. It is these kinds of informal activities in particular that give employees the opportunity to get to know each other better. As work relationships become closer, there are more possibilities to sanction cooperative behaviour positively and opportunistic behaviour negatively.

Good formal and informal relations with colleagues and with the supervisor are important for employees. For instance, acceptance in a group is one of the most important informal rewards in the workplace (Pfeffer, 1982). Compliance to group norms may be rewarded with social support from the group. In this sense group norms influence the behaviour of the group members (Coleman, 1994), resulting in positive and negative behaviour towards the organization (Roethlisberger & Dickson, 1939). Research on informal and formal network embeddedness shows that long-term, stable and close formal and informal relationships among employees, and informal activities within and outside the organization, have the ability to enhance one's willingness to behave cooperatively (Flache, 1996; Flache & Macy, 1996).

Network embeddedness can be related to cohesiveness. It can be expected that members of cohesive groups may interact more frequently. In this case they enjoy being together and therefore have more opportunities for co-worker control. A cohesive group will have a strong impact on its members, who will strive to keep the group intact and to remain in the group, conform to the group's norms and demands, and regard the group's interest above their own. Research shows positive relationships between group cohesiveness and employee satisfaction (Dobbins & Zaccaro, 1986), and cooperative behaviours (Kidwell Jr, Mossholder & Bennett, 1997).

Research shows that the leadership style of the supervisor or team leader can be related to the cohesiveness of his or her team, and as a consequence to the cooperative behaviour of employees. Koster and Sanders (2006b) and Koster et al. (2007) showed that supervisors play a key role in eliciting cooperative behaviours from their employees. They can do this directly by initiating cooperative behaviour towards their team. Since cooperative behaviour is reciprocal, a good move from the supervisor will be answered by a cooperative move from the subordinates. In addition, supervisors can also play a role in creating cooperative relationships among team members.

Sanders and Schyns (2006b, see also Sanders, Schyns, Koster & Rotteveel, 2003) extend on the results of Koster and Sanders (2006) and focus on the relationship between the perception of the leadership style of a supervisor and cooperative behaviour towards colleagues and to the supervisor. In this study it was found that consensus among employees regarding how the leader is evaluated or perceived, is an important stimulus for creating a cohesive in-group that will enhance cooperative behaviour among team members. But cohesiveness and consensus within a team is only related to cooperative behaviour towards the supervisor if the supervisor is perceived as 'high transformational'. In transformational leadership style, the supervisor asks employees to transcend their own self-interest for the good of the group, and to consider their long-term needs to develop themselves, rather than their needs of the moment. When employees perceive their supervisor as 'low transformational', there is no clear relationship between group cohesiveness and cooperative behaviour towards the supervisor.

Network embeddedness inside the organization can be influenced by circumstances outside the organization. For instance, the decline of the 'single breadwinner' family and the rising number of dual-earner families means that both male and female employees are confronted, to an ever-increasing degree, with conflicting responsibilities and duties from their organization, their households and their children. A growing proportion of employees report experiencing significant time pressures on the job and complain of burn out. Schor (1992) remarks that *'the quality of life is threatened as relatively short working hours, relaxing daily life and appreciation for the "finer things" are giving way in a number of countries to longer hours of work, a faster pace of life, and American style of consumption'*. The question can be asked whether it is true that those employees who are under time pressure with regard to work and households show less cooperative behaviour in organizations. In a study of 1347 people from 17 Dutch organizations, Sanders and Van Emmerik (2004) found that having children was positively related to cooperative behaviour towards other team members but was not significantly related to cooperative behaviour towards the supervisor. Furthermore, working overtime was positively related to cooperative behaviour to the supervisor, while it was not related to cooperative behaviour toward team members.

In this section we elaborated on the effects of network embeddedness on cooperative behaviour. Both informal and formal organizational networks were considered, as well as network embeddedness outside the organization. In the next section the effects of the third form of social embeddedness, institutional embeddedness, on the cooperative behaviour of employees is discussed.

Institutional embeddedness

Relationships are influenced by institutions, which provide the formal rules that govern the interactions between employers and employees and the interactions among employees; i.e., workplace relationships are *institutionally embedded* (North, 1990). Governance structures constitute the settings in which employees weigh alternatives and make decisions concerning the duration and timing of efforts expended for the organization. In this sense, the traditional bureaucratic-Tayloristic workplace presented a different context for making decisions than the modern firm does today. The content of an organization's governance structures are evident in human resource policies. Elements of formal governance structures are remuneration policies, monitoring and control systems.[8] Governance structures may also provide incentives to engaging social relations.

Characteristics of governance structures in most modern organizations compared to traditional firms include lower job security, a larger contingent workforce, the use of more performance-related pay and promotion systems, and the replacement of predictable career paths with

---

[8]An example of modern formal governance is project careers, a career system used widely by Dutch banks (see for instance Sanders, Van Emmerik and Raub, 2002). In a project career, employees have a permanent contract but they are placed in successive short-term projects in order to increase their flexibility and experience, and thus their value for the employer.

more uncertain and competitive promotion systems. These characteristics not only increase incentives for competition between employees but they also make promotion and pay rise more uncertain and less transparent.

It is well known from earlier research that differentiated and unpredictable reward systems may negatively affect employees' sense of fairness with respect to the employers' behaviour (Van Emmerik, Hermkens & Sanders, 1998). Denison and Mishra (1995), and Tyler (2001) found that a certain degree of predictability of resources and rewards is essential for meaning and satisfaction in work. Such predictability is also essential for the establishment of trust between workers and management (Fox, 1974; Granovetter, 1985). It can be assumed that the more supervisors show the presence of explicit fair pay rules, the more employees perceive predictability of rewards and resources.

According to the human resource management literature (Boselie, Dietz & Boon, 2005), investing in training and promotion are two central rewards that an organization can provide in order to enhance employees' performance. Employers can give their employees the prospect of a career in their organization. A career may be a way to achieve personal development, changing job demands so that their work stays interesting and provides a way to learn new skills, thereby creating more opportunities for interesting jobs. Career development could imply that employees perceive the prospect of an interesting career path with sufficient challenges and variation within the organization. For the employer, this could result in a stable workforce with motivated and committed people who are willing to work a bit harder than they have to, help their supervisor and colleagues, use their skills, and who are willing to acquire new firm-specific expertise; in short, employees who cooperate with the organization. To explain this mutual investment model, an application of social exchange theory of Blau (1964) and Homans (1961) for the employment relation can be used, that is, the relation between supervisor and employee. Tsui, Pearce, Porter and Tripoli (1997) argue that the employer (in this case the supervisor) is able to show the employee that he or she cares about the employee's wellbeing by investing in the employee's career. In turn, the employee may become willing to take on more tasks than formally stated in the contract or where agreed upon beforehand.

Lambooij, Flache, Sanders and Siegers (2007; see also Lambooij, 2005) examined whether training and promotion (possibilities) influence the willingness of employees to work overtime. Voluntarily working overtime can particularly be seen as a form of cooperation because it is costly. The employee has to give up spare time in order to be able to cooperate and the (short-term) costs only affect the employee and not the employer. In return, those who directly benefit when an employee completes a task because of working overtime (either colleagues or the supervisor), are then enabled to return the cooperation by finishing any postponed tasks for the employee. Directly compensating for cooperation may be harder when someone has worked overtime. Outside of work, employees can spend time with their loved-ones, spend time on a hobby or do something else which cannot be adequately compensated by the organization.

Multi-level analyses of a vignette experiment (N=338 in five organizations; 1531 vignettes) show that employees are more willing to work overtime when their employer has provided training, when the employee had been recently promoted, when the supervisor was supportive in the past and when colleagues approved of working overtime and behaved similarly. Future promotions, however, did not affect the willingness to overwork (Lambooij et al., 2007; Lambooij, 2005).

Human resource management (HRM) is assumed to affect knowledge, skills, abilities (Schuler & Jackson, 1995), attitudes and behaviour of employees (Guest, 1997) and may therefore affect performance of the organization (Boselie et al., 2005). The alignment of HRM with the organization strategy (*strategic fit*) and the alignment of the various HRM practices, such as career opportunities, training and appraisal within the organization (*internal fit*) are assumed to be important factors in explaining the link between HRM and organizational performance (Baron & Kreps, 1999). When HRM within an organization is well aligned, the employees know what is expected of them, they may act similarly, and their expectations about work and behaviour may be uniform. In line with Baron and Kreps (1999) it can be expected that when the internal and strategic fit are better, employees in an organization will cooperate more and that this will enhance the productivity of the organization. Baron and Kreps (1999) emphasize the importance of consistent HRM policy and provide a number of explanations. Consistent HRM practices are beneficial because it helps the individual to understand what is expected of them. The same argument can be found in the theoretical work of Bowen and Ostroff (2004). Employees develop expectations on how they will be treated in the future. When HRM practices are inconsistent, this will negatively affect the learning process.

An empirical study by Dorenbosch, Sanders & De Reuver (2006) shows that when HR practices are perceived to be more consistent, this leads to more effective commitment of the employees.

Conclusions

Recent developments both inside and outside organizations have sparked new research questions about the behaviour of supervisors and employees within modern work organizations. One of the characteristics of the modern organization is that employees bear a much larger responsibility for attaining production goals than in classical hierarchical firms, and employees are often working in teams or groups, such as management teams, project groups or self-management teams (Goodman, 1986; Cohen & Bailey, 1967). In this chapter we focused on the cooperative behaviours of employees needed to attain the production goals of such teams.

In addition to the description of the nature of cooperative behaviours and the assumption that cooperative behaviours in relationships are characterized by a norm of reciprocity (Gouldner, 1960; Hechter, 1987; Sanders, Emans & Koster, 2004), and since employee–employee and employee–manager relationships are quite different (Smith et al., 1995) we distinguish theoretically and empirically between cooperative behaviour from employees towards other employees (horizontal cooperative behaviour) and cooperative behaviour from employees towards their supervisor (vertical cooperative behaviour).

Given this norm of reciprocity it was argued that cooperative behaviours of employees should be examined as a result of the relationships employees have with different people within the organization. The *social embeddedness* of relationships is seen an important perspective to understand cooperative behaviour of employees. Social embeddedness of relationships was described in terms of three kinds of embeddedness within organizations: temporal embeddedness, network embeddedness and institutional embeddedness (Raub, 1997; Raub & Weesie, 1990; 2000). The three forms of social embeddedness were discussed and results of empirical research were outlined. In addition to the focus on the emergence of cooperative behaviour in terms of becoming friends, attention was paid to the emergence of non-cooperative behaviour likely to result in enmity.

References

Appelbaum, E. & Batt, R. (1994). *The New American Workplace*. Ithaca: ILR Press.

Aquino, K. (1998). A social dilemma perspective on cooperative behaviour in organisations: The effects of scarcity. *Group & Organisation Management, 23*, 390–414.

Axelrod, R. (1984). *The Evolution of Cooperation*. New York: Basic Books.

Azariadis, C. (1987). Implicit contracts. In: J. Eatwell, M. Milgate & P. Newman (eds). *The New Palgrave: Allocation, Information and Markets.* London: Macmillan, 132–140.

Barnard, C. I. (1938). *The Functions of the Executive.* Cambridge: Harvard University Press.

Baron, J. N. & Kreps, D. M. (1999). *Strategic Human Resources. Framework for General Managers.* New York: Wiley and Sons.

Bateman, T. S. & Organ, D. W. (1983). Job satisfaction and the good soldier: The relationship between affect and employee citizenship. *Academy of Management Journal, 26,* 587–595.

Batenburg, R., Raub, W. & Snijders, C. (2002). Contacts and contracts: Dyadic embeddedness and the contractual behaviour of firms. In V. Buskens, W. Raub & C. Snijders (eds) *The Governance of Relations in Markets and Organizations, Research in the Sociology of Organization,* pp. 135–188. Oxford: JAI/Elsevier.

Blau, P. (1955). *The Dynamics of Bureaucracy.* Chicago, Il: University of Chicago Press.

Blau, P. (1964). *Exchange and Power in Social Life.* New York: Wiley.

Blyton, P. & Morris, J. (1992). HRM and the limits of flexibility. In P. Blyton & P. Turnbull (eds) *Reassessing Human Resource Management.* Thousand Oaks: Sage.

Boselie, P., Dietz, G. & Boon, C. (2005). Commonalities and contradictions in research on Human Resource Management and Performance. *Human Resource Management Journal, 15,* 67–81.

Borman, W. C. & Motowidlo, S. J. (1993). Expanding the criterion domain to include elements of contextual performance. In Schmit, N. and Borman, W. C. (eds), *Personnel Selection,* San Francisco. Jossey-Bass, 71–98.

Bowen, D. E. & Ostroff, C. (2004). Understanding HRM-Firm performance linkages: The Role of the 'strength' of the HRM system. *Academy of Management Review, 29*(2), 203–221.

Cohen, S. G. & Bailey, D. E. (1997). What makes team work: Group effectiveness research from the shop floor to the executive suite. *Journal of Management, 23,* 239–290.

Coleman, J. S. (1990). *Foundations of Social Theory.* Cambridge, MA: Harvard University Press.

Coleman, J. S. (1994). A rational choice perspective on economic sociology. In N. J. Smelser & R. Swedberg (eds) *The Handbook of Economic Sociology* (pp. 166–180). Princeton, N.J.: Princeton University Press.

Cooper, C. L. & Lewis, S. (1999). Gender and the changing nature of work. In G. N. Powell (ed.). *Handbook of Gender and Work.* Thousands Oaks, California: Sage Publications, 37–46.

Denison, D. R. & Mishra, K. (1995). Toward a theory of organisational culture and effectiveness. *Organisation Science, 6,* 204–223.

Dobbins, G. R. & Zaccaro, S. J. (1986). The effects of group cohesion and leader behaviour on subordinate satisfaction. *Group and Organisational Studies, 11,* 203–219.

Dorenbosch, L., Sanders, K. & De Reuver, R. (2006). Getting the HR message across: The linkage between line – HR consensus and 'commitment strength' among hospital employees. *Management Revue, 17,* 274–291.

Flache, A. (1996). *The Double Edge of Networks: An Analysis of the Effect of Informal Networks on Cooperation in Social Dilemmas.* Amsterdam: Thesis Publishers.

Flache, A. & Macy, M. W. (1996). The weakness of strong ties: Collective action failure in a highly cohesive group. *Journal of Mathematical Sociology. 21*, 3–28.

Gouldner, A. W. (1960), The norm of reciprocity: A preliminary statement. *American Sociological Review, 25*, 161–178.

Goodman, P. S. (1986). The impact of task and technology on group performance. In P. Goodman (ed.) *Designing Effective Work Groups*. San Francisco: Jossey-Bass, 120–167.

Granovetter, M. S. (1985). Economic action and social structure: The problem of embeddedness. *American Journal of Sociology, 91*, 481–510.

Guest, D. E. (1997). Human resource management and performance: A review and research agenda. *International Journal of Human Resource Management, 8*(3), 263–276.

Guttman, L. (1952). Multiple group methods for common-factor analysis: Their basis, computation and interpretation. *Psychometrika, 17*, 209–222.

Hage, J. (1980). *Theories of Organisations: Form, Process, and Transformation*. New York: Wiley.

Handy, Ch. (1995). Trust and the virtual organisation. *Harvard Business Review, May–June*, 40–50.

Hart, O. (1987). Incomplete contracts. In J. Eatwell, M. Milgate & P. Newman. *The New Palgrave: Allocation, Information and Market*. London: Macmillan, 16–79.

Hechter, M. (1987). *Principles of Group Solidarity*. Berkeley: University of California Press.

Hendriks, P. & Kiers, H. A. L. (1999). Confirmatory factor analysis methods compared: The multiple group method and maximum likelihood confirmatory factor analysis. *Research Report*, Department of Psychology, Groningen.

Hinds, P.J., Carley, K. M., Krackhardt, D. & Wholey, D. (2000). Choosing work group members: Balancing similarity, competence and familiarity. *Organizational Behaviour and Human Decision Processes, 81*, 226–251.

Hirschman, A. O. (1970). *Exit, Voice, and Loyalty: Responses to Decline in Firms, Organisations, and States*. Cambridge: Harvard University Press.

Hodson, R. (1999). Organisational anomie and worker consent. *Work & Occupation, 26*, 292–313.

Homans, G. C. (1961). *Social Behaviour: Its Elementary Forms*. London: Routledge & Kegan Paul.

Kidwell, Jr, R. E., Mossholder, K. W. & Bennett, N. (1997). Cohesiveness and organisational citizenship behaviour: A multilevel analysis using work groups and individuals. *Journal of Management, 23*, 775–793.

Koster, F. (2005). For the time being. Accounting for inconclusive findings concerning the effects of temporary employment relationships on solidary behaviour of employees. Veenendaal: Universal Press.

Koster, F., Hodson, R., Stokman, F. & Sanders, K. (2007). Solidarity through networks: The effects of task and informal interdependence on cooperation within teams. *Employee Relations, 29*, 117–137.

Koster, F. & Sanders, K. (2006a) Serial solidarity: The effects of experiences and expectations on cooperative behaviour of employees. *International Journal of Human Resource Management, 18*, 568–585.

Koster, F. & Sanders, K. (2006b). Organisational Citizens or Cooperative Relationships? A social dilemma approach to solidary behaviour of employees. *Personnel Review, 35*, 519–537.

118   *Friends and Enemies in Organizations*

Koster, F., Sanders, K. & Van Emmerik, H. (2003). Solidarity of Temporary Workers: The effects of temporal and network embeddedness on solidary behaviour of Ph.D. students. *The Netherlands Journal of Social Sciences, 38,* 65–80.

Lambooij, M. (2005). Promoting cooperation. Studies into the effects of long-term and short-term rewards on cooperation of employees. Veenendaal: Universal Press.

Lambooij, M., Flache, A., Sanders, K. & Siegers, J. (2007). Encouraging employees to cooperate. The effects of sponsored training and promotion practices on employees' willingness to work overtime. *International Journal of Human Resource Management, 18,* 1748–1767.

LePine, J. A., Erez, A. & Johnson, D. E. (2002). The nature and dimensionality of organisational citizenship behaviour: A critical review. *Journal of Applied Psychology, 87,* 52–65.

Macaulay, S. (1963). Non-contractual relations in business. *American Sociological Review, 28,* 55–66.

Macneil, I. R. (1980). *The New Social Contract.* New Haven, CT: Yale University Press.

Maier, M. (1999). On the gendered substructure of organisation: Dimensions and dilemmas of corporate masculinity. In G. N. Powell (ed.). *Handbook of Gender and Work.* Thousands Oaks, California: Sage Publications, 69–83.

Morrison, E. W. & Phelps, C. C. (1999). Taking charge at work: Extra-role efforts to initiate workplace change. *Academy of Management Journal, 42,* 403–419.

Motowidlo, S. J., Borman, W. C., & Schmit, M. J. (1997). A theory of individual differences in task and contextual performance. *Human Performance, 10,* 71–83.

Motowidlo, S. J. & Van Scotter, J. R. (1994). Evidence that task performance should be distinguished from contextual performance. *Journal of Applied Psychology, 79,* 475–480.

MacKenzie, S., Podsakoff, P. & Fetter, R. (1991). Organisational citizenship behaviour and objective productivity as determinants of supervisorial evaluations of salespersons' performance. *Organisational Behaviour and Human Decision Processes, 50,* 123–150.

Miller, G. J. (1992). *Managerial Dilemmas: the Political Economy of Hierarchy.* Cambridge: Cambridge University Press.

Motowidlo, S. J. (2000). Some basic issues related to contextual performance and organisational citizenship behaviour in human resource management. *Human Resource Management Review, 10,* 115–127.

Mowday, R. T., Steers, L. W. & Porter, R. M. (1982). *Employee-Organisation Linkages: The Psychology of Commitment, Absenteeism, and Turn Over.* New York, NY: Academic Press.

North, D. C. (1990). *Institutions, Institutional Change and Economic Performance.* Cambridge: Cambridge University Press.

Organ, D. W. (1988).*Organisational Citizenship Behaviour: The Good Soldier Syndrome.* Lexington: Lexington Books.

Organ, D. W. (1990). *The Motivational Basis of Organisational Citizenship Behaviour.* In Staw, B. M. and Cummings, L. L. (eds), *Research in Organisational Behaviour.* Greenwich: JAI Press, 43–72.

Organ, D. W. (1997). Organizational citizenship behaviour: It's construct clean-up time. *Human Performance, 10,* 85–97.

Organ, D. W. & Lingl, A. (1995). Personality, satisfaction, and organisational citizenship behaviour. *Journal of Social Psychology, 135,* 339–350.

Pfeffer, J. (1982). *Organisation and Organisation Theory.* Boston: Pitman.

Piore, M. J. (2002). Thirty years later: Internal labor markets, flexibility and the new economy. *Journal of Management and Governance, 6,* 271–279.

Podsakoff, P. M., MacKenzie, S. B., Paine, J. B. & Bachrach, D. G. (2000). Organisational citizenship behaviours: A critical review of the theoretical and empirical literature and suggestions for future research. *Journal of Management, 26,* 513–563.

Pond, S. B., Nacoste, R. W., Mohr, M. F. & Rodriguez, C. M. (1997). The measurement of organisational citizenship behaviour: Are we assuming too much? *Journal of Applied Social Psychology, 27,* 1527–1544.

Probert, B. (1999). Mothers and the labourforce. *Family Matters, 54,* 60–64.

Raub, W. (1997). *Samenwerking in Duurzame Relaties en Sociale Cohesie.* [Cooperation in long-term relationships and social cohesiveness]. Amsterdam: Thesis Publishers.

Raub, W. & Weesie, J. (1990). Reputation and efficiency in social interactions: An example of network effects. *American Journal of Sociology, 96,* 626–654.

Raub, W. & Weesie, J. (2000). The management of durable relations. In J. Weesie & W. Raub (eds) *The Management of Durable Relations. Theoretical Models and Empirical Studies of Households and Organisations.* Amsterdam: Thela Thesis, 1–32.

Rholes, W. S., Newman, L. S. & Ruble, D. N. (1990). Understanding self and other: Developmental and motivational aspects of perceiving others in terms of invariant dispositions. In E. T. Higgins & R. Sorrentino (eds) *Handbook of Motivation and Cognition: Foundations of Social Behavior: Vol II* (pp. 369–407). New York: Guilford Press.

Roethlisberger, F. J. & Dickson, W. J. (1939). *Management and the Worker: An Account of a Research Program Conducted by the Western Electric Company.* Mass.: Harvard University Press.

Sanders, K. (2004). Playing truant within organisations: Informal relationships, work ethics and absenteeism. *Journal of Managerial Psychology, 19,* 136–155.

Sanders, K., Emans, B. & Koster, F. (2004). Determinanten van solidair gedrag binnen organisaties: Een terugblik. [Determinants of solidary behaviour within modern organisations: A review]. *Gedrag & Organisatie, 17,* 120–129.

Sanders, K., Seminara, J. & Koster, F. (2006). Solidarity of women and men in the workplace: Individual characteristics or quality of relationships? In L. den Dulk, T. van der Lippe & J. Schippers (ed.) *Emancipatie als Kwestie. Liber Amicorum voor Anneke van Doorne-Huiskes rond het thema vrouwen en beroepsparticipatie.* Amsterdam: Dutch University Press, 79–94.

Sanders, K. & Schyns, B. (2006a). Introduction: Trust, conflict and cooperative behaviour: Considering reciprocity within organisations. *Personnel Review, 35,* 508–518.

Sanders, K. & Schyns, B. (2006b). Leadership and solidarity behaviour: Consensus in perception of employees within teams. *Personnel Review, 35,* 538–556.

Sanders, K., Schyns, B., Koster, F. & Rotteveel, C. (2003). Het stimuleren van solidair gedrag: Een kwestie van leiderschap [Stimulating solidarity: A matter of leadership]. *Gedrag & Organisatie, 16,* 237–254.

Sanders, K. & Van Emmerik, H. (2004). Does modern organisations and governance threat solidarity? *Journal of Management and Governance, 8,* 351–372.

Sanders, K., Van Emmerik, I. J. H. & Raub, W. (2002). Nieuwe vragen voor onderzoek naar solidair gedrag binnen moderne organisaties [New questions for research into solidary behaviour within modern organisations]. *Gedrag & Organisatie, 15*, 184–201.

Sanders, K., Van Emmerik, I. J. & Raub, W. (2005). Solidarität am arbeitsplatz: Fiktion, fakten und kräfte. In J. Berger. (Hg). *ZerreiBt das Soziale Band. Beiträge zu einer aktuellen gesellschaftpolitischen Debatte.* Frankfurt/New York: Campus Verlag, 121–142.

Sanders, K. & Hoekstra, S. K. (1998). Informal networks and absenteeism within an organisation. *Computational and Mathematical Organisation Theory, 4*, 149–163.

Schor, J. B. (1992). *The Overworked American. The Unexpected Decline of Leisure.* New York: Basic Books.

Singh, V. & Vinnicombe, S. (2000). Gendered meanings of commitment from high technology engineering supervisors in the UK and Sweden. *Gender, Work and Organisation, 7*, 1–19.

Schuler, R. S. & Jackson, S. E. (1995). Understanding human resource management in the context of organisations and their environment. *Annual Review of Psychology, 46*, 237–264.

Seashore, S. E. (1954). *Group Cohesiveness in the Industrial Work Group.* Ann Arbor: Institute for Social Research, University of Michigan.

Smith, K. G., Carroll, S. & Ashford, S. (1995). Intra- and interorganisational cooperation: Toward a research agenda. *Academy of Management Journal, 38*, 7–23.

Smith, C. A., Organ, D. W. and Near, J. P. (1983). Organisational citizenship behaviour: Its nature and antecedents. *Journal of Applied Psychology, 68*, 653–663.

Tsui, A. S., Pearce, J. L., Porter, L. W. & Tripoli, A. M. (1997). Alternative approaches to the employee-organisation relationship: Does investment in employees pay off? *Academy of Management Journal, 40*, 1089–1121.

Tyler, T. R. (2001). Why do people rely on others? Social identity and social aspects of trust. In K. S. Cook (ed.) *Trust in Society.* New York: Russell Sage Foundation.

Torenvlied, R. & Velner, G. (1998). Informal networks and resistance to organisational change. *Computational and Mathematical Organisation Theory, 4*, 165–188.

Van Dyne, L., Cummings, L. L. & Parks, J. M. (1995). Extra-role behaviours: In pursuit of construct and definitional clarity (A bridge over muddied waters), in Staw, B. M. and Cummings, L. L. (eds), *Research in Organisational Behaviour.* Greenwich: JAI Press, 215–285.

Van Dyne, L. L., Graham, J. W. & Dienesch, R. M. (1994). Organisational citizenship behaviour: Construct redefinition, measurement and validity. *Academy of Management Journal, 37*, 765–802.

Van Emmerik, H., Hermkens, P. & Sanders, K. (1998). Personeelsbeleid en rechtvaardigheidsgevoelens van medewerkers. [HRM practices and feelings of justice of employees]. *Gedrag en Organisatie, 11*(6), 385–400.

Wickens, P. D. (1995). *The Ascendant Organisation: Combining Commitment and Control for Long-Term, Sustainable Business Success.* Basingstoke: Macmillan.

Williams, L. J. & Anderson, S. E. (1991). Job satisfaction and organizational commitment as predictors of organizational citizenship and in-role behaviors. *Journal of Management, 17*, 601–617.

Williamson, O. E. (1975). *Market and Hierarchies: Analysis and Antitrust Implications.* New York: Free Press.

Williamson, O. E. (1996). *The Mechanism of Governance.* New York: Oxford University Press.

7

The Double Edged Sword: Organizational Outcomes of Workplace Friendships

Rachel L. Morrison

Introducing Olivia, Jason and Emily

Olivia and Jason were close friends at University and shared student accommodation for some years; Olivia began working within Org X eight years ago and recommended Jason for a role when Org X was recruiting and Jason was hired. They have been within the same department for two years. Emily also works in the department and, over the past five years, she and Olivia have become increasingly close. They now work together on projects whenever they can and, more importantly to both of them, they have developed a strong friendship which is maintained outside the workplace. They meet for lunch on the weekend, baby-sit each other's children and holiday together.

Olivia really enjoyed Jason's first six months in Org X; it was wonderful to work with someone who shared part of her past and with whom she could reminisce about old times and old friends. However, since his arrival in Org X, Jason has become more and more difficult to work with. He has made no effort to make friends and does not lunch with his colleagues. He is not happy in his work, and not particularly good at his job. To compensate, he tries to delegate as much of it as he can, and often complains about his workload in order to appear busy and productive to others. He has been embroiled in conflict with several people in the department and frequently spends time at Olivia's desk complaining loudly about management and colleagues. Jason believes that, because they had a prior friendship, Olivia's loyalty will be with him rather than people he perceives as nothing more than her co-workers (as opposed to 'real' friends).

Jason will often ask Olivia for favours such as extending deadlines, assistance with his work and covering for him when he misses meetings

or pulls 'sickies'. Olivia has been trying to carefully manage her rela-
tionship with Jason. She wants to distance herself from him but is
very worried that he will turn on her as he has on others in the
department. Although she genuinely likes Jason, she has become
increasingly uncomfortable with his requests and with him using their
prior friendship as reason to expect special treatment.

Olivia has been leaning on Emily a great deal for emotional
support. But, even with Emily's support, Olivia's work is suffer-
ing. She has become aware that some in Org X perceive her and
Jason to be close friends and his bad behaviour is reflecting poorly on
her. She wishes she had never recommended Jason for a role in her
department.

The brief case above goes some way towards illustrating the very different outcomes friendships can have in the workplace. Both Emily and
Jason are Olivia's friends but the organizational outcomes of these
two relationships will be poles apart. Having friends is almost uni-
versally considered to be a good thing and, both outside and within
the work context, friends can enrich the environment, providing
support and sociability (Kenny & Kashy, 1994). Given that research
also generally links a friendly workplace with positive organizational
outcomes (Morrison, 2004; Nielsen, Jex & Adams, 2000; Richer,
Blanchard & Vallerand, 2002; Riordan & Griffeth, 1995), it is reasonable to assume that friends at work benefit all concerned. However
this situation may not be as clear-cut as it seems (Morrison & Nolan,
2007). The current interest in the concept of social support and the
potential benefits that may be provided often ignores or downplays
the notion that social relations entail costs as well as rewards (Blau,
1964; Rook, 1984). In addition the form, function and interactions
within relationships will be almost as varied as the people engaging
in them. Thus the outcomes of friends at work are likely to range
from positive and constructive (Olivia and Emily, above), to negligible
or neutral, to negative and difficult to manage (Olivia's relationship
with Jason).

Previous research (Morrison, 2004; Morrison, 2005a; Morrison, 2005b;
Morrison, 2005c; Morrison, 2006b; Morrison, 2008; Nielsen et al., 2000)
investigated the interrelationships among the opportunities and prevalence of friendship at work, workgroup cohesion, job satisfaction, organizational commitment and intentions to leave the organization. The
present chapter explores these findings, discussing the notion that the

organizational outcomes of friendship are complex and cannot easily be measured or assessed. This chapter queries whether friendships at work can be consistently or reliably linked to key organizational outcomes. Points made within this chapter will be linked to the case of Olivia and her friends (above).

Why study friendship?

Teams and workgroups are becoming more and more prevalent in the workplace, which makes the study of workplace friendships increasingly salient (Nielsen et al., 2000). Generally individuals who perceive that they have better workplace relationships report higher job satisfaction (Robinson, Roth & Brown, 1993; Winstead, Derlega, Montgomery & Pilkington, 1995) and an improved experience of work. Duck (1983) states that employees who are friendlier work well together and a link has been found between relationship factors such as cooperation/ social support and team productivity (Campion, Medsker & Higgs, 1993). The empirical studies on friendship generally highlight the positive outcomes of these relationships (e.g., Morrison, 2004; Richer et al., 2002; Riordan & Griffeth, 1995). Positive outcomes of friendship include improved worker wellbeing, providing increased communication (Kramer, 1996), support (Buunk, Doosje, Liesbeth, Jans & Hopstaken, 1993), trust, respect, cooperation and energy, which can in turn influence work related attitudes and behaviours (Foote, 1985; Krackhardt & Stern, 1988; Riordan & Griffeth, 1995). Thus, friendships developed within the workplace represent a key element in the informal structure of an organization, potentially facilitating organizational effectiveness.

Defining workplace friendship

Definitions of friendship are extremely variable. This is a complicating factor in any study of friendship, as one person may consider a colleague with whom they occasionally socialize a friend; while another may use the term only for people with whom they are very intimate. Friendships are voluntary relationships that exist primarily for enjoyment and satisfaction, rather than for the fulfilment of a particular function or role (Sapadin, 1988).

Jason believes that the term 'friend' should be reserved for someone who you have a relationship with outside of work; perhaps partly because he has not developed any strong friendships at work. He considers Olivia to

be his friend because they had a prior relationship, but does not per-
ceive the collegial relationships of those in his department to be true
friendships.

The friendship relationship is one which is seen as somehow special by
the participants, and which is rewarding. A seminal definition by
Wright (1974) incorporates the *context* in which friendships occur.
Wright defines friendship as a relationship involving voluntary interaction, in which '... the commitment of the individuals to one another
usually takes precedence over their commitment to the contexts in
which the interaction takes place' (p. 94). This is important when con-
ceptualising workplace relationships as it implies that the boundaries
of genuine friendships supersede the role boundaries that may exist in
a particular context.

Olivia's relationship with Emily meets the criteria for genuine friendship;
voluntariness *is exemplified by the time they spend together outside of*
work. This relationship would likely continue if one of them left Org X
*because they **enjoy** each other's company and get benefits over and above*
the tangible rewards obtained from working together on projects. In addi-
*tion the relationship is **reciprocal**; Olivia and Emily help each other and*
feel they can rely on one another.

It is worth distinguishing between formal and informal relationships
within organizations. The workplace relationships which have received
by far the most research attention are those of superior-subordinate (or
supervisor-supervisee) (e.g., Allen, 1995; Largent, 1987; Murphy & Ensher,
1999; Vecchio & Bullis, 2001) and mentor-protégé (e.g., Beans, 1999;
Higgins & Kram, 2001; Kram & Isabella, 1985; Kram, 1983). These relationships lack the voluntary aspect of friendships as they are prescribed
by the organization; they are an example of *formal* relationships and are
therefore not a direct focus of the current volume. This is not to say
however that a true friendship cannot evolve from an existing formal
organizational relationship. This chapter focuses on informal organizational relationships; those not prescribed by the organization.

Friendship as a multi-dimensional construct

Friends have long been recognized as important sources of affection,
pleasure, companionship and support. Aristotle described a multi-
dimensional conceptualization of friendship, outlining three functions,

or characteristics, of friendship; the qualities of *goodness, enjoyableness* and *utility*. Aristotle believed that perfect friendships would be characterized more by goodness (or beneficence), than by either utility or enjoyableness (Bukowski, Nappi & Hoza, 1987). There has been empirical research in social psychology that examines the validity of the multi-dimensional model first proposed by Aristotle. Murstein and Spitz (1974) conducted research with college women, testing Aristotle's theory. The authors found that the three friendship factors they identified, related closely to the three components of friendship proposed by Aristotle, thereby supporting his model. Bukowski et al. (1987) also assessed the validity of Aristotle's model, addressing some of the limitations of Murstein and Spitz's study by researching both men and women. Bukowski et al. also found support for Aristotle's conceptualization of friendship, establishing that the three components could be measured reliably, and also supporting the validity of the model as a means of understanding friendships.

The idea that all friendships are not alike (i.e., that different friendships will be characterized by various degrees of goodness, enjoyableness and/or utility) is an important one. It highlights the importance of defining and characterizing relationships under study; considering the context, antecedents, functions and consequences of the relationship for individuals. It also highlights the notion that different friendships at work (or in any other context) will not necessarily serve similar functions or have similar outcomes.

Jason's relationship with Olivia is characterized primarily by utility. He relies on her for favours and expects her to offer tangible help and support in the workplace. His behaviour demonstrates a lack of respect for her as an individual. In addition, the relationship lacks reciprocity. He does not offer very much in return for the assistance that Olivia provides. Goodness and enjoyableness are lacking in this relationship.

Gender differences in friendships

Research into friendship suggests that, not only will friends have different functions for different people in general, but also that there will be gender differences, with men and women utilizing their friends in different ways (refer also to Barbara Winstead and Valerie Morganson's chapter in this volume). While friendship relationships for men and women are similar in many respects (Hyde, 2005; Wright, 1988) and there are large variations *within* the genders in terms of their behaviour in same-sex friendships (Walker, 1994), there have been consistent findings in both the social psychology and organizational psychology literature of gender differences in friendships. Women's friendships have been described as communal, and tend to involve more self-disclosure, supportiveness and complexity than do friendships between men (Markiewicz, Devine & Kausilas, 2000; Winstead, 1986; Wright, 1988; Wright & Scanlon, 1991). Men's friendships can be described as instrumental; they tend to be organized around shared interests and activities, the exchange of tangible rewards and favours and be action-oriented rather than person-oriented (Markiewicz et al., 2000; Messner, 1992; Winstead, 1986; Wright, 1988, 1991). While men achieve and define closeness through the sharing of activities, women define and achieve closeness through the sharing of feelings and emotions (Odden & Sias, 1997; Wood & Inman, 1993). Similarly, Ashton and Fuerhrer (1993) found that males are generally less likely than females to seek emotional support when stressed or anxious. Flaherty and Richman (1989) also state that the provision of social and emotional support was more likely to be a function of women's relationships, with women both receiving and providing more emotional social support than men in times of unhappiness or distress.

> *Olivia has been leaning on Emily for support, Emily not only works well with Olivia on organisational tasks, but will listen to her problems and provide counsel and encouragement to her when she is distressed by Jason's behaviour.*

In an organizational context, Morrison (2008) found a significant gender difference in the extent to which job satisfaction was related to friendships in the workplace. Job satisfaction was not significantly correlated with friendship prevalence for women but was for men. That is, men who reported having more friends at work also reported relatively higher job satisfaction; while the prevalence of friends at work was not related to job satisfaction for women. In addition it was found that women were significantly more likely than men to perceive the benefits of friendship to be those involving social and/or emotional support (or perhaps to be more likely to utilize their workplace friendships in this way). Men, on the other hand, were more likely than women to perceive workplace friendships as having functional, task or career related benefits (Morrison, 2008). Morrison argues that the fact that women utilized their friends for emotional support when distressed helps explain the somewhat counter-intuitive finding that having friends at work was not significantly linked to job satisfaction for women. When women are *dissatisfied* with their jobs they may make *more* friends through leaning on their colleagues for social, emotional and instrumental support (Morrison, 2008; Odden & Sias, 1997; Wood & Inman, 1993).

The notion that women will seek support from friends when they are distressed links in, both with the qualitative responses in Morrison's study, and with previous findings that women will *tend and befriend* (rather than fight or flee) when distressed and/or dissatisfied (Taylor et al., 2000; Turton & Campbell, 2005). If women's friendships strengthen in situations where they are dissatisfied with their jobs or unhappy with their boss, a significant positive relationship between satisfaction and friendship prevalence will not be found, even if having more friends at work improves job satisfaction in other situations. The example below illustrates how women's work friendships may increase in number or deepen in intensity in times of dissatisfaction or distress.

Jason's terrible behaviour has become material for discussion in the tea room. Susan has to work with Jason and is annoyed with his attitude and behaviour, she has also noticed Olivia's distress. Although Susan and Olivia do not work closely with each other, they have recently spent time talking about Jason's conduct, and Susan has offered some good ideas and strategies to help. Olivia feels that she has really got to know Susan as a result of their informal chats and she appreciates the social support that Susan has offered.

Women define and achieve closeness through the sharing of feelings and emotions (Odden & Sias, 1997), perhaps using their friends at work as an outlet for venting work-related frustrations and emotional expression. Men, on the other hand, may use their friends more for discussion of other (possibly less negative and/or emotional) topics (Ashton & Fuerhrer, 1993). A positive relationship between friendships at work and job satisfaction will be more apparent for men because they are less likely than women to seek emotional support from their colleagues when times are bad. In Morrison's (2008) study this explanation was supported by the types of answers respondents gave to the question asking how friends benefit them in the workplace. Women were, indeed, significantly more likely than men to focus on the social and emotional support provided by their colleagues when they were stressed. Many responses specifically described this function of workplace friendships. For example:

'helped alleviate stress' (female), 'Being able to let off hot air in a trusted conversation' (female), '...made each other laugh during hard times'

(female), and '*Having friendships at work provide an outlet for venting frustrations over the current work environment*' *(female)*.

A further possible gender difference in the relationship between workplace friendships and job satisfaction relates to findings by Markiewicz et al. (2000) who found that, while research generally supports the notion that friendships involving women outside the work environment are consistently evaluated as more satisfying, this is not always the case in an organizational setting. Instead Markiewicz et al. found that friendships with women sometimes provided less rewards and were less satisfying. It is possible that the work context may influence the nature of relationships between men and women. Factors that might account for this include women's relatively lower status in many professions, making them less desirable as friends, and sex-role stereotypes leading to unfavourable attributions about work-related competencies. In addition, the relative proportion of women in a given occupation may mean their token status might make women less able to provide salient rewards, as they tend to have less power (Ibarra, 1993).

Measuring friends at work

The measurement of friendships at work is still relatively new. There is only one published, validated scale that specifically measures friendship prevalence and friendship opportunities in the workplace (Nielsen et al., 2000). The authors of this scale found both friendship prevalence and friendship opportunities to be significantly correlated at the bivariate level to job satisfaction, affective commitment, and turnover intention ($p < 0.01$). In addition, friendship prevalence and friendship opportunities were significantly correlated with each other and the authors stated that, given the substantial correlation between scores on the two subscales (opportunities and prevalence), '...future studies should investigate whether having two dimensions is, indeed useful.' (p. 640). Thus one purpose of the present chapter is to explore the relative contribution of *opportunities* for friendship and the actual *presence* of friends at work, to outcomes such as organizational commitment, job satisfaction and intention to leave the organization.

Morrison (2006a) compared the relative impact of friendship prevalence (the actual friends an employee has) and friendship opportunities (more related to the friendliness of the workplace). Respondents who reported having opportunities for friendship in their work environments also reported being more satisfied with their jobs and more committed to their organization, being part of more cohesive workgroups and being less likely to intend to leave the organization. Individuals' perceptions of friendliness at work accounted for significant variance in all the desirable organizational outcomes measured in the study.

The actual prevalence of friends at work, on the other hand, did not contribute significantly to the variance of any of the organizational variables that were measured, over and above that which was accounted for by friendship opportunities. This is not to say that friendships at work were not associated with an increase in satisfaction, cohesion, commitment, etc., but simply suggests that friendship opportunities is a far stronger predictor of these variables.

All friends are not created equal

One possible reason friendship prevalence had no apparent relationship with individuals' experiences of work in Morrison's (2006a) study may relate to variations in the types and functions of organizational relationships. Research examining these variations generally indicates that different friendships will not relate to organizational outcomes in the same, or even similar, ways. For instance the types of co-worker communication relationships and the quality of co-worker information have been found to differently predict perceptions of organizational support for men and women (Amason & Allen, 1997). Similarly, the level of intimacy individuals have with their peers (i.e., information peers, collegial peers and special peers) has been found to differently enhance people's experiences of work (Kram & Isabella, 1985). The maintenance difficulty, or dual role tension, in a relationship has been found to be related to organizational formalization and to predict the closeness of organizational relationships and the type of communication individuals engage in (Bridge & Baxter, 1992). Finally, there are gender differences both in the functions of organizational relationships (Fritz, 1997; Winstead, 1986; Winstead et al., 1995), and in people's motives to communicate and initiate relationships with their colleagues (Anderson & Martin, 1995).

Given that people are frequently motivated to make friends at work for reasons other than enjoyableness (e.g., for work avoidance, utility or social support), it is perhaps not surprising that having, or not having, workplace friendships does not reliably predict other organizational outcome variables. Although it seems intuitively likely that having friends will positively impact on individuals' experiences of work, the various

functions of workplace friendships mean that the impact of these relationships will be far more complex than can be measured with a single
"friendship prevalence" variable.

*Jason is motivated to maintain his relationship with Olivia because she
has been helpful to him, both in getting the job at Org X and since he has
been there. The time he spends at her desk chatting about their colleagues
is preferable to working (to him). Jason uses the relationship to bide time
and for utilitarian support. The outcome of this same relationship for
Olivia, however, is that she is distracted and much of her precious time is
wasted. Although the relationship works well for Jason, it is detrimental
to Olivia's experience of work.*

Initiating relationships and communicating with co-workers in order to
bide time or avoid work has been shown to *reduce* commitment and job
satisfaction (Anderson & Martin, 1995). Winstead et al. (1995) also found
that making a special effort to spend time with a workplace friend was
associated with a reduction in job satisfaction, perhaps related to the
desire to avoid work. On the other hand, individuals may need functional
support from colleagues in order to do their jobs. Although they may be
strongly motivated to engage in friendly relations with their co-workers
for this utilitarian support they may not genuinely like or admire them.
In addition, if employees find themselves in an unusually toxic work
environment, or one where they believe their supervisor or colleague
is treating them unfairly, a response may be to seek social and emotional support at work and consequently make more friends (such as
in the example above where Susan and Olivia have "bonded" over
their shared frustration with Jason) (Odden & Sias, 1997; Sias & Jablin,
1995).

   If one is lucky enough to find a true friend in the workplace, even
these relationships may not have clear, positive organizational outcomes. By definition a genuine friendship will supersede the role
boundaries of the workplace; it will fit the definition of a 'special peer'
(Kram & Isabella, 1985). For special peers, formal workplace roles are
ignored or downplayed in favour of high levels of self-disclosure and
self-expression. Special peers will be loyal to their friends rather than
to their organization so positive organizational outcomes may not
necessarily result from these relationships either. This is particularly
true where an individual or friendship dyad is experiencing dual role
tension (Bridge & Baxter, 1992), where there are potentially incompat-
ible demands associated with the role of 'friend' and the role of 'work

associate'. Thus the variety of both antecedents and consequences of workplace friendships will greatly compromise any direct, measurable outcomes friendships might have at work.

Although Olivia is occasionally very angry with the way the Jason behaves at work, the fact that they have a shared history and many mutual friends means that she is reluctant to compromise their relationship. By covering for him when he takes time off and giving positive evaluations of his work to their supervisor she is demonstrating loyalty to him over loyalty to her organization or workgroup.

An alternative explanation for the apparent differences in the way the two friendship variables (opportunities and prevalence) relate to organizational outcomes may be that friendship opportunities is clearly an organizational or contextual variable (i.e., a friendly workplace). Friendship prevalence (actually making friends), on the other hand, may be an individual difference variable (i.e., a friendly person). Thus a relationship between two organizational variables (e.g., friendship opportunities and job satisfaction) will be more easily determined than one between an individual difference variable and a workplace variable (e.g., friendship prevalence and job satisfaction).

Collaboration and performance outcomes

A recent study by Nolan and Morrison (2009) presents an insight into friendly workplace relationships from the perspectives of those involved. Short qualitative responses provided insights into the intentions, behaviours, and actions that characterize friendly relationships within the workplace, thus adding clarity to this complex topic. Different approaches to collaboration at work were explored: how collaboration both draws upon friendships and simultaneously nourishes the relationship. People naturally tend towards friendships at work because they also offer the prospect of rewards. There are many reasons people are motivated to engage in friendships with co-workers; the first being the prospect of a better, more enjoyable working environment, with friends providing gratification of social needs and support at times of stress. Further rewards accrue from the sharing of information and knowledge in the completion of tasks. The conclusion here is that, with most people not only enjoying their friendship, but also utilizing friendships to improve their functional performance, both the individual and the organization can benefit from workplace friendships.

Emily and Olivia work well together because they are friends; they understand each other's points of view and can receive criticism about work related issues without taking offence. Conversely they became friends partly because they worked well together and had collaborated successfully on several projects early in their collegial relationship.

Other, less benign, outcomes of workplace friendship identified in Nolan and Morrison's (2009) study were the more selfish rewards sometimes obtained from friendships. Employees may use friendly networks to leverage better jobs for themselves by manipulating friendships with others who work outside of their immediate work environment.

Jason sought out the recommendation from Olivia. It is unlikely he would have got the job at Org X without Olivia's support.

Although the data is by no means conclusive on this issue, this form of behaviour may indicate a self-interested motive which breaches the doctrine of 'reciprocity' essential for maintaining a friendship and thus could well lead to the breakdown of the relationship. A number of respondents in Nolan and Morrison's (2009) study provided clues to behaviours such as offloading work on to friends and demanding favours from them which were likely to create dialectical tensions (Bridge & Baxter, 1992) in the relationship, putting a strain upon friendships. Thus, although largely supportive of the previous literatures promoting the 'happy workplace', the investigation also illustrated possible negative outcomes. Friendships at work operate at the boundary between the social norms governing friendship and the expectations surrounding organizational work roles. The findings from Nolan and Morrison's study provide qualitative accounts to support the positive side to friendships, but also illustrate the dilemmas and contradictions which people face when confronted by this boundary.

Earlier work by Bridge and Baxter (1992) and more recent investigations such as that conducted by Nolan and Morrison (2009), suggest that most people, when faced with dual-role dilemmas, will prioritize their friendship above their responsibilities to the organization. This notion is consistent with Kram and Isabella's (1985) definition of the 'special peer' in which formal workplace roles are ignored or downplayed and Wright's (1974) definition where the commitment of the individuals to one another is prioritized over their commitment to the context or situation (their workplace in this instance). Thus, as well as potentially providing a great deal of benefit to individuals and organizations, workplace friendships can present a significant distracting influence, both to those in the friendship dyad and to those on the periphery of friendly relationships. It is possible that these distractions are as likely to hinder workplace performance as to enhance it.

Conclusion

This chapter has discussed whether friendships at work can be reliably linked to key organizational outcomes. The *opportunities* to make friends at work can make workplaces more collegial and more satisfying, and may reduce turnover intentions of employees at work. However, the impact of actual friends at work may be less straightforward. It could be argued that individuals are only minimally affected by their workplace relationships and that simply providing a friendly workplace is sufficient to improve individuals' experiences of work, whether or not people actually made friends. An alternative, and perhaps more likely, explanation is that existing measures of friendship prevalence simply do not adequately reflect the complexity of adult friendship. In all probability the organizational correlates of friendships will be different for various types of friends, for the various functions friendships have, for the degree of closeness in the friendship, and for the difficulty experienced maintaining the relationship in the workplace. Thus, in order to measure any organizational outcomes that may arise from having friendships at work, the various facets of the relationship must first be evaluated.

Suggestions for future research

The most obvious direction for future research is to develop a measure of the types, functions, maintenance difficulty and intensity of organizational friendships. Another worthwhile area of study would be to examine what makes a genuinely friendly workplace; one where friendships can flourish. According to findings by (Morrison, 2006a), the factors facilitating workplace friendships themselves are probably not as important as those that would create perceptions of the *opportunities* for friendship or collegiality at work.

This chapter highlights the importance of defining and characterizing relationships under study and considering the context, antecedents, functions and consequences for individuals in these relationships. There is a crucial distinction between having friends at work and working in a friendly environment. Whereas the former situation is undoubtedly important and 'natural' at certain times and for certain individuals, the latter situation does not require a deep emotional involvement between individuals and may perhaps prove more beneficial overall in terms of organizational performance.

Recommendations

The importance of situational factors may be good news for management as, although there are limits to what an organization can do in terms of planning interventions aimed at improving informal relationships at work, one thing that organizations *can* do is alter the work environment and associated 'office policy' or 'house rules' in ways which can increase opportunities for friendships. The behavioural facets underlying the friendship opportunities construct include the opportunity to communicate with and get to know co-workers and the opportunity to collectively solve problems. Interventions aimed at increasing opportunities for friendships in the workplace could include changes that would allow employees to engage in these behaviours.

References

Allen, E. (1995). Should you be friends with your boss? *Working Woman, 20*(11), 72–74.

Amason, P. & Allen, M. W. (1997). Intraorganizational communication, perceived organizational support, and gender. *Sex Roles, 37*(11–12), 955–977.

Anderson, C. M. & Martin, M. M. (1995). Why employees speak to coworkers and bosses: Motives, gender, and organizational satisfaction. *The Journal of Business Communication, 32*(3), 249.

Ashton, W. A. & Fuerhrer, A. (1993). Effects of gender and gender role identification of participant and type of social support resource on support seeking. *Sex Roles, 28*(7–8), 461–476.

Beans, B. (1999). Protégés want mentors 'sympatico' not paternal. *APA Monitor Online, 30*(10).

Blau, P. (1964). *Exchange and Power in Social Life.* New York: John Wiley.

Bridge, K. & Baxter, L. A. (1992). Blended relationships: Friends as work associates. *Western Journal of Communication, 56*(3), 200–225.

Bukowski, W. M., Nappi, B. J. & Hoza, B. (1987). A test of Aristotle's model of friendship for young adults' same-sex and opposite-sex relationships. *Journal of Social Psychology, 127*(6), 595–603.

Buunk, B. P., Doosje, B. J., Liesbeth, G., Jans, J. M. & Hopstaken, L. E. M. (1993). Perceived reciprocity, social support, and stress at work: The role of exchange and communal orientation. *Journal of Personality and Social Psychology, 65*, 801–811.

Campion, M. A., Medsker, G. J. & Higgs, A. C. (1993). Relations between work group characteristics and effectiveness: Implications for designing effective work groups. *Personnel Psychology, 46*(4), 823–850.

Duck, S. (1983). *Friends for Life: The Psychology of Close Relationships.* New York: St. Martin's.

Flaherty, J. & Richman, J. (1989). Gender differences in the perception and utilization of social support: Theoretical perspectives and an empirical test. *Social Science and Medicine, 28,* 1221–1228.

Foote, N. N. (1985). *The Friendship Game.* New York: Image Books.

Fritz, J. H. (1997). Men's and women's organizational peer relationships: A comparison. *The Journal of Business Communication, 34*(1), 27–46.

Higgins, M. C. & Kram, K. E. (2001). Reconceptualizing mentoring at work: A developmental network perspective. *Academy of Management Review, 26*(2), 264–288.

Hyde, J. S. (2005). The gender similarities hypothesis. *American Psychologist, 60*(6), 581–592.

Ibarra, H. (1993). Personal networks of women and minorities in management: A conceptual framework. *Academy of Management Review, 18*(1), 56–87.

Kenny, D. A. & Kashy, D. A. (1994). Enhanced co-orientation in the perceptions of friends: A social relations analysis. *Journal of Personality and Social Psychology, 67*(6), 1024–1033.

Krackhardt, D. & Stern, R. N. (1988). Informal networks and organizational crises: An experimental simulation. *Social Psychology Quarterly, 51*(2), 123–140.

Kram, K. & Isabella, L. (1985). Mentoring alternatives: The role of peer relationships in career development. *Academy of Management Journal, 28*(1), 110–132.

Kram, K. E. (1983). Phases of the mentor relationship. *Academy of Management Journal, 26*(4), 608–625.

Kramer, M. W. (1996). A longitudinal study of peer communication during job transfers. The impact of frequency, quality, and network multiplexity on adjustment. *Human Communication Research, 23*(1), 59–86.

Largent, R. N. (1987). *The Relationship of Friendship with a Supervisor to Job Satisfaction and Satisfaction with the Supervisor.* Unpublished Masters Thesis, University of North Dakota, Grand Forks, North Dakota.

Markiewicz, D., Devine, I. & Kausilas, D. (2000). Friendships of women and men at work: Job satisfaction and resource implications. *Journal of Managerial Psychology, 15*(1–2).

Messner, M. A. (1992). *Power at Play: Sports and the Problem on Masculinity.* Boston: Beacon Press.

Morrison, R. (2004). Informal relationships in the workplace: Associations with job satisfaction, organisational commitment and turnover intentions. *New Zealand Journal of Psychology, 33*(3), 114–128.

Morrison, R. (2005a, 12–13 November). *Friendships at Work, Job Type and Needs: The Impact on Organisational Outcomes.* Paper presented at the Australian Psychological Society: Psychology of Relationships Special Interest Group 5th Annual Conference, Melbourne.

Morrison, R. L. (2005b). *Informal Relationships in the Workplace: Associations with Job Satisfaction, Organisational Commitment and Turnover Intentions.* Unpublished Doctoral Thesis, Massey University, Albany.

Morrison, R. L. (2005c). Testing for the invariance of a causal model of friendships at work: An investigation of job type and needs. *Enterprise and Innovation Research Paper Series, 19–2005,* 1–30.

Morrison, R. L. (2006a, 1–4 July). *All Friends are not Created Equal. An Evaluation of the Workplace Friendship Scale: Is There Ecological Validity in Measuring the 'Prevalence of Friends' at Work?* Paper presented at the Australian Centre for Research in Employment and Work (ACREW) Conference. 'Socially responsive, socially responsible approaches to employment and work', Monash University Prato Centre, Italy.

Morrison, R. L. (2006b, 26–30 September). *Men Like their Workplace Friends… but Women Need Theirs: Gender Differences in the Relationship between Workplace Friendships and Organisational Outcomes.* Paper presented at the joint conference of the Australian Psychological Society and the New Zealand Psychological Society. 'Psychology: Bridging the Tasman', Auckland, New Zealand.

Morrison, R. L. (2008). Are women tending and befriending in the workplace? Gender differences in the relationship between workplace friendships and organisational outcomes. *Sex Roles,* DOI 10.1007/s11199-11008-19513-11194.

Morrison, R. L. & Nolan, T. (2007). Too much of a good thing? Difficulties with workplace friendships. *University of Auckland Business Review, 9*(2), 33–42.

Murphy, S. E. & Ensher, E. A. (1999). The effects of leader and subordinate characteristics in the development of leader-member exchange quality. *Journal of Applied Social Psychology, 29*(7), 1371–1394.

Murstein, B. & Spitz, L. (1974). Aristotle and friendship: A factor analytic study. *Interpersonal Development, 4,* 21–34.

Nielsen, I. K., Jex, S. M. & Adams, G. A. (2000). Development and validation of scores on a two dimensional workplace friendship scale. *Educational and Psychological Measurement, 60*(4), 628–643.

Nolan, T. & Morrison, R. L. (2009). I get by with a little help from my friends… at work. *Kōtuitui: New Zealand Journal of Social Sciences Online, 14*(4), 330–344.

Odden, C. M. & Sias, P. M. (1997). Peer communication relationships, psychological climate, and gender. *Communication Quarterly, 45,* 153–166.

Richer, S. F., Blanchard, U. & Vallerand, R. J. (2002). A motivational model of work turnover. *Journal of Applied Social Psychology, 32*(10), 2089–2113.

Riordan, C. M. & Griffeth, R. W. (1995). The opportunity for friendship in the workplace: An underexplored construct. *Journal of Business and Psychology, 10*(2), 141–154.

Robinson, S. E., Roth, S. L. & Brown, L. L. (1993). Morale and job satisfaction among nurses: What can hospitals do? *Journal of Applied Social Psychology, 23,* 244–251.

Rook, K. S. (1984). The negative side of social interaction: Impact on psychological well being. *Journal of Personality and Social Psychology, 46,* 1097–1108.

Sapadin, L. A. (1988). Friendship and gender: Perspectives of professional men and women. *Journal of Social and Personal Relationships, 5,* 387–403.

Sias, P. M. & Jablin, F. M. (1995). Differential superior/subordinate relations, perceptions of fairness, and coworker communication. *Human Communication Research, 22,* 5–38.

Taylor, S. E., Klein, L. C., Lewis, B. P., Gruenewald, T. L., Gurung, R. A. R. & Updegraff, J. A. (2000). Biobehavioral responses to stress in females: Tend-and-befriend, not fight-or-flight. *Psychological Review, 107*(3), 411–429.

Turton, S. & Campbell, C. (2005). Tend and befriend versus fight or flight: Gender differences in behavioral response to stress among university students. *Journal of Applied Biobehavioral Research, 10*(4), 209–232.

Vecchio, R. P. & Bullis, R. C. (2001). Moderators of the influence of supervisor/ subordinate similarity on subordinate outcomes. *Journal of Applied Psychology, 86*(5), 884–896.

Walker, K. (1994). Men, women, and friendship – What they say, what they do. *Gender and Society, 8*(2), 246–265.

Winstead, B. A. (1986). Sex differences in same sex friendships. In J. Derlega & B. A. Winstead (eds), *Friendship and Social Interaction* (pp. 81–99). New York: Springer-Verlag.

Winstead, B. A., Derlega, V. J., Montgomery, M. J. & Pilkington, C. (1995). The quality of friendship at work and job satisfaction. *The Journal of Social and Personal Relationships, 12*(2), 199–215.

Wood, J. T. & Inman, C. C. (1993). In a different mode: Masculine styles of communicating closeness. *Journal of Applied Communication Research, 21*, 279–295.

Wright, P. H. (1974). The delineation and measurement of some key variables in the study of friendship. *Representative Research in Social Psychology, 5*, 423–436.

Wright, P. H. (1988). Interpreting research on gender differences in friendship: A case for moderation and a plea for caution. *Journal of Social and Personal Relationships, 5*, 367–373.

Wright, P. H. & Scanlon, M. B. (1991). Gender role orientations and friendship: Some attenuation, but gender differences abound. *Sex Roles, 14*, 551–566.

8
Gender and Relationships at Work

Barbara A. Winstead and Valerie Morganson

Despite the lack of an extensive research literature on the topic, the intersection of gender and relationships is an everyday occurrence in the workplace and it is worthy of greater empirical and theoretical attention. The presence and importance of gender in the workplace is widely acknowledged. Gender affects type of occupation, position in the organizational hierarchy, salary, work values, work behaviours and many other facets of work. Relationships too have captured the attention of organizational researchers (e.g., Allen, McManus & Russell, 1999; Bauer, Morrison & Callister, 1998; Graen & Uhl-Bien, 1995; Kram & Isabella, 1985; McDougall & Beattie, 1997), but in many cases workplace friendships and social networks have been studied with little or no attention paid to the dynamics of gender in those relationships (Gibbons, 2004; Ibarra, 1993; Ibarra & Andrews, 1993; Winstead, Derlega, Montgomery & Pilkington, 1995). The mentoring literature appears to be an exception. Although mentoring literature has extensively considered gender dynamics (e.g., Dreher & Cox, 1996; Ragins & Cotton, 1991, 1999; Olian, Carroll & Giannantonio, 1993), many more aspects have yet to be explored (cf., Young, Cady & Foxton, 2006); and the empirical work is in need of updating. The tendency to report on sex differences without conceptualizing the 'links between gender identity and organizational structures and practices' has recently been noted by Ely and Padavic (2007). An effort to contextualize the influence of gender on relationships at work will be a major focus of this chapter.

Perhaps the complexities of gender and relationships in the context of an organization have slowed progress in this area. Consider the following factors that affect gender and relationships at work. First, in a relationship, gender is both a person variable and a stimulus variable. In relationship research the gender of the participant may affect outcomes and the gender of the participant's relationship partner may also affect outcomes. Second, the actions of any individual are interpreted by others within the context of their gender. A woman and man engaging in the same behaviour are not necessarily perceived or evaluated similarly by others. Third, the workplace is gender segregated. A woman or man may work in a setting with many same-sex others (e.g., a female nurse, a male engineer) or few same-sex others (e.g., a male nurse, a female engineer). As workplace friendships tend to develop from sharing a physical space and work-related problems or tasks (Sias & Cahill, 1998), the availability of women or men in the work setting may affect whether one's friend is female or male. Fourth, workers may occupy positions of more or less power, autonomy, control, and prestige and these occupational/professional characteristics affect workplace relationships. Power and prestige are generally linked to gender. These four factors, at minimum, affect gender and relationships at work.

Consider this scenario: Pat asks Terry out for a cup of coffee during a break in the workday. Now, imagine:

1. Pat and Terry are both women account managers in an investment company.
2. Pat and Terry are two men working on the assembly line at the automobile plant.
3. Pat is a male manager and Terry is his female secretary.
4. Pat is a female nurse supervisor and Terry is her female nurse supervisee.
5. Pat is the male director of marketing and Terry is a female intern.
6. Pat is a male computer operator and Terry is his female supervisor.
7. Pat and Terry are a female and a male math teacher in a high school.

This hardly exhausts the possibilities. But if we were to write a script of this coffee break or try to predict the nature of these relationships we would certainly find substantial differences in our perceptions based on organizational factors and the sex of the workers. Look at the first two scenarios which are examples of the most common friendship found in the workplace, same-sex peer relationships. Even so did you think of Pat and Terry in the first scenario as seeking one another out as a source of female support in a predominantly male environment? What kinds of conversations would Pat and Terry in scenario #2 have? Did you think of them as just passing the time, maybe talking about sports? In addition to their positions within their companies and the gendered nature of their work, there is also the question of whether or not gender differences in same-sex friendships (Fehr, 1996; Winstead, Derlega & Rose, 1997) might affect these relationships. Do the women share more intimate information with one another than the men? What about scenario #3? Can we imagine this relationship across the divides of occupational levels and sex as a mutual friendship? Might the 'boss' be offering coffee in exchange for good work? Is there a potential sexual connotation to this invitation? What if the gender of the characters was reversed: A female manager asks her male secretary to join her for coffee? Consider scenario #4. Is this likely to be a friendship? Is there a possibility that this is a mentoring relationship? Do we see scenario #5 as similar to #4? Does the gender of the supervisor and supervisee make the dynamics of a mentoring relationship different? What about scenario #6? Now the sex difference does not match the stereotypical male-female status difference. Does this matter? Does it matter that the supervisee is the person who initiates the social encounter? Do we imagine that Pat the male supervisee has a concern or complaint and is hoping to address it in a 'friendly' context? Do we think this because his position is inferior or because he is a male with a female 'boss'? Can we imagine that these two are just friends? What about scenario #7? How easy is it to imagine that Pat and Terry, two math teachers at the same school, have a cross-sex friendship? Are they as likely as other work friends to engage in activities outside of work? Are there barriers to cross-sex friendship even when workers occupy the same position (cf., Elsesser & Peplau, 2006)?

Our example is a simple behaviour: 'Can you join me for a coffee break?' But our interpretation of the meaning of this invitation may vary greatly depending on the gender and position of the actor and the recipient and also on their context within the organization. No wonder social scientists have been reluctant to pursue this line of research; and, as we will see, those who have are always faced with the dilemma of being unable to account for all of these sources of influence on outcomes.

This chapter will review the empirical literature on gender and relationships at work. Although any interaction between workers could imply relationship, we are focusing on those relationships that are voluntary and more than casual. Excluded from this discussion are studies of non-voluntary or 'official' interactions, such as teamwork and interactions that occur between leader and follower, supervisor and supervisee. Included are relationships that workers choose and nurture. These include friendships, mentoring relationships, and social networks. Clearly these may involve individuals on teams or in supervisor-supervisee relationships. The distinction is that research focusing on the necessary interactions between these individuals (e.g., task-focused interactions among team members or feedback interactions between supervisor and supervisee) would not be included; but research on voluntary interactions (e.g., friendships or mentoring relationships between supervisor and supervisee) would be.

To understand gender and relationships in the workplace we begin with a discussion of how best to understand gender. Gender has been used to represent biological categories, socialization processes, sociocultural stereotypes, or an interactional performance (i.e., 'doing gender,' West & Zimmerman, 1987). Thus, the first section is a discussion of the complexities of studying gender, gender and relationships, and gender and relationships in the workplace. The subsequent sections present research on gender and workplace friendships, mentoring and social networks. We then consider the special status of cross-sex relationships in the workplace and negative relationships. In conclusion we discuss the need for additional research and fresh perspectives on the study of gender and personal relationships in the workplace.

Studying gender and personal relationships in the workplace

Studying gender

Is it gender or sex? In an influential article Unger (1979) presented an argument for differentiating between sex (as a designation of the biological distinction between women and men) and gender (as the designation of psychological, social, and cultural differences associated with women and men). Yet in most studies, researchers use the female vs. male grouping but do not further explore the reasons or causes of any differences discovered. They generally do not measure the gender role identity of their participants (i.e., the degree to which these individuals adhere to socially prescribed feminine or masculine prototypes), leaving only participants' willingness to designate themselves as female or male as the operational definition of sex/gender. Researchers may implicitly or explicitly discuss observed sex/gender differences in terms of their biologically determined naturalness or in terms of their basis in a history of gender socialization, but the research itself is rarely designed to delve into the question of origins of these differences.

We choose to use gender as the term referring to this categorization of individuals into female or male. We recognize that this term privileges sociocultural views of these differences and although none of the research reviewed explicitly addresses the question of the causes of differences observed, we are nevertheless comfortable with the assumption that socialization and cultural factors play an important role.

Gender, however, does not simply reside in the person as a biological entity with a history of gender socialization. Gender also resides in the current interaction. In any interpersonal exchange being female or male is a stimulus variable, as well as a person variable. Perceptions and expectations, based on gender, influence the responses of others which in turn affect the actor (Skrypnek & Snyder, 1982). When gender is salient individuals may also perform or behave in ways that conform to gender stereotypes even without 'prodding' from others (Ambady, Shih, Kim & Pittinsky, 2001; Steele, Spencer & Aronson, 2002). Individuals acting against the gender stereotype are also noticed and judged in the context of this conscious or unconscious act of resistance. According to Ely and Padavic (2007), 'gender identity is a profoundly social process ... rather than being an essential property of the self, gender identity is developed and maintained socially' (p. 1130) and not just as a result of past experience but very much in the moment.

Gender is also related to power and status and these have implications for individual women and men (Ely & Padavic, 2007). Men continue to be overrepresented in organizational and political positions of power and status. Our cultural stereotypes link masculinity with strength and agency and femininity with compliance, communality, and nurturance. In the U.S. we constantly ask citizens if they would be willing to vote for a woman as president (cf., Eagly, 2007), but would we ask such a question about a male as candidate for president? The gender of the individual conveys information about their likely position in society. A man in a position of power is the rule; a woman in a position of power is usually an exception.

Studying gender and personal relationships

The definition of personal relationships, like gender, is a complex topic. We will simplify our topic somewhat by asserting that we are interested in non-kin and non-sexual relationships. The personal relationships under study are those that are considered voluntary and mutual. They are generally regarded as sources of help, companionship and acceptance. Generally, these personal relationships are considered friendships, but in the workplace we have extended this definition to include mentorships and social networks. Numerous empirical studies have examined gender and friendships. Research on gender differences in same-sex friendships has repeatedly yielded results that are consistent with Wright's description of women's friendships as 'face-to-face' and men's as 'side-by-side'

(Wright, 1982). Women compared to men describe their same-sex friend-ships as more intimate and affectionate (Aukett, Ritchie & Mill, 1988; Floyd, 1995; Mazur, 1989). Friendships can of course be same-sex (female-female or male-male) or cross-sex (female-male). In a sample of profes-sionals, Sapadin (1988) found that men rated their cross-sex friendships as higher in overall quality, enjoyment, and nurturance and they reported more acceptance, intimacy, and emotional support from their women friends. Women, on the other hand, rated their same-sex friend-ships higher in overall quality, enjoyment, and nurturance. Both women and men are more comfortable confiding in and disclosing to women (Dindia & Allen, 1992).

These findings are comfortably in line with our cultural stereotypes of women as communal and relationship-oriented. Stereotypes encourage us to think of relationships as 'women's work' while other, task-oriented or instrumental activities are 'men's work'. It is notable that both women and men were more comfortable disclosing and confiding to women, sug-gesting that gender as a stimulus is also a factor. If others confide in a woman based on her gender, she may be drawn into a closer relationship with them whether she is very relationship-oriented or not.

Studying gender and personal relationships at work

There is perhaps a natural tension between the constructs of personal relationships and work. Remarking on the absence of research on co-worker friendships in the sociological literature, Marks (1994) noted, 'It is as if the category "worker" denudes workers from the rest of their lives while they are working, as if all they should be attending to at work is work' (p. 150). Fletcher (2004) also points out that relational activities at work are 'disappeared' because we think of these as per-taining to the private sphere and not to the public sphere of work. Thus, personal relationships and work are not seen as overlapping or compat-ible. Furthermore, gender itself has associations with the public vs. private (work vs. home spheres, respectively). Despite their longstanding and increasing presence in the workforce, women are still stereotyped as com-munal, relationship-oriented and as belonging in the private sphere as keepers of family and relationships, whereas men continue to assume the mantle of the agentic breadwinner (Fletcher, 2004). Clearly studying the intersection of work, personal relationships and gender, challenges our social construction of each of these concepts.

Perhaps the cultural and historical segregation of personal and public spheres that Fletcher (2004) discusses explains why there is no 'friend-ship' or 'relationship' theme that emerges in reviews and textbooks about organizational psychology. Instead, interpersonal relationships are interspersed in various places throughout the literature as an explicit or implicit aspect of theories and research domains. For example, interpersonal relationships are a component of organizational socialization (Bauer et al., 1998) and Leader-Member Exchange Theory (Graen & Uhl-Bien, 1995). Perhaps because of the relational aspects of social support and social coping, research in these domains is often gendered (e.g., González-Morales, Perió, Rodríguez & Greenglass, 2006; Greenglass, 2002; Somech & Drach-Zahavy, 2007). Examining interpersonal relationships and gender directly offers a new and broader lens for viewing organizational phenomena.

In studying relationships at work, we also have to move beyond the confines of the actor and her or his partner to the gender composition of the larger social context of the workplace. Relational demography (i.e., the demographic characteristics of the workplace; Tsui & O'Reilly, 1989) plays a significant role. Whether a worker's relationships are with females or males will certainly depend on whether the available others are 10% female, 50% female, or 90% female. Indeed whether or not a woman's workplace friendship is with another woman may be less a matter of choice than of the demographics of her workplace.

The nature of the work, stereotyped as female or male, the structure of the organizational hierarchy, and one's position in it are also influential. An emphasis on gender as an individual difference vs. an emphasis on structural or organizational variables that influence gender differences have been identified as the two prevailing explanatory approaches to understanding gender and relationships (Ely & Padavic, 2007). In this review we will remain mindful of the organizational context for relationships.

Workplace friendships

Fundamental to understanding the role of gender in social relationships is the concept of homophily or the similarity-attraction paradigm (Byrne, 1971). Simply put, 'similarity breeds connection' (McPherson, Smith-Lovin & Cook, 2001, p. 415) and homophily refers to the tendency to prefer and form relationships with similar others. Being the same sex is one type of similarity that can be a basis for choosing another for a personal relationship. The preference for same-sex ties at work was confirmed in the 1985 General Social Survey using a representative national sample of 1534 U.S. adults. Respondents were asked to name others with whom they discussed important matters over the past six months. Twenty percent (20%) of women and 39.5% of men named at least one co-worker as a discussion partner. Both women and men were likely to name same-sex others, but this was truer for males; 88% of men's choices were same-sex compared to 69% of women's choices. Women in this sample were more likely to be in mixed gender occupations, whereas males tended to be in male-dominated occupations, leading the authors to conclude that both structural (gender composition) and personal factors of the workplace influenced these homophilous choices (Straits, 1996). The advantages of homophily in work relations have been found to include liking, satisfaction, commitment, performance, and decreased turnover (Williams & O'Reilly, 1998). Regardless of outcomes, the phenomenon of choosing same-sex others for personal relationships at work is real (Brass, 1985; Ibarra, 1992, 1993; Moore, 1992; but see Gibbons & Olk, 2003).

Much organizational research has focused on the work-related functions of social relationships, such as information or influence obtained through social networks, rather than on workplace friendship *per se*. In research combining measures of social network variables and quality of closest friend at work, Markiewicz, Devine and Kausilas (2000) studied work relations in three distinct settings (information technology workers, lawyers, and managers). Results revealed, as expected, that homophily characterized networks and closest friendships. Results also showed that participants' salaries were higher when there were more men with whom they shared work activities and more men in their friendship network. Finally, women had smaller informal or friendship networks and fewer men in their networks. The friendship quality measures revealed that workplace friends tend not to be best friends (as stated by 90% of the sample), but that 75% were rated as close friends. Having a higher quality friendship with one's closest male colleague was associated with a higher salary, while reporting more voluntary interdependence with one's closest female friend was associated with a lower salary. Being closer to a man who is likely to have higher status, legitimacy, and power in the organization leads to better outcomes (higher salary) while being closer to a woman has the opposite effect. On the other hand, a female friend rated high in utility value (willingness to provide time, resources and assistance) predicted a higher salary. Finally, maintenance difficulty with one's closest male friend was related to lower job satisfaction for both women and men. Neither the sex of the participant nor the sex of the friend influenced ratings of the work friendship and there was no evidence that women's same-sex friendships were considered closer than men's same-sex friendships, a finding discrepant with other research on adult friendships. In fact, results showed that men were even more likely than women to say they would make a special effort to seek out their closest male friend at work. The results support several points. The association between salary and both having men in one's workflow or friendship network and having a higher quality friendship with a man may represent the advantages of being male in the workplace but may also represent the opportunities that association with higher status (i.e., male) others provide. Difficulties in relations with a male co-worker also had important negative effects.

Examining the development of friendships with peer co-workers, Sias, Smith and Avdeyeva (2003) asked participants to identify one peer co-worker who was a good or close friend and then to rate factors that influenced the development of that relationship from acquaintance to friend, friend to close friend, and close friend to very close/almost best friend. Consistent with other research on homophily, 78% of the co-worker friendships were same-sex (e.g., male-male or female-female). Just less than half of these relationships, 44%, were identified as friends, 36% were 'close friends,' and 20% were 'very close/almost best friends,' suggesting that, as Markiewicz et al. (2000) found, workplace relations are close but not frequently that of best friends. Confirming previous qualitative research, Sias et al. (2003) found that individual factors (personality and similarity) and workplace factors (proximity and shared tasks) were important in moving a relationship from an acquaintance to a friend, whereas extra organizational factors (socializing together and life events) were more influential as relationships became close and very close/ best friends. Women reported higher communication frequency in their friendships at all levels, but higher communication intimacy scores only in the transition from acquaintance to friend.

These studies of workplace friendships show strong evidence for homophily but otherwise suggest that gender similarities are greater than gender differences. Women report higher communication frequency, as is often found in research on same-sex friendships, but other measures of friendship quality show no gender differences. Friendships with men, however, may be advantageous for work outcomes (e.g., higher salary).

Mentor relationships

Mentorships are a specific kind of workplace relationship wherein a more experienced employee guides, advises, counsels and otherwise enhances the professional development of another employee. Mentoring has been associated with increased salary and promotion rate, job satisfaction, and organizational commitment (e.g., Allen, Eby, Poteet, Lentz & Lima, 2004; Chaos, Waltz & Gardner, 1992; Payne & Huffman, 2005; Scandura, 1992). Given the constellation of positive outcomes with which mentoring has been associated, it is no wonder that it has been lauded in the work psychology literature as a key to overcoming work stress and barriers to the career development of women (e.g., Noe, 1988; Olian, et al., 1993; Ragins, 1989, 1999; Young et al., 2006).

Kram (1986) suggested that mentors serve two functions, career support and psychosocial support. *Career support* refers to behaviours that focus on the organization and the protégé's career; it entails providing sponsorship, serving as a source of information and advice, making the protégé visible to influential others and protecting the protégé from political situations. Similar to a friend, mentors may also provide *psychosocial support*. Psychosocial functions are the interpersonal aspects of the mentorship. They enhance and develop the protégés competence, self-efficacy and personal and professional development. Kram (1985) defined four psychosocial functions including acceptance and confirmation, counselling, friendship, and role modeling.

Mentorships can be formal or informal (Ragins & Cotton, 1999) and may occur either within or across organizations (Ragins, 1997). In formal mentorships, mentors and protégés are assigned to work together for a specified time period. Typically, dyads are created by a programme coordinator on the basis of application forms. By contrast, informal mentoring relationships develop on the basis of mutual identification and evolve naturally over time without an official obligation or commitment. Informal mentorships are likely to be more intense and evolve over time to meet the needs of the mentor and protégé. Informal mentors provide greater psychosocial functions including friendship, social support, role modelling and acceptance (Ragins & Cotton, 1999). Because formal mentorships are synthetic rather than truly voluntary, they are excluded from this segment to the extent that they are distinguishable in the samples under study.

Mentoring researchers have examined the roles of gender similarity-attraction in mentoring dyads (e.g., Dreher & Cox, 1996; Ensher & Murphy, 1997). Research has repeatedly found that same-gender mentorships are more common than mixed-dyads (cf., Ragins & Cotton, 1999; Sosik & Godshalk, 2000; Turban, Dougherty & Lee, 2002). Some researchers have suggested that female mentors are better suited to mentor women because they may be better equipped to deal with issues of sexual discrimination and harassment and/or the issues that face women whose career path is altered by family work and responsibilities (Kalbfleisch &

Keyton, 1995). Women may also prefer to be mentored by individuals who are demographically similar to themselves (Ragins, 1997).

In a study of 104 summer intern protégés and their volunteer mentors who were part of a training programme designed to prevent minority youth joblessness, Ensher and Murphy (1997) found that liking, satisfaction, and contact with one's mentor were higher when protégés' perceived themselves to be similar to their mentors. A study of 220 doctoral student-faculty advisor relationships found the duration of the relationship moderated the effects of gender similarity and perceived similarity on mentoring received. While gender similarity predicted outcomes at the beginning of the relationship, its effect dissipated as the relationship developed (Turban et al., 2002). This finding is consistent with the notion that shared demographics serve as proxies for shared experiences and outcomes that may facilitate a higher quality interaction (Jackson et al., 1991).

As women enter predominantly male occupations and professions and move into managerial and leadership positions traditionally held by men, the availability of mentors for women has been a concern (e.g., Noe, 1988; Ragins & Cotton, 1991, 1999). In a sample of 550 men and women in both formal and informal mentorships from various departments and hierarchical levels within three research and development firms, Ragins and Cotton (1991) found that women reported a greater need for mentoring than men did. They found, however, that women perceived more barriers to obtaining a mentor than their male counterparts even after controlling for protégé experience, age, rank and tenure. Despite higher barrier perceptions, women were just as likely as men to report taking an assertive role to initiate mentoring relationships. Thus, the authors concluded that women apparently overcome the barriers they encounter in obtaining a mentor.

Several studies have examined mentor-protégé attraction from the perspective of the mentor. Gender itself does not appear to prevent mentors from taking on female subordinates (e.g., Allen, Poteet, Russell & Dobbins, 1997; Ragins & Cotton, 1991). However, gender stereotypes continue to be a mentoring barrier for female protégés. Researchers have suggested that female protégés are sometimes viewed as not taking their professional goals as seriously as male protégés (Noe, 1988; Schwiebert, Deck, Bradshaw, Scott & Harper, 1999). This is consistent with Olian et al.'s (1993) finding that the combination of marital status and gender predicted how willing mentors were to engage in behaviours to enhance the careers of their protégés. Mentors anticipated the greatest rewards from a relationship when working with a married male protégé or a single female protégé. The implication of this study is that stereotypes concerning women with family obligations may interfere with the mentoring women receive.

Research regarding gender differences in the quality of mentoring provided to and experienced by protégés has been mixed. In a study of 94 mentors across 7 high technology firms Burke, McKeen and McKenna (1993) found that mentors reported giving more psychosocial support to female protégés, but providing equal amounts of career support to female and male protégés. In a sample of health-care professionals male protégés reported greater career-related mentoring than females, but there were no differences in psychosocial mentoring (Koberg, Boss, Chappel & Ringer, 1994). Other studies have found no gender differences in the procurement of psychosocial support from a protégé's perspective (e.g., Ensher & Murphy, 1997; Noe, 1988; Koberg, Boss & Goodman, 1998). In a sample of engineering and accounting workers, Allen and Eby (2004) examined gender differences in mentoring from the perspective of the mentor and found that mentors reported providing female protégés with more psychosocial support than males; there were no gender differences in their provision of career mentoring. Where gender effects do occur the associations are between being female and receiving psychosocial support and being male and receiving career support.

Research examining the gender of the mentor in relation to mentoring suggests that female mentors provide more emotional or psychosocial support whereas male mentors provide more instrumental career-related mentoring. This was the case in the engineering and accounting sample discussed above (Allen & Eby, 2004). The authors attribute these findings to gender differences in position within the organizational hierarchy and familiarity with the organizational power structure and to gender role ideology.

The gender of both the protégé *and* the mentor are important predictors of the levels of psychosocial and career support exchanged in the mentoring relationship. In Burke et al.'s (1993) study, the interaction of mentor and protégé gender was not tested, but perceived similarity was; mentors provided more career and psychosocial functions to those that they perceived as similar to themselves. Allen and Eby (2004) noted that the gender interaction has been a common omission in mentoring research. They found that female mentors provided more psychosocial support to female protégés but male mentors reported providing the same amount of psychosocial support regardless of the protégé's gender. Psychosocial mentoring was greatest in female-female mentorships and least in the case of female mentors and male protégés.

Beyond the issue of the type of mentoring provided by women or men, research has also found that just having a male mentor is instrumental in obtaining financial and career outcomes. In a sample of 3623 MBA graduate students who were part of a consortium mentorship programme, graduates who established mentoring relationships with white men earned an average of $16,840 more than graduates with mentors who were not white men (Dreher & Cox, 1996). In the study with the large American sample mentioned earlier (Ragins & Cotton, 1999), protégés with a history of male mentors received significantly greater compensation and more promotions over the past ten years than protégés with a history of female mentors. As with research on the association between having male workplace friendships and salary, the monetary advantages of having a white male mentor may reflect being in a setting where white men predominate and salaries are high or they may reflect the opportunities that the privileged can confer on others.

Social networks

There is a long and rich history of research on social networks in organizations. Brass, Galaskiewicz, Greve and Tsai (2004) define a network simply as nodes and the ties between the nodes. Although this definition is flexible enough to include networks of persons, work units or organizations, it is interesting to note the impersonal terms used to denote networks which, when applied to individual actors, really are social relationships. One's social network can serve different functions, but the research literature tends to distinguish between instrumental or advice networks (that are work or performance focused) and expressive, personal, or friendship networks (that provide socializing and social support; Gibbons, 2004; Ibarra & Andrews, 1993).

The focus of research on social networks in organizations has generally been on their role in individual work-related outcomes (e.g., promotions, salary, influence, commitment; Brass, 1985; Ibarra, 1992; Morrison, 2002) or in organizational outcomes (e.g., interunit and interorganizational information exchange, changing professional values; Gibbons, 2004; Hansen, 2002). Constructs that capture influential aspects of an individual's position in the social network include, among others, centrality (i.e., the degree of access to and integration with interaction webs), social inclusion (i.e., the extent of informal ties with co-workers and the feeling of belonging) and brokering (i.e., bridging structural or network holes in the organization and becoming the person through whom information is passed). Centrality has been positively related to power (Burkhardt, 1994;

Ibarra, 1993) and to leaders' objective group performance and reputation for leadership (Mehra, Dixon, Brass & Robertson, 2006); social inclusion has been positively related to individual work performance (Pearce & Randel, 2004; Prusak & Cohen, 2001); and structural holes in the networks of men (but not women, see below) have been related to earlier promotion, better job evaluations, and higher compensation (Burt, 1998). The advantage of social relationships among workers to individuals or organizations is generally labelled social capital, a resource that one can accrue and invest and that might be more available to some than to others.

Gender and ethnicity were discovered to influence network relationships in some of the earliest research on the topic. Studying five professional organizations, Lincoln and Miller (1979) found that gender and race tend to influence personal and instrumental ties in these organizations but had a greater influence on personal ties. Education and authority, the other attributes studied, were also related to network ties, leading the authors to conclude: 'With very few exceptions, these four attributes are shown to be status determinants: White males with high education in formal positions of authority have high probabilities of occupying the most central locations in the network space' (p. 193). This rather unsurprising result from the 1970s led others to consider the special role of gender in social networks, but should also encourage us to ask if in the next 30 years we might expect to see some changes in this pattern.

In an examination of interaction patterns and influence in an organization, Brass (1985) studied a publishing company where women made up 40% of the employees. He found that women and men were both involved in informal networks; but that these tended to be gender segregated (men listed other men in their interaction network 75% of the time, and women listed women 68% of the time). The implication is that women were non-central in the men's network and in the network of the 'dominant coalition' which was entirely male. These findings, however, may be due in large part to the gender segregation of workgroups within the organization. When looking at workers in integrated workgroups, women were as central to the dominant coalition and to the general men's network as men in these groups were. While women overall were perceived as less influential (a perception strongly related to networking with the dominant coalition), in the integrated workgroups women were not different from men in ratings of influence. The results of this study reinforce the importance of gender segregation vs. integration as a context in which social networking occurs.

In another study of gender and social networks, Ibarra (1992) found, after controlling for availability, that men were more likely to choose homophilous networks, while women made differentiated choices, choosing more men for advice and influence and more women as friends. Since men occupied more prestigious and higher level positions in the organization, these patterns make sense: for men both advantageous and homophilous choices are the same (other men), but for women, more powerful individuals (men) were selected for advice and influence, whereas similar others (women) were selected for friends. Ibarra raises concerns about the exclusion of women from social networking: 'the dilemma for women, however, may lie in men's reciprocation of their choices: If network contacts are chosen according to similarity and/or status considerations, they [women] are less desirable network choices for men on both counts' (p. 440). Interestingly, the results also indicate that although men primarily network with other men, when they do include women it is more likely in their friendship and support networks than in their advice and influence networks. This result parallels findings from the friendship literature that suggest that relationships with women have benefits (nurturance, acceptance, mutual disclosure) for both women and men.

Stackman and Pinder (1999) examined gender differences in expressive networks, instrumental networks and the overlap in these networks in a sample of managers and supervisors. Consistent with Ibarra's findings, their results showed that expressive, or friendship networks were highly homophilous and equally so for women and men but that women's instrumental networks were significantly less homophilous (47%) than men's (67%). There were no gender differences in size of the overlap in these networks but men's overlap was also more homophilous than women's. They also found, as predicted, that these female managers and supervisors had expressive networks with greater locational and functional range than men's expressive networks, indicating that women have to go outside their immediate work setting to form homophilous work friendships. Women's expressive networks also showed less density (fewer connections among others in their network) and less frequency of contact, also suggesting that women's expressive ties were less interconnected and less available to them than men's expressive ties. Stackman and Pinder conclude that structural factors (fewer women in these managerial positions) play an important role in these outcomes.

Examining information and career networks, Ibarra (1997) found that women in managerial positions had less homophilous networks than men, as expected given women's underrepresentation in managerial positions in the companies studied. Interestingly, however, women with high advancement potential were found to have more homophilous networks than women with low advancement potential and closer and more wide-ranging ties than high potential men. Ibarra (1997) suggested that women in management may benefit from seeking out information and career advice from other women (as the mentoring literature indicates) and that high potential women, compared to high potential men, may need the additional advocacy and/or sponsorship that close and diverse ties can provide in order to advance in the organization.

Network researchers tend to discuss these results in terms of how social networks can be advantageous, or not, to work performance and advancement. Ibarra (1992) interprets women's failure to include men in their affective networks as not fully taking 'advantage of a potential "opening" by the dominant group' (p. 441). We should consider, however, that friendships at work may serve functions other than job or career advancement (e.g., stress reduction, pleasurable work environment).

In a study of MBA students, Mehra, Kilduff and Brass (1998) found that women and minorities were more likely than men and whites to make within-group friendship choices. They argue that this reflects not only homophily but also the distinctiveness of one's group, that is the proportion of others like you. Being fewer means one's gender or race is more salient and more likely to influence relationship choices. They also found, however, that exclusionary pressures (not being included by the network of white men) also played a role and significantly contributed to the marginalization of both women and minorities.

In an important counter-example to the numerous gender homophily findings, Gibbons and Olk (2003) failed to find that gender had any impact on friendship development in two samples of MBA students. This sample and Mehra et al.'s (1998) did not differ in distinctiveness for sex. Thirty-four percent of the Mehra et al. sample was female compared to 36% of the Gibbons and Olk sample. The researchers suggest that the efforts of the MBA programmes they studied to create heterogeneous groups and the peer status of all participants were important factors in this outcome. They conclude that 'when status is equal, and the individuals are familiar with members of both genders, gender does not necessarily affect friendship selections' (p. 349). On the other hand, ethnicity (being Asian in this sample) did influence friendship ties and social structures. It is also possible that advances women have made in the workplace, despite their similarity in proportionality in MBA programmes, may nevertheless have had some impact on their being perceived as legitimate and welcome colleagues.

The influence of the proportionality of women in the positions of power in the workplace and its influence on women's relationships with one another was the focus of Ely's (1994) research. Drawing on social identity theory and organizational demography, Ely hypothesized that fewer women at the top of the organization will lead women to be viewed as having lower status, which would in turn make them less likely to have positive relationships with other women in the organization. To test these ideas, Ely (1994) interviewed junior women in law firms that were male-dominated (4–11% women partners) or sex-integrated (15–29%) female partners. The percentage of women associates in these firms was higher and similar in both types of firms (40–50% in male-dominated and 38–47% in sex-integrated). Female associates were asked about their relationships with senior women and female peers. As expected, junior women in male-dominated firms were critical of senior women and did not rely on them for support or regard them as role models; whereas junior women in more sex-integrated firms identified with senior women and saw them as a source of validation and support. The number of women at the top also affected women's relationships with same-sex peers. Women in male-dominated firms were more likely to view female peers in competitive terms; they were also likely to compare themselves negatively with them. Women in sex-integrated firms viewed their female peers as a source of support and collaboration and generally had a more positive view of other women in the firm. Thus, the status of women within the organization, not just their presence or absence, has a profound effect on women's same-sex work relationships.

The status of women within the organization was also an issue in Burt's work on the value of a social network rich in opportunities to facilitate contact between individuals who would otherwise be disconnected, that is, being the bridge across structural holes. In a major study of senior managers in a large American firm, Burt (1998) found that men built social capital when they took advantage of the information and control benefits of bringing people from opposite sides of structural holes together. A social network with more structural holes paid off in earlier promotions for men but not for women. In this study the women who gained early promotion did so by 'borrowing social capital,' that is, by having a strong tie with someone in a position of power and influence. Burt (1998) concluded that this occurs because women were not considered 'one of us;' they were not considered legitimate members of management. These findings reinforce the notion that women's social networks and their outcomes are as much influenced by how women are regarded by others as by their own relational actions.

Considering organizational demography and the gender identity of workers, Bird (2003) examined the experiences of men in predominantly and exclusively male workgroups (75–100% male) and in mixed-sex (14–74% male) workgroups. She focused on how many close friends men reported, how often they spent social evenings with co-workers, and how cohesive their workgroup was. She also measured multiple aspects of individual male workers' gender ideology and identification with masculine stereotypes. She found no differences in number of close friends or social evenings based on workgroup gender composition. Men in predominantly-male groups felt more able to be themselves, compared to men in mixed-sex groups, but men in mixed-sex groups reported higher workgroup cohesion. Men's identification with masculine stereotypes had complex relations with these outcomes. The workgroup cohesion difference was explained largely by men with less traditional gender ideologies experiencing less cohesion in predominantly-male groups and more in mixed-sex groups. Gender composition of the workgroup does not appear to affect men's workplace friendships, but may affect their perceptions of themselves in relation to the group or their perceptions of the group. The outcomes also suggest that gender identity plays a role in the complex intersection of gender, relationships and work.

Social networks are not only affected by gender segregation and the status of women in the workforce, but may also help to maintain women's segregation and status. Even among college students (who might arguably be less embedded in gender segregated arenas due to less work experience and no spouse or children), Straits (1998) found that personal contacts for information or assistance in finding jobs tended to be same-sex (70–72% for male and 60–69% for female participants). Male students were also more likely to report using personal contacts in learning about and getting a job. When asked about a future search for a permanent job, males were far more likely than females to name a same-sex facilitator. This was in part due to the greater proportion of males in the prestigious jobs to which these college students aspired. But even controlling for the estimated proportion of females in the future occupation both males and females were still more likely to name a same-sex facilitator. To the extent that these facilitators carry gender attributes with them (e.g., type of job, status in the organization) they may inadvertently steer these young adults into positions that perpetuate the gendered nature of work.

Finally there is much evidence that men are more likely than women to use their social networks for work-related outcomes. Men are more likely than women to use personal contacts in finding work (Campbell & Rosenfeld, 1985; Straits, 1998) and they are more likely than women to use informal networks to seek promotions (Cannings & Montmarquette, 1991).

Cross-sex relationships at work

The data clearly demonstrate that individuals generally choose same-sex others for their workplace relationships. Explanations of this homophily phenomenon have focused on the benefits of and/or comfort with same-sex others. It is possible, however, that these choices are also driven by issues particular to forming cross-sex relationships at work.

Friendships

In their study of the development of peer workplace friendships, Sias et al. (2003) found that, whereas female and male same-sex friendships were similar in their developmental influences, cross-sex friendships (accounting for 22% of the reported-on friendships) were different. Socializing was less important for cross-sex dyads than for men's same-sex friendships, proximity was more important and communication intimacy was less frequent in cross-sex than in women's same-sex friendships, and life events were less important in cross-sex than in women's or men's same-sex relations. These findings suggest that women and men in same-sex friendships engage in activities away from work or bring outside experiences into the work friendships, while cross-sex friends are more often kept in the work context.

Individuals may in fact experience obstacles to developing and maintaining cross-sex friendships in the workplace. Elsesser and Peplau (2006) collected information from interviews and questionnaires with 21 female and 20 male professionals to explore barriers to maintaining cross-sex friendships at work. Participants identified their three closest friends at work. Consistent with previous research, 69% of these friends were same-sex; only 31% were cross-sex. Although most participants worked in predominantly male organizations women were as likely as men to name same-sex friends. On the other hand, with the exception of one male participant all of the participants had one cross-sex friend.

The major concern about cross-sex friendships was the possibility that someone, (e.g., other co-workers, the friend, one's partner) might misperceive the friendship as a romantic relationship. Questions from co-workers about the nature of the relationship were reported by 30% of the participants. Given presumptions of heterosexuality it is also possible that the friend might misperceive one's intentions in forming a relationship and this can lead to awkwardness and even the termination of the friendship. Heightened awareness about sexual harassment as a workplace issue was frequently mentioned, especially by men (75%). Men reported watching what they say and how they act around women, constraints that may limit their comfort around their female colleagues and their willingness to develop a friendship. Although women did not feel constrained in their behaviour towards men, 66% reported observing such inhibitions in men. Ratings by participants of sexual tension as a barrier to cross-sex friendship between peers was lower for married participants compared to single participants. Jealousy from a romantic partner, however, was considered a moderate barrier by both women and men.

Elsesser and Peplau (2006) label these barriers the 'glass partition' and speculate that it 'may differentially disadvantage women who work in predominantly male organizations' (p. 1094). They conclude that 'phenomena which create even small barriers to cross-sex friendships could have a large impact on the career advancement of women' (pp. 1096–1097). Indeed the barriers to cross-sex friendships may account in part for the exclusion of women from the social networks of men noted in other research.

Mentorships

Gender composition of the mentoring dyad has been widely explored in research. Perhaps due to the availability of mentors, women and minorities are more likely than men to be in non-homophilous mentoring relationships (Ragins, 1997). Research indicates that cross-gender mentor dyads are more difficult to establish and sustain (Dreher & Cox, 1996; Ragins & Cotton, 1991). As with organizational friendships, mentorships between opposite sex parties are challenged by sexual undercurrents. In cross-gender mentorships, both parties may be reluctant to pursue a mentorship for fear that mentoring relationships would develop sexual overtones or that others would make sexual attributions about the nature of the relationship (e.g., Kram, 1983; Noe, 1988). Bowen (1985) used a sample of 32 mentor/protégé pairs from a variety of fields. Comparing male-female dyads to female-female dyads, they found that female mentors with male protégés perceived problems including a jealous spouse, office gossip, and family resentment due to the fact that the relationship was cross-gendered. This study did not explore cross-gender relationships with female mentors and male protégés. Ragins and Cotton (1999), however, found that female protégés with male mentors were significantly less likely to report engaging in social activities with their mentors than female protégés with female mentors. Clawson and Kram (1984) argued that cross-gender dyads are challenged by a developmental paradox; on one hand, closeness of the mentor and protégé is essential for the development of the mentorship, but on the other hand the closeness needed to nurture the relationship can lead involved parties to maintain distance as a precaution to avoid romantic or intimate entanglement. Fears of sexual tensions apparently lead to self-imposed constraints on the relationship (e.g., limiting interaction to work hours, avoiding meetings behind closed doors, not having lunch together, Clawson & Kram, 1984; Kram, 1985; Ragins & McFarlin, 1990).

Negative relationships

Several recent studies have emerged examining the dark side of workplace relationship including lateral work relationships and social networks (LaBianca & Brass, 2006) and dysfunctional and negative mentorships (Eby & Allen, 2002; Eby, Butts, Lockwood & Simon, 2004; Eby & McManus, 2004; Eby, McManus, Simon & Russell, 2000; Ragins, Cotton & Miller, 2000; Scandura, 1998). Although these studies have generally neglected to consider the role of gender, there are a number of reasons to suspect gender differences in exposure to and type of dysfunctional relationship. Maintenance difficulty (the experience of tension or strain) with a male friend or friends has been shown to be negatively related to job satisfaction for both women and men (Markiewicz et al., 2000; Winstead et al., 1995). The overall effects of negative interpersonal work relationships may be more severe for women. A meta-analysis of 31 studies showed that women place greater importance than men on having friendly and sociable coworkers and supervisors (Konrad, Corrigal, Lieb & Ritchie, 2000). Markiewicz et al. (2000) found that women have smaller friendship networks, which suggests that a negative tie may have a greater impact (cf., LaBianca & Brass, 2006). If the negative relationship is with a more powerful other, an experience that may be more frequent for women than for men, a worker may feel pressured to stay in the relationship for fear of social repercussions.

Studies of dysfunctional mentorships often involve abuse of power and a negative relationship with someone of a more powerful status and is associated with greater negative consequences. Individuals who lack resources are at greater risk of having power exerted against them, and as Cortina, Magley, Williams and Langhout (2001) pointed out '..."femaleness" traditionally confers less sociocultural and physical power' (p. 66). Indeed, research findings indicate that women are more likely to be targets of various types of workplace aggression (e.g., incivility, sexual harassment; Cortina et al., 2001; Lapierre, Spector & Leck, 2005; Magley, Waldo, Drasgow & Fitzgerald, 1999). Women may have less power than men to influence and prevent aggression against them (Barling, 1996). Furthermore, unmarried status and underrepresentation in one's workgroup have been related to vulnerability to sexual harassment (Gutek, Cohen & Konrad, 1990).

Sexual harassment has emerged as a potential problem for female protégés in dysfunctional mentorships (Scandura, 1998). As Scandura pointed out 'Persons involved in these intense personal relationships sometimes lose sight of the fact that these are working relationships between professionals first and foremost. Issues of sexual harassment, when they emerge in mentoring, are clearly dysfunctional since sexual harassment is more about power than it is about sex' (p. 458). On the other hand, in an article about toxic protégés, Eby and McManus (2004) also discussed the risk of harassment as a dysfunctional relationship hazard for female mentors.

Stereotypes about gender roles can also affect protégés. Scandura (1998) described a hypothetical situation that illustrates how even with good intentions mentorships can be dysfunctional. She describes a mentor (male or female) who suggests that a female protégé not have children to devote more time to her career. This situation puts the female protégé in an anxiety-provoking situation where she feels that she must make a choice between her career and family. Note the findings of Olian et al. (1993) which show that mentors anticipated more rewards from mentoring a single female or married male compared to married females or single males.

Summary and directions for future research

The research reviewed here illustrates the point that understanding gender and relationships in the workplace is challenging. One consistent finding is that women and men seek out same-sex others with whom to form friendships, mentorships, and social networks. Women and men form expressive or friendship networks that are similarly homophilous, but, because men generally hold positions of greater power and authority in the workplace, women tend to form instrumental or advice networks that are less homophilous than men's. To whatever degree homophily in work relationships is advantageous (cf., William & O'Reilly, 1998) women are missing out on these benefits in their instrumental networks. Structural issues in the workplace (e.g., the gender composition of the workforce, the number of women in positions of power) are consistently shown to influence outcomes in research on gender and relationships (Brass, 1985; Ely, 1994; Ibarra, 1992; Stackman & Pinder, 1999). As long as there are occupational segregation and glass ceilings, we can expect women and men to have differing experiences of workplace relations and mentoring. On the other hand, studies of workplace friendships and expressive social networks find more gender similarities than is the case in research on adult friendships in general. The workplace may, in fact, be a context in which gender differences in some behaviours are reduced.

Despite the complexities, research on gender and relationships at work might proceed in several exciting directions. First, we were surprised to discover numerous studies of relationships in the workplace that did not consider gender at all. Gender was often used as a control variable, so the possibilities of gender differences or gender as a moderating variable were never explored. We urge researchers to investigate gender rather than controlling for it. Second, the numbers of women in the workplace and in previously male-dominated occupations continue to increase. Although occupational segregation and low proportions of women in top managerial levels are not yet close to disappearing, research that invest-igates gender and relationships and mentoring in occupations where gender composition is shifting or has shifted and in settings where women share managerial power is needed. To the degree that structural factors do affect work relationships, we need studies that can advance our understanding of how these factors operate. Third, in the studies reviewed here, gender is nearly always operationalized simply as being female or male. Studies that incorporate gender identity (the degree to which an individual sees themselves as fitting gender roles) and gender ideology (individual beliefs about gender and gender roles) will advance our understanding of how individual differences affect work relationships (cf., Bird, 2003). Fourth, any review of organizational research finds that all or nearly all studies are based on North American samples. Studies of gender and relationships in the workplace in other cultures would provide opportunities to understand how cultural beliefs and practices relevant to gender influence the experiences of women and men forming relationships at work.

Finally, nearly all of the research on work friendships, mentoring, and social networks has situated the research in the context of the possible positive, or negative, work-related outcomes of relationships. For exam-ple, are friendships related to job satisfaction or commitment; does men-toring predict salary and promotion or do social networks lead to career opportunities? Missing from this perspective is the notion that relation-ships might contribute to relational competence, personal growth and development, and life satisfaction. For example, using a relational framework, Ragins and Verbos (2007, p. 96) define mentoring as 'an interdependent and generative developmental relationship that promotes mutual growth, learning and development within the career context.' This relational perspective may encourage researchers to examine variables such as social support, coping, teamwork and even transformational leadership as plausible outcomes of positive workplace relationships (Allen & Eby, 2004).

References

Allen, A. D. & Eby, L. T. (2004). Factors related to mentor reports of mentoring functions provided: Gender and relational characteristics. *Sex Roles, 50,* 129–139.
Allen, A. D., Eby, L. T., Poteet, M. L., Lentz, E. & Lima, L. (2004). Career benefits associated with mentoring protégés: A meta-analytic review. *Journal of Applied Psychology, 89,* 127–136.
Allen, A. D., Poteet, M. L., Russell, J. E. A. & Dobbins, G. H. (1997). A field study of factors related to supervisors' willingness to mentor others. *Journal of Vocational Behaviour, 50,* 1–22.
Allen, T. D., McManus, S. E. & Russell, J. E. A. (1999). Newcomer socialization and stress: Formal peer relationships as a source of support. *Journal of Vocational Behaviour, 54,* 453–470.
Ambady, N., Shih, M., Kim, A. & Pittinsky, T. L. (2001). Stereotype susceptibility in children: Effects of identity activation on quantitative performance. *Psychological Science, 12,* 385–390.
Aukett, R., Ritchie, J. & Mill, K. (1988). Gender differences in friendship patterns. *Sex Roles, 19,* 57–66.
Barling, J. (1996). Prediction, experience and consequences of violence. In G. R. VandenBos & E. Q. Bulatao (eds), *Violence on the Job: Identifying Risks and Developing Solutions* (pp. 29–49). Washington, DC: American Psychological Association.
Bauer, T. N., Morrison, E. W. & Callister, R. R. (1998). Organizational socialization: A review and directions for future research. In G. R. Ferris (ed.), *Research in Personnel and Human Resources Management* (Vol. 16, pp. 149–214). Greenwich, CT: JAI.
Bird, S. R. (2003). Sex composition, masculinity stereotype dissimilarity and the quality of men's workplace social relations. *Gender, Work and Organization, 10,* 579–604.
Bowen, D. D. (1985). Were men meant to mentor women? *Training and Development Journal, 39,* 30–34.
Brass, D. J. (1985). Men's and women's networks: A study of interaction patterns and influence in organizations. *Academy of Management Journal, 28,* 327–343.
Brass, D. J., Galaskiewicz, J., Greve, H. R. & Tsai, W. (2004). Taking stock of networks and organizations: A multilevel perspective. *Academy of Management Journal, 47,* 795–817.
Burke, R. J., McKeen, C. A. & McKenna, C. (1993). Correlates of mentoring in organizations: The mentor's perspective. *Psychological Reports, 72,* 883–896.

Burkhardt, M. (1994). Social interaction effects following a technological change: A longitudinal investigation. *Academy of Management Journal, 37,* 869–898.

Burt, R. S. (1998). The gender of social capital. *Rationality and Society, 10,* 5–46.

Byrne, D. (1971). *The Attraction Paradigm.* New York: Academic Press.

Cannings, K. & Montmarquette, C. (1991). Managerial momentum: A simultaneous model of the career progress of male and female managers. *Industrial and Labor Relations Review, 44,* 212–228.

Campbell, K. E. & Rosenfeld, R. A. (1985). Job search and job mobility: Sex and race differences. *Research in the Sociology of Work, 3,* 147–174.

Chaos, G. T., Waltz, P. & Gardner, P. (1992). Formal and informal mentorships: A comparison on mentoring functions and contrast with nonmentored counterparts. *Personnel Psychology, 45,* 618–636.

Clawson, J. G. & Kram, K. E. (1984). Managing cross-gender mentoring. *Business Horizons, 27,* 22–32.

Cortina, L. M., Magley, V. J., Williams, J. H. & Langhout, R. D. (2001). Incivility in the workplace: Incidence and impact. *Journal of Occupational Health Psychology, 6,* 64–80.

Dindia, K. & Allen, M. (1992). Sex differences in self-disclosure: A meta-analysis. *Psychological Bulletin, 12,* 106–124.

Dreher, G. F. & Cox, T. H., Jr. (1996). Race, gender and opportunity: A study of compensation attainment and the establishment of mentoring relationships. *Journal of Applied Psychology, 8,* 297–308.

Eagly, A. H. (2007). The female leadership advantage and disadvantage: Resolving the contradictions. *Psychology of Women Quarterly, 31,* 1–12.

Eby, L. T. & Allen, T. D. (2002). Further investigation of protégés negative mentoring experiences: Patterns and outcomes. *Group Organization Management, 27,* 456–479.

Eby, L., Butts, M., Lockwood, A. & Simon, S. A. (2004). Protégés' negative mentoring experiences: Construct development and nomological validation. *Personnel Psychology, 57,* 411–447.

Eby, L. T. & McManus, S. E. (2004). The protégé's role in negative mentoring experiences. *Journal of Vocational Behaviour, 65,* 255–275.

Eby, L. T., McManus, S. E., Simon, S. A. & Russell, J. E. A. (2000). An examination of negative mentoring experiences from the protégé's perspective. *Journal of Vocational Behaviour, 57,* 42–61.

Elsesser, K. & Peplau, L. A. (2006). The glass partition: Obstacles to cross-sex friendships at work. *Human Relations, 59,* 1077–1100.

Ely, R. (1994). The effects of organizational demographics and social identity on relationships between professional women. *Administrative Science Quarterly, 39,* 203–238.

Ely, R. & Padavic, I. (2007). A feminist analysis of organizational research on sex differences. *Academy of Management Review, 32,* 1121–1143.

Ensher, E. A. & Murphy, S. E. (1997). Effects of race, gender, perceived similarity, and contact on mentor relationships. *Journal of Vocational Behaviour, 50,* 460–481.

Fehr, B. (1996). *Friendship Processes.* Thousand Oaks, CA: Sage.

Fletcher, J. K. (2004). Relational theory in the workplace. In J. Jodran, M. Wlaker & L. Hartling (eds), *The Complexity of Connection: Writings from the Stone Center's Jean Baker Miller Training Institute.* New York, NY: Guilford Press.

Floyd, K. (1995). Gender and closeness among friends and siblings. *Journal of Psychology: Interdisciplinary and Applied, 129*, 193–202.

Gibbons, D. E. (2004). Friendship and advice networks in the context of changing professional values. *Administrative Science Quarterly, 49*, 238–262.

Gibbons, D. E. & Olk, P. M. (2003). Individual and structural origins of friendship and social position among professional. *Journal of Personality and Social Psychology, 84*, 340–351.

González-Morales, M. G., Perió, J. M., Rodríguez, I. & Greenglass, E. R. (2006). Coping and distress in organizations: The role of gender in work stress. *International Journal of Stress Management, 13*, 228–248.

Graen, G. B. & Uhl-Bien, M. (1995). Relationship-based approach to leadership: Development of leader-member exchange (LMX) theory of leadership over 25 years: Applying a multi-level multi-domain perspective. *The Leadership Quarterly, 6*, 219–247.

Greenglass, E. R. (2002). Work stress, coping, and social support: Implications for women's occupational well-being. In D. L. Nelson & R. J. Burke (eds), *Gender, Work, Stress and Health* (pp. 85–96). Washington, DC: APA.

Gutek, B. A., Cohen, A. G. & Konrad, A. M. (1990). Predicting social-sexual behaviour at work: A context hypothesis. *Academy of Management Journal, 33*, 560–577.

Hansen, M. T. (2002). Knowledge networks: Explaining effective knowledge sharing in multiunit companies. *Organization Science, 13*, 232–248.

Ibarra, H. (1992). Homophily and differential returns: Sex differences in network structure and access in an advertising firm. *Administrative Science Quarterly, 37*, 422–447.

Ibarra, H. (1993). Network centrality, power, and innovation involvement: Determinants of technical and administrative roles. *Academy of Management Journal, 18*, 56–87.

Ibarra, H. (1997). Paving an alternative route: Gender difference in managerial networks. *Social Psychology Quarterly, 60*, 91–102.

Ibarra, H. (1993). Race, opportunity, and diversity of social circles in managerial networks. *Academy of Management Journal, 38*, 673–703.

Ibarra, H. & Andrews, S. B. (1993). Power, social influence, and sense making: Effects of network centrality and proximity on employee perceptions. *Administrative Science Quarterly, 38*, 277–303.

Jackson, S., Brett, J., Sessa, V., Cooper, D., Julin, J. & Peyronnin, K. (1991). Some differences make a difference: Individual dissimilarity and group heterogeneity as correlates of recruitment, promotions, and turnover. *Journal of Applied Psychology, 76*, 675–689.

Kalbfleisch, P. J. & Keyton, J. (1995). Power and equality in mentoring relationships. In P. J. Kalbfleisch & M. J. Cody (eds), *Gender, Power, and Communication in Human Relationships*. Hillsdale, NJ: Lawrence Erlbaum Publishers.

Koberg, C. S., Boss, R. W., Chappel, D. & Ringer, R. C. (1994). Correlates and consequences of protégé mentoring in a large hospital. *Group and Organization Management, 19*, 219–239.

Koberg, C. S., Boss, W. & Goodman, E. (1998). Factors and outcomes associated with mentoring among health-care professionals. *Journal of Vocational Behaviour, 53*, 58–72.

Konrad, A. M., Corrigal, E., Lieb, P. & Ritchie, J. E., Jr. (2000). Sex differences in job attribute preferences among managers and business students. *Group and Organization Management, 25*, 108–131.

Kram, K. E. (1983). Phases of the mentor relationship. *Academy of Management Journal, 26,* 608–625.

Kram, K. E. (1985). *Mentoring at Work.* Glenview, IL: Scott, Foresman.

Kram, K. E. (1986). Mentoring in the workplace. In D. T. Hall (ed.), *Career Development in Organizations* (pp. 160–201). San Francisco: Jossey Bass.

Kram, K. E. & Isabella, L. A. (1985). Mentoring alternatives: The role of peer relationships in career development. *Academy of Management Journal, 28,* 110–132.

LaBianca, G. & Brass, D. J. (2006) Exploring the social ledger: Negative relationships and negative asymmetry in social networks in organizations. *Academy of Management Review, 31,* 596–614.

Lapierre, L. M., Spector, P. E. & Leck, J. D. (2005). Sexual versus nonsexual workplace aggression and victims' overall job satisfaction: A meta-analysis. *Journal of Occupational Health Psychology, 10,* 155–169.

Lincoln, J. R. & Miller, J. (1979). Work and friendship ties in organization: A comparative analysis of relational networks. *Administrative Science Quarterly, 24,* 181–199.

Magley, V. J., Waldo, C. R., Drasgow, F. & Fitzgerald, L. F. (1999). Impact of sexual harassment on military personnel: Is it the same for men and women? *Military Psychology, 11,* 283–302.

Markiewicz, D., Devine, I. & Kausilas, D. (2000). Friendships of women and men at work: Job satisfaction and resource implications. *Journal of Managerial Psychology, 15,* 161–184.

Marks, S. R. (1994). Studying workplace intimacy: Havens at work. In D. L. Sollie & L. A. Leslie (eds), *Gender, Families and Close Relationships.* California: Sage Publications.

Mazur, E. (1989). Predicting gender differences in same-sex friendships from affiliation motive and value. *Psychology of Women Quarterly, 13,* 277–291.

McDougall, M. & Beattie, R. S. (1997). Peer mentoring at work: The nature and outcomes of non-hierarchical developmental relationships. *Management Learning, 28,* 423–437.

McPherson, M., Smith-Lovin, L. & Cook, J. M. (2001). Birds of a feather: Homophily in social networks. *Annual Review of Sociology, 27,* 415–444.

Mehra, A., Dixon, A. L., Brass, D. J. & Robertson, B. (2006). The social network ties of group leaders: Implications for group performance and leader reputation. *Organization Science, 17,* 64–79.

Mehra, A., Kilduff, M. & Brass, D. J. (1998). At the margins: A distinctiveness approach to the social identity and social networks of underrepresented groups. *Academy of Management Journal, 41,* 441–452.

Moore, G. (1992). Gender and informal networks in state government. *Social Science Quarterly, 73,* 46–61.

Morrison, E. W. (2002). Newcomers' relationships: The role of social network ties during socialization. *Academy of Management Journal, 45,* 1149–1160.

Noe, R. A. (1988). Women and mentoring: A review and research agenda. *Academy of Management Review, 13,* 65–78.

Olian, J. D., Carroll, S. J. & Giannantonio, C. M. (1993). Mentor reactions to protégés: An experiment with managers. *Journal of Vocational Behaviour, 43,* 266–278.

Payne, S. C. & Huffman, A. H. (2005). A longitudinal examination of the influence of mentoring on organizational commitment and turnover. *Academy of Management Journal, 48,* 158–168.

Pearce, J. L. & Randel, A. E. (2004). Expectations of organizational mobility, workplace social inclusion and employee job performance. *Journal of Organizational Behaviour, 25*, 81–98.

Prusak, L. & Cohen, C. (2001). How to invest social capital. *Harvard Business Review, 79*, 86–93.

Ragins, B. R. (1989). Barriers to mentoring: The female manager's dilemma. *Human Relations, 42*, 1–22.

Ragins, B. R. (1997). Antecedents of diversified mentoring relationships. *Journal of Vocational Behaviour, 51*, 90–109.

Ragins, B. R. (1999).Gender and mentoring relationships: A review and research agenda for the next decade. In G. Powell (ed.), *Handbook of Gender and Work* (pp. 347–370). Thousand Oaks, CA: Sage.

Ragins, B. R. & Cotton, J. L. (1991). Easier said than done: Gender differences in perceived barriers to gaining a mentor. *The Academy of Management Journal, 34*, 939–951.

Ragins, B. R. & Cotton, J. L. (1999). Mentor functions and outcomes: A comparison of men and women in formal and informal mentoring relationships. *Journal of Applied Psychology, 84*, 529–550.

Ragins, B. R., Cotton, J. L. & Miller, J. S. (2000). Marginal mentoring: The effects of type of mentor, quality of relationship, and program design on work and career attitudes. *Academy of Management Journal, 43*, 1177–1194.

Ragins, B. R. & McFarlin, D. (1990). Perception of mentor roles in cross-gender mentoring relationships. *Journal of Vocational Behaviour, 37*, 321–339.

Ragins, B. R. & Verbos, A. K. (2007). Positive relationships in action: Relational mentoring and mentoring schemas in the workplace. In J. Dutton & B. R. Ragins (eds), *Exploring Positive Relationships at Work: Building a Theoretical and Research Foundation* (pp. 91–116). Mahwah, NJ: Lawrence Erlbaum.

Sapadin, L. A. (1988). Friendships and gender: Perspectives of professional men and women. *Journal of Social and Personal Relationships, 5*, 387–403.

Scandura, T. A. (1992). Mentorship and career mobility: An empirical investigation. *Journal of Organizational Behaviour, 13*, 169–174.

Scandura, T. A. (1998). Dysfunctional mentoring relationships and outcomes. *Journal of Management, 24*, 449–467.

Schwiebert, V. L., Deck, M. D., Bradshaw, M. L., Scott, P. & Harper, M. (1999). Women as mentors. *Journal of Humanistic Counseling, Education and Development, 37*, 241–254.

Sias, P. M. & Cahill, D. J. (1998). From coworkers to friends: The development of peer friendships in the workplace. *Western Journal of Communication, 62*, 273–299.

Sias, P. M., Smith, G. & Avdeyeva, T. (2003). Sex and sex-composition differences and similarities in peer workplace friendship development. *Communication Studies, 54*, 322–340.

Skrypnek, B. J. & Snyder, M. (1982). On the self-perpetuating nature of stereotypes about women and men. *Journal of Experimental Social Psychology, 18*, 277–291.

Somech, A. & Drach-Zahavy, A. D. (2007). Strategies for coping with work-family conflict: The distinctive relationships of gender role ideology. *Journal of Occupational Health Psychology, 12*, 1–19.

Sosik, J. J. & Godshalk, V. M. (2000). The role of gender in mentoring: Implications for diversified and homogeneous mentoring relationships. *Journal of Vocational Behaviour, 57*, 102–122.

Stackman, R. W. & Pinder, C. C. (1999). Context and sex effects on personal work networks. *Journal of Social and Personal Relationships, 16*, 39–64.

Steele, C. M., Spencer, S. J. & Aronson, J. (2002). Contending with group image: The psychology of stereotype and social identity threat. *Advances in Experimental Social Psychology, 34*, 379–440.

Straits, B. C. (1996). Ego-net diversity: Same- and cross-sex coworker ties. *Social Networks, 18*, 29–45.

Straits, B. C. (1998). Occupational sex segregation: The role of personal ties. *Journal of Vocational Behaviour, 52*, 191–207.

Tsui, A. S. & O'Reilly, C. A. (1989). Beyond simple demographic effects: The importance of relational demography in superior-subordinate dyads. *Academy of Management Journal, 32*, 402–423.

Turban, D. B., Dougherty, T. W. & Lee, F. K. (2002). Gender, race, and perceived similarity effects in developmental relationships: The moderating role of relationship duration. *Journal of Vocational Behaviour, 61*, 240–262.

Unger, R. (1979). Toward a redefinition of sex and gender. *American Psychologist, 34*, 1085–1094.

West, C. & Zimmerman, D. H. (1987). Doing gender. *Gender and Society, 1*, 125–151.

Williams, K. Y. & O'Reilly, C. A. (1998). Demography and diversity in organizations: A review of 40 years of research. *Research in Organizational Behaviour, 20*, 77–140.

Winstead, B. A., Derlega, V. J., Montgomery, M. J. & Pilkington, C. (1995). The quality of friendships at work and job satisfaction. *Journal of Social and Personal Relationships, 12*, 199–215.

Winstead, B. A., Derlega, V. J. & Rose, S. (1997). *Gender and Close Relationships*. Thousand Oaks, CA: Sage.

Wright, P. (1982). Men's friendships, women's friendships and the alleged inferiority of the latter. *Sex Roles, 8*, 1–20.

Young, A. M., Cady, S. & Foxton, M. J. (2006). Demystifying gender differences in mentoring: Theoretical perspectives and challenges for future research on gender and mentoring. *Human Resource Development Review, 5*, 148–175.

9
Rudeness and Incivility in the Workplace

Janie Harden Fritz

Incivility may be defined as low intensity deviant behaviour that violates workplace norms for mutual respect. The effects of intra-organizational incivility are considerable, and resolving conflicts among co-workers can account for much of managers' time. This chapter details the nature of incivility and its consequences. The chapter provides keys to recognizing and dealing with habitual instigators and offers remedies that are being used effectively by organizations to curtail and correct employee-to-employee incivility.

Introduction

Scholarly attention to problematic workplace interaction has increased over the last decade, yielding conceptualization and development of constructs defining and describing the contours of a number of both intense and low-level problematic organizational behaviours known as misbehaviour in the workplace (Vardi & Weitz, 2004) or antisocial work behaviour (O'Leary-Kelly, Duffy & Griffin, 2000). Workplace aggression (Baron & Neuman, 1996, 1998), bullying (Tracy, Lutgen-Sandvik & Alberts, 2006), social undermining (Duffy, Ganster & Pagon, 2002), abusive supervision (Tepper, 2007), petty tyranny (Ashforth, 1994), problematic work relationships (Fritz & Omdahl, 2006), interactional injustice (Skarlicki & Folger, 1997), and toxic management in organizations (Appelbaum & Roy-Girard, 2007; Kimura, 2003) are receiving long-needed attention, and research continues to differentiate and identify specific features of these interrelated constructs (O'Leary-Kelly et al., 2000). This scholarly attention intersects with practitioner recognition of the costly toll of problematic workplace interaction and the need for intervention to prevent and/or curtail it (Gonthier, 2002; Johnson & Indvik, 2001a, 2001b; Pearson, Andersson & Porath, 2005; Sutton, 2007).

Although incidents such as violent aggression in the workplace garner headlines for their intensity and vivid nature, much problematic work behaviour is less obtrusive – verbal, passive, indirect, and relatively subtle (Baron & Neuman, 1996). In a typical workplace, employees may find themselves targets – or senders – of intentional or unintentional slights, negative comments, insults, rudeness, and other lapses of common courtesy that are less intense than overt aggression or violence but that are nonetheless distressing, distracting, and disruptive. Such messages, which may come from and be directed toward anyone at any level of the organizational hierarchy, disregard workplace norms for interaction necessary to constructive coordination of action and rob the receiver of dignity and respect. These breaches of consideration have been conceptualized formally over the past decade as workplace incivility (Andersson & Pearson, 1999; Pearson, Andersson & Wegner, 2001; Pearson et al., 2005), defined as 'low-intensity deviant (rude, discourteous) behaviour with ambiguous intent to harm the target in violation of workplace norms for mutual respect' (Pearson et al., 2005, p. 179).

Workplace incivility not only violates implicit and explicit organizational norms for respect, but strikes at the fundamental human integrity of persons. According to Zauderer (2002), 'Incivility is disrespectful behaviour that undermines the dignity and self-esteem of employees and creates unnecessary suffering. In general, behaviours of incivility indicate a lack of concern for the well-being of others and are contrary to how individuals expect to be treated' (p. 38). The term 'incivility' captures the philosophical heart of rudeness (Johnson & Indvik, 2001a, 2001b; Porath & Erez, 2007), breaches of propriety (Miller, 2001), and related problematic behaviours through its contrast with the necessary consideration of others with whom we dwell and interact in the public realm. As Andersson and Pearson (1999) point out, incivility runs counter to civility, the upholding of practices of respect and restraint that permit social interaction to run smoothly. A key pragmatic concern with incivility at the organizational level is its role as a distraction in the workplace; when the focus of attention is drawn away from necessary tasks, the organization – the 'civitas' – suffers through the incivilities inflicted upon and endured by its members. Incivility affects both those who suffer directly and observers of such behaviour.

Workplace incivility is an interactive event (Andersson & Pearson, 1999) that is communicative in nature, with its caustic power residing in the relational dimension of the message (Watzlawick, Beavin, & Jackson, 1967). The relational dimension of messages carries meaning about the relationship between two persons and the sender's perception of the recipient of the message. Once articulated verbally, the spoken words construct or frame the recipient for those within the interaction and for observers, and they also become part of the ambient work environment itself, producing, maintaining, or altering the organizational climate (Guzley, 1992). Workplace incivility is harmful to persons, to the organization, and to the work performed in the organization (Andersson & Pearson, 1999; Pearson et al., 2005).

Workplace incivility as a problematic communicative work behaviour demands a communicative remedy: professional civility (Arnett, 2006; Arnett & Fritz, 2003; Arnett & Fritz, 2001; Fritz & Arnett, 2007), a communicative ethic grounded in the good of respect for persons, those with whom one works; for the place – the local organizational home or 'dwelling' (Arnett, Fritz & Bell, 2009); and for productivity, the 'between' that emerges among members of an organization engaged in coordinated labor around a common centre (Arnett, 1986). Professional civility frames and extends current recommendations for managing incivility in the workplace and offers a philosophical and pragmatic ground for these remedies. A communicative ethic of professional civility creates and supports an organizational culture and climate that functions within the realm of public discourse, invites clear, recognized guidelines for behavioural expectations in the public interpersonal arena, and requires accountability at all organizational levels, particularly from those in formal leadership roles.

Contextualizing workplace incivility

Workplace incivility is part of a larger group of related concepts emerging in management and related literatures over the last fifteen years that have been characterized as the 'dark side of organizational behaviour' (Griffin & O'Leary-Kelly, 2004). These behaviours are parallelled by similar and convergent phenomena in the communication field (e.g., Cupach & Spitzberg's 1994 volume, *The Dark Side of Interpersonal Communication*; Spitzberg & Cupach's 1998 volume, *The Dark Side of Close Relationships*; see also Fritz & Omdahl's 2006 edited volume *Problematic Relationships in the Workplace*). Workplace incivility is noted for both its deceptive banality, given its seemingly innocuous, low-level nature (Sypher, 2004), and its prevalence (Buhler, 2003; Cortina, Magley, Williams & Langhout, 2001; Pearson & Porath, 2004). For example, in Cortina et al.'s (2001) research on 1,180 public sector employees, 71% of the respondents reported experiencing incidents of incivility during the last five years. Incivility, sometimes defined operationally as one of its defining attributes, rudeness (Johnson & Indvik, 2001a, 2001b; Porath & Erez, 2007), damages persons and organizations through direct and indirect means, creating a toxic work climate (Kimura, 2004) and affecting productivity through distractions that take the focus of attention away from work (Pearson & Porath, 2005; Pearson, Andersson & Porath, 2000; Sutton, 2007). Incivility gathers broad interest, given its connection to its opposing term, civility (Andersson & Pearson, 1999; Sypher, 2004), the domain of manners, constructive dialogue in the public domain (Arnett, 2001), and issues connected to the functioning of diverse communities in a world that has lost a sense of shared common good or purpose (e.g., Arnett, 2001; Arnett & Arneson, 1999; Bellah, Madsen, Sullivan, Swidler & Tipton, 1985; Carter, 1998; MacIntyre, 1981; Putnam, 2000).

The concept of workplace incivility has recently emerged from a developmental stage of conceptual introduction and elaboration (Wanous, Reichers & Austin, 2000), earning a theoretical and psychometric place as part of a larger nomological network of constructs addressing interpersonal life in organizations. The definition of incivility appears to have achieved established conceptual status; Andersson and Pearson's (1999) definition (i.e., low-intensity deviant behaviour with ambiguous intent to harm the target in violation of workplace norms for mutual respect) is the most frequently used and is the one cited most often by researchers (Hutton, 2006). Current research on workplace incivility is exploring correlates such as status and gender (e.g., Porath, Overbeck & Pearson, 2008) and the role of mediating variables such as negative affectivity (Penney & Spector, 2005) on outcomes associated with workplace incivility. Although emerging from the management literature in its initial development and elaboration, the nature of incivility as an interactive public interpersonal communication behaviour has been addressed insightfully by communication scholars (e.g., Alberts, Lutgen-Sandvik & Tracy, 2005; Darr, 2005; Heinemann, 1996; Sypher, 2004; Tracy & Tracy, 1998) and scholars within in a number of other fields, including health care (Hutton, 2006) and public administration (Vickers, 2006). The communication field is a natural home for research on incivility and its potential remedy, professional civility (Arnett, 2006; Arnett & Fritz, 2003; Arnett & Fritz, 2001), and can contribute to further understanding of this multidisciplinary concept and effective means of addressing it.

History of the concept of workplace incivility

Workplace, incivility received its initial impetus from the social interactionist work of Andersson and Pearson, whose theoretical framework

(Andersson & Pearson, 1999) and subsequent exploratory research (Pearson et al., 2001) are cited as foundational in subsequent research on workplace incivility and established its definition and conceptual status as a construct. In a comprehensive review, Pearson, et al. (2005) cite several conceptualizations of workplace incivility and related terms that offer further facets of the concept, including Miller's (2001) impropriety, Winters and Duck's (2001) aversive behaviour, Johnson and Indvik's (2001a, 2001b) low-level workplace abuse, and Zauderer's (2002) framing of incivility as 'disrespectful behaviour' characterized by 'undermining' (p. 38). Blau and Andersson (2005), Cortina et al. (2001) and Vickers (2006) refer to workplace incivility as a form of mistreatment in organizations; Vickers equates it with 'obnoxious behaviour' (p. 74). The work of Kane and Montgomery (1998) on 'dysempowerment' in organizational settings was a precursor to the concept of workplace incivility, describing behaviours that fall within its operational domain.

Theoretical frameworks and conceptual development

Andersson and Pearson (1999) and Pearson et al. (2001) originally framed workplace incivility as falling within the scope of antisocial behaviour in organizations (with Cortina et al., 2001, and Thau, Crossley, Bennett and Sczesny, 2007, following suit), which also included deviance, violence, and aggression. Within this approach, incivility formed a subset of organizational deviance and overlapped with aggression, but not with violence. Pearson et al. (2005) reframed incivility within the scope of the newly-extant term counter-productive work behaviour (Fox & Spector, 2005), behaviour that harms an organization and/or its members, where it remained as a subset of organizational deviance with some overlap with both aggression and the recently emergent 'dark side' behaviour known as bullying/emotional abuse, but not overlapping with another recently emergent 'dark side' behaviour, mobbing, nor with violence.

Subsequent reviews and empirical research helped define and differentiate incivility from related problematic interpersonal workplace interaction such as aggression, violence, and petty tyranny, along several dimensions: (1) to whom the behaviour is directed (from and to whom hierarchically; to/from others inside or outside the organization), (2) clarity of intent, (3) intensity, (4) whether physical contact takes place, and (5) pattern of incidence (one-time or occasional occurrence vs. repeated and/or systematic). Incivility includes behaviours directed at another individual, but not at the organization (Pearson & Porath, 2004, pp. 404–405); organizational deviance includes behaviours directed toward the organization and toward persons within the organization. Petty tyranny (Ashforth, 1994) takes the form of negative behaviour directed toward subordinates by leaders who abuse their authority; incivility, in contrast, can take place between members at any level of the organization (Andersson & Pearson, 1999). Workplace incivility takes place between members of an organization rather than between employees and persons external to the organization (Cortina et al., 2001).

Andersson and Pearson's (1999) definition of incivility as a deviant behaviour involving ambiguous intent to harm and as of low intensity distinguishes the concept from the more deliberate behaviour of workplace violence and suggests its partial overlap with the highly intense behaviour of aggression (see also Pearson et al., 2005). Blau and Andersson's (2005) investigation of instigated workplace incivility confirmed both the distinction between workplace incivility and aggression and this partial overlap. Workplace incivility differs from violence in that it does not involve physical contact (Pearson & Porath, 2004), although it holds the potential to spiral into aggressive and/or violent behaviours (Andersson & Pearson, 1999; Pearson et al., 2000; Pearson & Porath, 2005). Martin and Hine (2005) differentiate workplace incivility from bullying and harassment, highlighting the latter as 'repeated and systematic attempts to harm someone by an individual or group,' with a perceived or actual power imbalance between victims and perpetrators (p. 477). The key differentiating factor here is the extent to which the behaviour is repeated and systematic, involves aggressive intent, and involves a power differential. Milder forms of bullying and harassment would fall within the definition of workplace incivility, according to Martin and Hine (see also Alberts et al., 2005). Pearson et al. (2005) further differentiate incivility from mobbing, which they classify as of moderate to high intensity, persistent, aggressive behaviour that is both physical and nonphysical, and bullying/emotional abuse, which they define as nonphysical, aggressive, persistent behaviour (see Table 9.1 for a summary of these distinctions).

Workplace incivility as a communicative phenomenon

Andersson and Pearson (1999) conceptualized workplace incivility as an interactive construct. The work by Cortina et al. (2001), as well as its initial conceptualization (Andersson & Pearson, 1999) and further development, points to a more specific understanding of incivility in the workplace as an interactive communication process consisting of direct and indirect, intentional or unintentional messages with rhetorical/

Table 9.1   Differentiation of constructs related to workplace incivility

	To/from whom behaviour directed	Clarity of intent	Intensity	Physical contact	Patterning
Workplace incivility	anyone within organization	ambiguous	low	no	not necessarily
Aggression	anyone	unambiguous	high	sometimes	not necessarily
Violence	anyone	unambiguous	very high	yes	not necessarily
Petty tyranny	boss/subordinate	varies	moderate	no	repeated/systematic
Bullying	power imbalance	unambiguous	low to moderate	not usually	repeated/systematic
Mobbing	power imbalance	unambiguous	moderate to high	not usually	
Harassment	power imbalance	unambiguous	low to high	sometimes	repeated/systematic
Organizational deviance	organization and persons within	varies	low to high	sometimes	not necessarily

persuasive shaping impact (e.g., Darr, 2005; Sypher, 2004) that violates workplace norms for respect and basic human integrity. These observations are consistent with those of Baron and Neuman (1998) who, in their review and study of workplace aggression, noted that the bulk of problematic work behaviours are not extreme, headline-grabbing events, but fall into the category of verbal comments and other behaviours not involving physically aggressive contact. For example, their three-dimensional model of workplace aggression included a dimension of hostility that consisted almost exclusively of verbal behaviours.

Incivility, as a violation of norms of respect and dignity of the person, sends a message, whether intended or unintended, that the recipient is less than deserving of ordinary courtesy and respect extended to members of the human community. In this sense, it excludes the receiver from status as a worthy human being; it also sends a message about the communicative identity of the sender as perpetrator. Furthermore, because the climate of an organization emerges through communicative inter-action (Guzley, 1992), incivility's effect on the construction of toxic work environments and problematic organizational climates takes place through the medium of communication. These powerful effects of incivility, to be discussed later in this chapter, are brought about by the shaping power of the relational dimension of uncivil messages. Sypher (2004) raised concerns about conceptualizing incivility in a broader way that recognizes its destructive communicative potential. Sypher's work resonates with that of Hannah Arendt, who notes the power of the banality of evil (Arnett, 2007): thoughtlessness, or lack of mindfulness, generates wickedness. Lack of attention and concern for the 'synovial' substance of social interaction can lead just as surely to the collapse of organizations and communities as more vivid instances of violence. Interestingly, research suggests that it is the 'everyday hassles' of life (DeLongis, Folkman & Lazarus, 1988) that eventually lead to illness and collapse; we are equipped to deal with the larger problems that we expect in life, but the everyday wearing away of our humanity is a far more insidious and destructive phenomenon. These concerns resonate with the literature on marital distress by Gottman (1994), which suggests that the type of message that is the most destructive is not the angry out-burst, but contempt, which shares conceptual identity with an incivility that fails to recognize the essential humanity and worth of another.

Communicating workplace incivility: operationalizations of the workplace incivility construct

Indicators of workplace incivility consist of behaviours manifested in explicit verbal or nonverbal behaviours – communicative actions in the form of messages sent about the (lack of) value and worth of others. Pearson et al. (2001) originally operationalized incivility in their qual-itative study as 'rude, insensitive, and disrespectful behavior' (pp. 1389, 1395). Cortina et al. (2001) provided additional theoretical and construct development with their development of a 7-item measure of incivility that related in expected ways to Donovan, Drasgow and Munson's (1998) Perceptions of Fair Interpersonal Treatment measure. This scale includes seven items, all communicative in form and function: putting some-one down/being condescending, paying little attention to someone's statements or showing little interest in someone's opinion, making demeaning or derogatory remarks about a person, addressing someone in unprofessional terms in public or private, ignoring or excluding someone from professional camaraderie, doubting someone's judgment in matters over which one has responsibility, and making unwanted attempts to draw someone into a discussion of personal matters (p. 70). Blau and Andersson (2005) employed a measure of 'instigated workplace incivility' consisting of uncivil behaviours enacted by the respondent in the workplace, and examined associated outcomes, building on the Cortina et al. scale. Sample items ask how often someone at work has exhibited these particular behaviours to the respondent during the past year: 'Put you down or was condescending to you in some way'; 'made rude, demeaning, or derogatory remarks about you'; 'addressed you in professional terms, either publicly or privately' (p. 604).

Martin and Hine (2005), building on the work of Cortina et al., developed a more extensive scale, identifying four factors, each indexed with communicative behaviours: hostility (a raised voice while speaking to the respondent; using an inappropriate tone when speaking to the respondent; speaking to the respondent in an aggressive tone of voice; rolling one's eyes at the respondent); privacy invasion (taking stationery from the respondent's desk without later returning it; taking items from the respondent's desk without prior permission; interrupting the respondent while the respondent was speaking on the telephone; reading messages addressed to the respondent, such as e-mails or faxes; opening the respondent's desk drawers without prior permission); exclusionary behaviour (failing to consult the respondent in reference to a decision the respondent should have been involved in; giving unreasonably short notice when cancelling or scheduling events for which the respondent was required to be present; failing to inform the respondent of a meeting the respondent should have been informed about; failing to consult the respondent when it would be expected to; excessive slowness in returning the respondent's phone messages or e-mails without good reason for the delay; intentionally failing to pass on information of which the respondent should have been made aware; being unreasonably slow in seeing to matters for which the respondent was reliant on the instigator without good reason); and gossiping (e.g., talking behind the respondent's back; sharing confidential information about the respondent in public; making snide remarks about the respondent) (see Table 9.2).

Vickers (2006) offers a summary of specific instances of incivility from several sources, almost all of which are explicitly communicative in nature, and the rest of which are implicitly communicative: 'sending a nasty or demeaning note or e-mail; undermining a colleague's credibility; treating another like a child; berating one for an action in which they played no part; giving people the silent treatment; giving public reprimands; making unfounded accusations; spreading gossip; excluding

Table 9.2   Uncivil workplace behaviour factors and items (from Martin & Hine, 2005, p. 411)

Hostility	A raised voice while speaking to respondent
	Using an inappropriate tone when speaking to the respondent
	Speaking to the respondent in an aggressive tone of voice
	Rolling one's eyes at the respondent
Privacy invasion	Taking stationery from the respondent's desk without later returning it
	Taking items from the respondent's desk without prior permission
	Interrupting the respondent while the respondent was speaking on the telephone
	Reading messages addressed to the respondent, such as e-mails or faxes
	Opening the respondent's desk drawers without prior permission)
Exclusionary behaviour	Failing to consult the respondent in reference to a decision the respondent should have been involved in
	Giving unreasonably short notice when cancelling or scheduling events for which the respondent was required to be present
	Failing to inform the respondent of a meeting the respondent should have been informed about
	Failing to consult the respondent when it would be expected to consult with the respondent
	Excessive slowness in returning the respondent's phone messages or e-mails without good reason for the delay
	Intentionally failing to pass on information of which the respondent should have been made aware
	Being unreasonably slow in seeing to matters for which the respondent was reliant on the instigator without good reason
Gossiping	Talking behind the respondent's back
	Sharing confidential information about the respondent in public
	Making snide remarks about the respondent
	Gossiping behind the respondent's back

someone from a meeting; neglecting to greet someone; cutting people off when they are speaking; not turning mobile phones off during meetings; leaving a jammed photocopier or printer for another to fix; leaving mess and untidiness in the kitchen; listening in on another's phone call; ignoring a colleague's request; using demeaning language; making inflammatory remarks; and writing rude or unnecessarily incendiary emails (Cortina et al., 2001; Johnson & Indvik, 2001a, p. 707; Johnson & Indvik, 2001b, p. 458; Pearson et al., 2000; Pearson, Andersson & Wegner, 2001)' (pp. 74–75).

Sypher (2004) summarizes a number of uncivil behaviours in the communicative realm: 'angry displays, rudeness, bad manners, discourteous behaviour, "workplace bullying", insensitivity, etiquette crises, interpersonal mistreatment, interactional injustice, inattentiveness, not listening, interrupting others, questioning intentions and motives, temper tantrums/emotional tirades, and behaviours as specific as phone slamming, snippy e-mails, yelling and harsh reprimands' (p. 260). Related work on rudeness and problematic work relationships sheds additional light on this communicative concept. For example, the work of Fritz (2002, 2006) identified factors related to incivility, directly touching some of the items identified by Cortina et al. (2001). For instance, 'The person badmouths me to others,' 'The person criticizes me/others,' and 'The person gossips or talks about others' were identified as unprofessional behaviours for peers.

Miller's (2001) study revealed individual and interactive behaviour defined as impropriety, which corresponds to instances of workplace incivility. These improper interactive behaviours constitute communicative manifestations of incivility: 'insufficient attention,' including behaviours of interrupting and ignoring others, not showing 'appropriate concern, respect, or sympathy for others' (p. 46); violations of privacy: 'snooping, prying, eavesdropping, spying, or gossiping' (p. 46); insufficient manners, defined as failing to show politeness, such as not offering thanks or providing 'other small courtesies to others' (p. 47); selfishness, defined as 'lazy irresponsibility' (p. 47), including actions such as 'shirking ... duties or tasks' (p. 47), which demonstrated 'some element of greed that was not present in a simple failure of manners' (p. 47), such as leaving dishes in the sink and changing the station on the radio or television without asking others first; rudeness, defined as 'straightforwardly discourteous' behaviours that aggravated others, such as 'thoughtless or intended criticism that disparaged others' (p. 48); intentional embarrassment or provocation when such behaviours proved to be 'so crude or obnoxious that they annoyed the target or others' (p. 48) and therefore judged to be improper (horseplay, pulling down someone's pants); maliciousness, defined as 'insults or sabotage that derisively demeaned or harmed others' (p. 49), such as urinating in someone's drink when the person is absent from the scene temporarily; drunkenness and associated annoying behaviour; boorishness, defined by Miller as 'excessive, needless vulgarity' (p. 49); playfulness, defined as 'rambunctious clowning or annoying impishness' (p. 50). One additional category was noted as 'other's sensitivity,' or a perceiver's having 'thin skin' (p. 50) or being easily offended despite an apparent lack of a breach of norms in the situation.

This review of operationalizations of workplace incivility shows this construct to consist of communicative 'sins' of omission and commission freighted with relational meaning. Workplace incivility sends a message of low worth, disdain, and inconsequentiality to the recipient. From a communicative perspective, the effects of workplace incivility are brought about by the power of the relational communicative dimension of uncivil messages repeated over time; these messages construct organizational climates, identities of others, and habitual patterns of instigators if not corrected and redirected.

Factors contributing to the incidence of workplace incivility

Causes of workplace incivility at the societal level are tied to changes in society's norms and subsequent lack of agreed-upon standards for discourse and behaviour in the civic sphere (Miller, 2001). A breakdown of shared expectations for public discourse began late in the 19th century, with challenges to norms of reticence regarding topics such as sexual behaviour and the private lives of public figures (Gurstein, 1996). Talk about topics that at one time had been withheld to protect and preserve their sacredness was touted as the earmark of liberation and enlightenment, reducing the social power of expectations for decorum in discourse. Explicit violence in the media since the 1960s (Miller, 2001) is a recent manifestation of this development of banality of exposure. An ethic of self-expression resists restraint as an infringement upon the rights of the self (Andersson & Pearson, 1999), while disagreement about appropriate public behaviour parallels lack of shared ethical standards in the workplace (Fritz, Arnett & Conkel, 1999). The rise of informality in organizational dress and behaviour (Andersson & Pearson, 1999; Arnett & Fritz, 2003) on the heels of a rejection of perceptions of the inauthenticity of public roles emerging from the social and sexual revolution of the 1960's stressed an individualism inattentive to the needs and concerns of others and an approach to interpersonal communication aimed at promoting and enhancing the self (Rawlins, 1985).

At the level of the organization, increased work demands in both quantity and pace and uncertainty from organizational change contribute to workplace incivility – workers are expected to do more with less, increasing stress and fraying tempers (Pearson et al., 2005). Many organizational technologies remove the human face, erasing the salience of accountability to another and increasing the likelihood of uncivil behaviour (Pearson et al., 2000). Furthermore, the immediacy and ease of use of technology decreases restraint (Fritz & Arnett, 2003) and contributes to a climate of informality (Lievrouw & Finn, 1996) conducive to workplace incivility. Blau and Andersson's (2005) longitudinal study of instigated workplace incivility – a measure of the extent to which one is the perpetrator of incivility – showed distributive justice and job satisfaction to be negative predictors and work exhaustion to be a positive predictor of instigated workplace incivility. These cultural and organizational causes are accompanied by individual differences, such as lack of knowledge of rules for culturally acceptable behaviour, lack of skill, lapse of control, lack of effort, lack of care, malevolence, and selfishness, which may contribute to impropriety or perceptions of impropriety characteristic of incivility (Miller, 2001).

How workplace incivility operates

Incivility can extend its reach throughout the organization through what Pearson et al. (2000) describe as spirals or cascades. Workplace incivility can affect organizational norms through non-escalating exchanges, when rude behaviour is exchanged in a 'tit for tat' fashion (Andersson & Pearson, 1999; Pearson et al., 2000) and is observed and imitated by others. Incivility spirals happen when an uncivil behaviour ('Move out of the way. I need the copier') is met by a reciprocal response of another uncivil behaviour because of the perceived unfairness, or interactional injustice, of the event and accompanying negative affect ('No, I was here first – can't you wait?'), which is then responded to with an increased level of incivility and rude remarks ('MY DEADLINE IS FIVE MINUTES AWAY!!'), which is followed by a stronger expression of incivility (moving very close to someone and yelling back: 'THAT'S TOO BAD!!!'), which then may be followed by stronger and more intense reactions and/or maligning insults (a shove to move the person away from the copier or calling the person a name) – in other words, the level of intensity of incivility may escalate, crossing the boundary into the more intense problematic workplace behaviour of aggression or even violence. Cascading incivility happens when the incivility spiral generates mimetic effects in the rest of the organization through direct observation and imitation of incivility by third parties to the interaction. Cascading incivility can occur indirectly, as well, when employees other than those involved directly in the uncivil interaction obtain second-hand information about the incivility event. Such information creates a perception that leads to availability of the behaviour for easy imitation under similar circumstances, or it may simply contribute, over the course of time, to an uncivil climate or to perceptions of the organization as one that is host to such behaviours, damaging the organization's internal and external reputation (Pearson et al., 2000).

Outcomes of workplace incivility

A growing body of research documents the deleterious effects of workplace incivility on a number of organizational and individual outcomes. Pearson et al. (2000) report that workplace incivility affects absenteeism, commitment, productivity, and turnover. Specifically, 1/3 of respondents in their questionnaire study reported reduced commitment, 50% reported thinking about quitting, and 12% actually did quit. Twenty-five percent of respondents decreased their work efforts. Such effects on employees decreases productivity, affecting the organization's viability. Workplace incivility leads to perceptions of unfairness and interactional injustice (Pearson & Porath, 2005), thereby jeopardizing the health of an organization's climate and increasing the likelihood of further incivility.

Workplace incivility generates negative effects on employee outcomes (Cortina et al., 2001; Lim & Cortina, 2005). Cortina et al. (2001) report that 'with more frequent experiences of disrespectful, insensitive, uncivil behaviour on the job, respondents were less satisfied with all aspects of their employment – their jobs, supervisors, co-workers, pay and benefits, and promotional opportunities. Further, they considered quitting more frequently. In addition to such numerous job-related effects, respondents who experienced more frequent incivility also endured greater psychological distress' (p. 75). Lim and Cortina (2005) found that increasing levels of experienced incivility, sexual harassment, and gender harassment generated additive negative effects on employee occupational, psychological, and physical health, though experiences of incivility alone produced significant negative effects on these outcomes. These findings are supported by subsequent research of Martin and Hine (2005), who suggest that 'being the target of incivility is associated with lower satisfaction with co-workers and supervisors, higher levels of job and work withdrawal, higher levels of psychological distress, and lower levels of psychological well-being and health satisfaction' (p. 488).

Workplace incivility as a job stressor was negatively associated with job satisfaction and positively associated with counter-productive work behaviours in research conducted by Penney and Spector (2005). This effect was moderated by negative affectivity, an individual-level variable that describes the tendency to experience negative mood states, to be especially sensitive to 'frustrations and irritations,' and to have a greater likelihood of experiencing 'negative emotions, such as anxiety, guilt, anger, rejection, sadness, and distress' (p. 781). Penney and Spector suggest that negative affectivity on the part of persons experiencing incivility may increase the likelihood of an incivility spiral.

Porath and Erez (2007), in a series of studies, found that rudeness, one of the manifestations of incivility and operationalized in their study by negative verbal statements, was associated with decreased task performance, creativity, flexibility, and helpfulness. These effects held whether rudeness was directed toward the participants in a subtle or direct way. Even imagining an incident of rudeness affected productivity through decreased performance. Porath and Erez explained this effect as a result of disruption of cognitive processes necessary for creative focus on task. They also found a 'spillover' effect in which recipients of rudeness decreased helping behaviour to innocent parties not involved in the rude interaction. This finding suggests that workplace incivility has the potential to 'chill' an organization's human environment, further evidence for workplace incivility's deleterious effect on organizational climate.

The instigator may suffer, likewise, from the effects of targets of incivility upon whom the instigator depends. Female recipients may avoid the instigator, potentially affecting the instigator's productivity if the instigator work depends upon the target's participation. Male targets may retaliate by spoiling the instigator's reputation (Porath & Pearson, 2000, reported in Pearson et al., 2005). Targets with less power may respond in passive ways, withdrawing support that might formerly have been provided behind the scenes for an instigator (Pearson & Porath, 2005).

Variables affecting workplace incivility

Several variables thought to mitigate or enhance effects or perceptions of workplace incivility have been investigated. In addition to the previously-discussed moderating variable of negative affectivity identified by Penney and Spector (2005), Montgomery, Kane and Vance (2004) found that women are more likely than men to perceive uncivil behaviours as inappropriate. Cupach, Huggins, Long and Metts (2002) found a tendency to experience embarrassment to be positively associated with judgments of offensiveness (rudeness, vulgarity, and inconsideration) and that women rated improprieties as more offensive than men. Whereas Pearson et al. (2000) found men and women equally likely to be targets of incivility, Cortina et al. (2001) found women to be the targets of incivility more often than men. Montgomery et al.'s (2004) study revealed that the extent to which an observer identified with a target of incivility predicted perceptions of inappropriateness. Cupach et al. (2002) found that older participants were more likely than younger participants to perceive vulgarity as offensive; a generational effect.

Current research on workplace incivility is turning to specific mechanisms by which incivility is generated and sustained in relation to other variables. Lim and Cortina (2005) found experiences of incivility to be correlated moderately with sexual harassment, speculating that sexual harassment takes place against the backdrop of generalized incivility at work, such that norms for inappropriate behaviour may encourage multiple types of problematic behaviours.

Porath et al. (2008) conducted a series of studies examining the influence of relative status and gender of target and instigator on responses to incivility. In the first two of three studies, incivility was framed as a challenge to status and operationalized as rude, insensitive or disrespectful behaviour directed toward the respondent. In both studies, higher status targets and male targets reported being more likely to respond with overt aggression in response to incivility than lower status and female targets, with higher status males more likely than lower status males to respond with overt aggression. Overt retaliation was more likely in male dyads, and higher status male targets were more likely than lower status male targets to retaliate with overt aggression. Lower status targets and female targets were more likely to report that they would avoid the instigator of incivility. Lower status female targets were more likely to avoid male instigators of incivility. The third study's results revealed that 'women showed a consistent linear pattern of decreasing resistance and increasing acquiescence to higher-status challengers, men tended to show the most resistance to peers, followed by lower- and then higher-status challengers' (p. 27). This study provides a close look at how status and gender may contribute to reproduction of hierarchical patterns, particularly how gender and status inequality may be reinforced by patterns of responses to incivility.

Disputes and debates

Residual theoretical dispute still exists with regard to the classification and nature of workplace incivility. Bies and Tripp (2005) argue for conceptualizing workplace incivility, counter-productive workplace behaviours, deviance, bullying, abuse, and revenge as subsets of workplace aggression. Sypher (2004), working from a communicative perspective, urges that we broaden the scope of incivility construct as anti-social behaviour, given its potential for damage to persons and environments, and recommends 'captur[ing] the differences along two continua of intensity and intentionality' (p. 259). She presents a table that captures a two-dimensional model of workplace incivility ranging from terms that move from low intensity and intentionality to high intensity and intentionality, beginning with ignoring and moving to not listening, interrupting, excluding others, using profanity, exhibiting rudeness, name-calling, humiliating, exhibiting desk rage, bullying, engaging in verbal aggression, engaging in verbal harassment, exhibiting verbal abuse, and enacting physical violence (p. 261). While these perspectives offer thoughtful reflection on the conceptualization of incivility, current research is following the conceptualization and theoretical framing originally laid out by Andersson and Pearson (1999), with recognition that alternative perspectives and conceptualizations can ensure 'that the stream [of research on workplace incivility] remains open to novel, broader, and more intricate conceptualizations and explanatory frameworks' (Pearson et al., 2005, p. 180).

Recommendations for preventing, curtailing, and managing workplace incivility

Within the matrix of unpleasant and erosive workplace interpersonal phenomena, incivility appears at the interactional interface of civil professional communication and aggressive and physically violent behaviour. Andersson and Pearson's (1999) model suggests that incivility can create a spiral that may lead to increased hostility or violence. In this sense, incivility defines the boundary between constructive social interaction and behaviour that destroys communities. At the level of the immediate interaction, the zone of incivility provides some 'reactional' latitude for the recipient's response to create a spiral of incivility or to diffuse the behaviour. Incivility can be understood as the most significant turning point for an organization's interactive climate. While it stays within this zone, incivility can be addressed and changed; left unchecked, it becomes a transition point for organizational dysfunction and eventual demise.

While decrying the adverse effects of workplace incivility, it is also important to recognize that human beings are subject to lapses in judgment, occasional breaches of propriety, and thoughtless remarks. Incivility is part and parcel of flawed human experience, requiring forbearance on the part of recipients, who will themselves, on occasion, be on the sending end of these slights and in need of interactional grace from co-workers. In many cases, responsible and thoughtful deflective action on the part of recipients of incivility may stop an incivility spiral (Pearson et al., 2000), defuse a potential argument, or heal an injury through forgiveness (Metts, Cupach & Lippert, 2006). The occasional lapse is of less concern than recurrent destructive practices resulting in patterned structures of and expectations for interaction that increase the likelihood of incivility spirals and toxic organizational climates. Halting and redirecting patterns of uncivil communication are possible only within a context that permits changing those patterns and attending factors that make such behaviour likely. Consider the previous example of the use of the photocopier. One way to deflect incivility is for the recipient to respond with calm assertiveness: 'If your need is urgent, I'll be glad to assist. Otherwise, I'll go ahead with my copies. It won't be a long wait.' Alternatively, the original instigator might reflect on the original utterance and reframe the request: 'I'm in a very tight spot – could you help out just this one time by letting me get these copies made? I'd be so grateful.' Recognizing the communicative nature of workplace incivility suggests a conceptual framing for this construct that rests within the domain of communication ethics. Incivility can be understood as unethical organizational communicative behaviour that fails to protect and promote the good of an organization as a 'dwelling place' for oneself and others (Arnett et al., 2009). An organizational communication ethic of professional civility responds to Andersson and Pearson's (1999) original conceptualization and subsequent theorizing and research on the workplace incivility construct and focuses attention on conditions conducive to ethical communicative behaviour in organizations, conditions that rest largely with organizational leadership.

An organizational communicative ethic of professional civility

Professional civility (Arnett & Fritz, 2001, 2003; Arnett, 2006; Fritz & Arnett, 2007) is a communicative ethic for interpersonal interaction in organizations that attends to the interrelated 'goods' of productivity, people, and place. Professional civility provides a framework addressing communicative conduct in organizations across a variety of domains, including hiring and socializing new employees, generating clear public guidelines for organizational behaviour, and enforcing managerial accountability for enacting organizational guidelines. Professional civility rejects a human relations model in which organizations attempt to meet individual needs as a technique to increase production. Professional civility embraces, instead, a human resource model, elevating ideas, creativity, and productivity as the focus of organizational life. Professional civility involves respect for others in the workplace and a willingness to work with those whom one may not like, engaging distance when necessary in order to permit constructive work to continue (Hess, 2006). Professional civility asks organizations to take responsibility for public articulation of a mission or guiding narrative that has fidelity, in which word and deed are connected, maintaining the identity of the institution with integrity for internal and external audiences.

In the most recent treatment of professional civility, Arnett (2006) draws on the work of Hannah Arendt to warn against the invasion of the public by the private as a danger to public and private life. Professional civility assumes an orientation to organizations as public places, the importance of coordinated roles, and the need for boundaries protecting public and private life, concerns implicit in the recommendations of Andersson and Pearson (1999) and Pearson et al. (2000) for curtailing workplace incivility. Professional civility assumes limits for expectations of persons and their employing organizations: organizations are not designed as places of self-fulfillment, and employees are not designed to give the totality of their lives to organizations such that the public replaces or overwhelms the private sphere.

Arnett's (2006) argument for differentiating public and private spaces recognizes the need to experience life that is balanced in multiple ways such that work does not bear the sole burden of fulfillment of a life, a condition likely to generate employee cynicism from unmet high expectations (Arnett & Arneson, 1999). This recommendation resonates with the concerns of Pearson et al. (2000), who note the increasingly demanding pace of work as an antecedent of incivility. Organizations, likewise, bear the responsibility of accountability within the public sphere, balancing the need for profit or continued service – survival – with the need to offer publicly fair and just procedures and protections for employees and communities, not demanding the soul of employees through invasion of their privacy and outside lives.

The dialectical tension between person and institution is managed by a public statement of expectations for employment, the dignity of organizational roles that permits focus of attention on work rather than the personal attributes of others, permitting others to do their work without the interference of those who think it should be done 'my' way, discourse that avoids social undermining of others, and avoidance of feigned intimacy with those one does not know well. This focus on roles and restraint moves away from a climate of informality conducive to workplace incivility (Andersson & Pearson, 1999), focusing attention on non-personalized expectations that move attention away from the person and toward public expectations. Ironically, this depersonalization holds the promise of greater civility, respect based on community standards for behaviour rather than personal preference, attacking workplace incivility at its heart.

A communicative ethic of professional civility suggests a number of guidelines for preventing and controlling workplace incivility. First, a framework of professional civility recognizes the importance of clear, public guidelines for professionally civil behaviour (Arnett & Fritz, 2003; Pearson et al., 2000). An organization must communicate a common centre (Arnett, 1986; Arnett & Fritz, 2003) that organizes and guides efforts of employees at all levels, putting in place clear expectations for organizational interpersonal interaction (Pearson et al., 2000, p. 133). Bandow and Hunter (2008), for example, report that PepsiCo defines uncivil behaviour as 'lying about another employee, forcing an employee do something illegal or against policy, applying pressure with unnecessary language, and disrespecting co-workers in any form or fashion' (p. 104). These specific behaviours provide public guidelines to assess conduct and reinforce an organizational mission devoted to the dignity of all workers and prevention of uncivil behaviour. Pearson and Porath (2005) suggest setting 'zero tolerance expectations' (p. 12) for uncivil behaviour.

As important as clear guidelines is the consistency of leader behaviour in adhering to those guidelines. Leaders who fulfill public expectations for organizational behaviour are an invaluable resource in combating workplace incivility. As Fritz et al. (1999) report, managers who walk the talk, exhibiting managerial behavioural integrity (Simons, 2002), play a critical role in making employees aware of standards for conduct and in establishing trust and commitment so important for constructive organizational functioning.

Recent work on *management citizenship behaviour* (MCB) (Hodson, 2002), which is defined as 'behaviour that conforms to prevailing norms for organizational leadership and for respecting workers' rights' (p. 75) and has been shown to support a productive workplace environment, offers additional insight into the role of managers as standard bearers of professional civility. MCB promotes workplace harmony and decreases conflict and problematic behaviour among employees, including behaviours, such as gossip, that characterize workplace incivility. Managers who exhibit MCB are modelling professional civility for employees, creating salient behavioural alternatives to workplace incivility.

MCB may be conducive to a constructive communication cycle that counters spirals of workplace incivility. Hodson (2002) reports that MCB promotes organizational citizenship behaviour on the part of employees, which suggests a similar operative mechanism to that of cascading workplace incivility, but in a constructive direction. Because of the strong effect of MCB on suppressing infighting, defined operationally as 'conflict, gossip, and interference within and between workgroups' (p. 83), and on encouraging organizational citizenship behaviours, constructive work practices are encouraged and amplified, while destructive ones are attenuated.

Incivility can be stopped before it begins by careful attention to hiring decisions. Managers who are conscientious and cautious with employee recruitment and selection, checking references to avoid hiring uncivil people (Pearson et al., 2000), for example, are protecting the culture and climate of the organization: the people make the place (Schneider, 1987). Once employees are hired, attentiveness to orientation and training ensures understanding of organizational expectations for behaviour (Pearson et al., 2000, p. 134), and understanding is translated into action upon observation of managerial adherence to these standards (Fritz et al., 1999; Hodson, 2002; Simons, 2002). Formal employee socialization and mentoring provide good opportunities for instilling the organization's expectations for civil interpersonal interaction, keeping the invitation to participate in the organization's project foremost rather than employee comfort (Arnett & Fritz, 2003).

Organizations show their commitment to policies through investment of resources. Communication skills training for interpersonal communication competencies grounded in civility (Gonthier, 2002; Troester & Mester, 2007) is one way to both demonstrate public commitment to an ethic of professional civility and offer concrete assistance to employees in their day-to-day interactions. Pearson and Porath (2005) recommend training in listening, conflict resolution, dealing with difficult people, and stress management and tying expectations for civil behaviour to career advancement. Uncivil behaviour can be prevented by appraisal training that focuses on making constructive attributions for others' behaviour (e.g., Omdahl, 2006). Supporting a workplace that is friendly but not intimate and encouraging employees to have meaningful lives outside of work can prevent envy and jealousy, which are likely to arise when the world of work is the only focus of a person's attention (Arnett, 2006; Arnett & Arneson, 1999) and accompanying uncivil outbursts arising from these emotions.

To monitor ongoing adherence to organizational standards for civility, managers can encourage and attend to feedback from employees about instances of uncivil behaviour (Pearson et al., 2000, pp. 134–135), particularly anonymous feedback from lower-level employees (Pearson & Porath, 2005), and respond by dealing with the instigator through corrective feedback (Pearson et al., p. 135), documenting the behaviour each time. Habitual offenders often 'get away with it' because they have talents and skills valued by upper-level administrators or access to organizational power, managers look the other way, or organizational leaders fail to deal with the problem in an effective manner (Pearson & Porath, 2005). Avoid giving repeat offenders authority over others by promoting them or moving them; lateral moves just shift the problem to another location and infests the rest of the organization (Pearson & Porath, 2005). If necessary, terminate uncivil employees if the behaviour doesn't stop. Finally, invest in post-departure interviews to determine whether unrecognized incivility is occurring (Pearson & Porath, 2005).

Summary

The quality of work life interaction is of significant consequence for employees and organizations. The growing body of research on workplace incivility is clear: the conditions of work can function as contributors to workplace incivility instigation, and workplace incivility damages organizations and employees. As organizational leadership seeks to create workplaces conducive to creativity and productivity, the steps needed to prevent and/or ameliorate the scourge of workplace incivility will become increasingly important.

Chronic understaffing, change that is poorly communicated, unclear guidelines for appropriate interpersonal behaviour, blurring of public and private boundaries, and lack of leadership response to incivility when it occurs appear to increase conditions under which incivility can take root and flourish. As organizations work to create healthier work settings, structural conditions set the stage for reduced incivility. A commitment to building a culture of professional civility generates long-term rewards. Organizations as productive workplaces require differentiation of public and private life with clear codes of conduct and expectations for behaviour. Careful hiring and socialization practices will assist in making these guidelines clear. It is imperative that managers model and enforce these guidelines, 'walking the talk,' and that consistent and patterned breaches of civility be taken seriously and acted upon when reported. Training in responses to the inevitable slights that will happen in the workplace can assist in navigating the landscape of inevitable human error and frailty.

As scholars in fields of management, communication, health care, public administration, and kindred areas continue their efforts to understand workplace incivility and its remedies from varied approaches, practitioners will put theory to the test, identifying best practices for further investigation and confirmation. Our body of knowledge will continue to grow, contributing to the larger picture of healthy work life and organizational structures. Through such efforts, both institutions and the persons who inhabit them will be enriched.

References

Alberts, J. K., Lutgen-Sandvik, P. & Tracy, S. J. (2005, May). Workplace bullying: A case of escalated incivility. Paper presented at the annual meeting of the International Communication Association, New York.

Andersson, L. M. & Pearson, C. M. (1999). Tit for tat? The spiraling effect of incivility in the workplace. *Academy of Management Review, 24,* 452–471.

Appelbaum, S. & Roy-Girard, D. (2007). Toxins in the workplace: Affect [*sic*] on organizations and employees. *Corporate Governance, 7*(1), 17–28.

Arnett, R. C. (1986). *Communication and Community: Implications of Martin Buber's Dialogue.* Carbondale: Southern Illinois University Press.

Arnett, R. C. (2001). Dialogic civility as pragmatic ethical praxis: An interpersonal metaphor for the public domain. *Communication Theory, 11,* 315–338.

Arnett, R. C. (2006). Professional civility. In J. M. H. Fritz & B. L. Omdahl (eds), *Problematic Relationships in the Workplace* (pp. 233–248). New York: Peter Lang.

Arnett, R. C. (2007). Hannah Arendt: Dialectical communicative labor. In P. Arneson (ed.), *Perspectives on Philosophy of Communication* (pp. 67–84). West Lafayette, IN: Purdue University Press.

Arnett, R. C. & Arneson, P. (1999). *Dialogic Civility in a Cynical Age: Community, Hope, and Interpersonal Relationships.* Albany, NY: SUNY Press.

Arnett, R. C. & Fritz, J. M. H. (2001). Communication and professional civility as a basic service course: Dialogic praxis between departments and situated in an academic home. *Basic Communication Course Annual, 13,* 174–206.

Arnett, R. C. & Fritz, J. M. H. (2003). Sustaining institutional ethics and integrity: Management in a postmodern moment. In A. S. Iltis (ed.), *Institutional Integrity in Healthcare* (pp. 41–71). Dordrecht: Kluwer Academic Publishers.

Arnett, R. C., Fritz, J. M. H. & Bell, L. M. (2009). *Communication Ethics Literacy: Dialogue and Difference.* Thousand Oaks, CA: Sage.

Ashforth, B. (1994). Petty tyranny in organizations. *Human Relations, 47,* 755–778.

Bandow, D. & Hunter, D. (2008). Developing policies about uncivil workplace behaviour. *Business Communication Quarterly, 71,* 103–106.

Baron, R. A. & Neuman, J. H. (1996). Workplace violence and workplace aggression: Evidence on their relative frequency and potential causes. *Aggressive Behaviour, 22,* 161–173.

Baron, R. A. & Neuman, J. H. (1998). Workplace aggression – The iceberg beneath the tip of workplace violence: Evidence on its forms, frequency and targets. *Public Administration Quarterly, 21,* 446–464.

Bellah, R., Madsen, H., Sullivan, W., Swidler, A. & Tipton, S. (1985). *Habits of the Heart: Individualism and Commitment in American Life.* Berkeley: University of California Press.

Bies, R. J. & Tripp, T. M. (2005). The study of revenge in the workplace: Conceptual, ideological, and empirical issues. In S. Fox & P. E. Spector (eds), *Counter-productive Workplace Behaviour: Investigations of Actors and Targets* (pp. 65–81). Washington, DC: American Psychological Association.

Blau, G. & Andersson, L. (2005). Testing a measure of instigated workplace incivility. *Journal of Occupational and Organizational Psychology, 78,* 595–614.

Buhler, P. (2003). Managing in a new millennium. *Supervision, 64*(4), 20–23.

Carter, S. L. (1998). *Civility: Manners, Morals, and the Etiquette of Democracy.* New York: Basic Books.

Cortina, L., Magley, V., Williams, J. & Langhout, R. (2001). Incivility in the workplace: Incidence and impact. *Journal of Occupational Health Psychology, 6,* 64–80.

Cupach, W. R., Huggins, J., Long, L. W. & Metts, S. (2002, March). Perceptions of impropriety: Role of embarrassability and perceiver sex. Paper presented at the annual meeting of the Western States Communication Association, Long Beach, CA.

Cupach, W. R. and Spitzberg, B. H. (eds) (1994). *The Dark Side of Interpersonal Communication.* Hillsdale, NJ: Lawrence Erlbaum.

Darr, C. R. (2005). Civility as rhetorical enactment: The John Ashcroft 'debates' and Burke's theory of form. *Southern Communication Journal, 70,* 316–328.

DeLongis, A., Folkman, S. & Lazarus, R. S. (1988). The impact of daily stress on health and mood: Psychological and social resources as mediators. *Journal of Personality and Social Psychology, 54,* 486–495.

Donovan, M. A., Drasgow, F. & Munson, L. J. (1998). The perceptions of fair interpersonal treatment scale: Development and validation of a measure of interpersonal treatment in the workplace. *Journal of Applied Psychology, 83,* 683–692.

Duffy, M. K., Ganster, D. C. & Pagon, M. (2002). Social undermining in the workplace. *Academy of Management Journal, 45,* 331–351.

Fox, S. & Spector, P. E. (eds) (2005). *Counter-Productive Work Behaviour: Investigations of Actors and Targets.* Washington, DC: American Psychological Association.

Fritz, J. M. H. (2002). How do I dislike thee? Let me count the ways: Constructing impressions of troublesome others at work. *Management Communication Quarterly, 15,* 410–438.

Fritz, J. M. H. (2006). Typology of troublesome others at work: A follow-up investigation. In J. M. H. Fritz & B. L. Omdahl (eds), *Problematic Relationships in the Workplace* (pp. 21–46). New York: Peter Lang.

Fritz, J. M. H. & Arnett, R. C. (2003, April). Organizational mission, 'spirit,' and organizational technology. Paper presented at the annual meeting of the Eastern Communication Association, Pittsburgh.

Fritz, J. M. H. & Arnett, R. C. (2007, November). Professional civility as communicative and rhetorical practice in organizations: Social style grounded in substance. Paper presented at the annual meeting of the National Communication Association, Chicago.

Fritz, J. M. H., Arnett, R. C. & Conkel, M. (1999). Organizational ethical standards and organizational commitment. *Journal of Business Ethics, 20,* 289–299.

Fritz, J. M. H. & Omdahl, B. (eds) (2006). *Problematic Relationships in the Workplace.* New York: Peter Lang.

Gonthier, G. (2002). *Rude Awakenings: Overcoming the Civility Crisis in the Workplace.* Chicago: Dearborn Trade.

Gottman, J. (1994). Why marriages fail. *Family Therapy Networker, 18*(3), 41–48.

Griffin, R. W. & O'Leary-Kelly, A. M. (eds) (2004). *The Dark Side of Organizational Behaviour.* San Francisco: Jossey-Bass.

Gurstein, R. (1996). *The Repeal of Reticence: A History of America's Cultural and Legal Struggles Over Free Speech, Obscenity, Sexual Liberation, and Modern Art.* New York: Hill and Wang.

Guzley, R. M. (1992). Organizational climate and communication climate: Predicators of commitment to the organization. *Management Communication Quarterly, 5,* 379–402.

Heinemann, R. L. (1996). Campus-wide communication incivility in the basic course: A case study. (ERIC Document Reproduction Service No. ED 404 701).

Hess, J. A. (2006). Distancing from problematic co-workers. In J. M. H. Fritz & B. L. Omdahl (eds), *Problematic Relationships in the Workplace* (pp. 205–232). New York: Peter Lang.

Hodson, R. (2002). Management citizenship behaviour and its consequences. *Work and Occupations, 29,* 64–96.

Hutton, S. A. (2006). Workplace incivility: State of the science. *Journal of Nursing Administration, 36,* 22–28.

Johnson, P. & Indvik, J. (2001a). Rudeness at work: Impulse over restraint. *Public Personnel Management, 30,* 457–465.

Johnson, P. R. & Indvik, J. (2001b). Slings and arrows of rudeness: Incivility in the workplace. *Journal of Management Development, 20,* 705–713.

Kane, K. & Montgomery, K. (1998). A framework for understanding dysempowerment in organizations. *Human Resource Management, 37,* 263–275.

Kimura, H. (2003). Overcome toxic management. *Nursing Management, 34,* 26–29.

Lievrouw, L. A. & Finn, T. A. (1996). New information technologies and informality: Comparing organizational information flows using the CSM. *International Journal of Technology Management, 11,* 28–42.

Lim, S. & Cortina, L. M. (2005). Interpersonal mistreatment in the workplace: The interface and impact of general incivility and sexual harassment. *Journal of Applied Psychology, 90,* 483–496.

MacIntyre, A. (1981). *After Virtue: A Study in Moral Theory.* Notre Dame, IN: University of Notre Dame Press.

Martin, R. J. & Hine, D. W. (2005). Development and validation of a measure of the uncivil workplace behaviour questionnaire. *Journal of Occupational Health Psychology, 10,* 477–490.

Metts, S., Cupach, W. & Lippert, L. (2006). Forgiveness in the workplace. In J. M. H. Fritz & Omdahl, B. L. (eds), *Problematic Relationships in the Workplace* (pp. 249–274). New York: Peter Lang.

Miller, R. S. (2001). Breaches of propriety. In R. Kowalski (ed.), *Behaving Badly: Aversive Behaviours in Interpersonal Relationships* (pp. 29–58). Washington, DC: American Psychological Association.

Montgomery, K., Kane, K. & Vance, C. M. (2004). Accounting for differences in norms of respect: A study of assessments of incivility through the lenses of race and gender. *Group and Organization Management, 29,* 248–268.

O'Leary, A. M., Duffy, M. K. & Griffin, R. W. (2000). Construct confusion in the study of anti-social work behaviour. *Research in Personnel and Human Resources Management, 18,* 275–303.

Omdahl, B. L. (2006). Towards effective work relationships. In J. M. H. Fritz & B. L. Omdahl (eds), *Problematic Relationships in the Workplace* (pp. 279–294). New York: Peter Lang.

Pearson, C., Andersson, L. & Porath, C. (2000). Assessing and attacking workplace incivility. *Organizational Dynamics, 29,* 123–137.

Pearson, C., Andersson, L. & Wegner, J. (2001). When workers flout convention: A study of workplace incivility. *Human Relations, 54,* 1387–1419.

Pearson, C., Andersson, L. & Porath, C. (2005). Workplace incivility. In S. Fox & P. E. Spector (eds), *Counter-Productive Workplace Behaviour: Investigations of Actors and Targets* (pp. 177–200). Washington, D.C.: American Psychological Association Press.

Pearson, C. M. & Porath, C. L. (2004). On incivility, its impact, and directions for future research. In R. W. Griffin & A. M. O'Leary-Kelly (eds), *The Dark Side of Organizational behaviour* (pp. 403–425). San Francisco: Jossey-Bass.

Pearson, C. M. & Porath, C. L. (2005). On the nature, consequences, and remedies of workplace incivility: No time for 'nice'? Think again. *Academy of Management Executive, 19,* 7–18.

Penney, L. M. & Spector, P. E. (2005). Job stress, incivility, and counter-productive work behaviour (CWB): The moderating role of negative affectivity. *Journal of Organizational Behaviour, 26,* 777–796.

Porath, C. L., Overbeck, J. R. & Pearson, C. M. (2008). Picking up the gauntlet: How individuals respond to status challenges. *Journal of Applied Social Psychology, 37,* 1945–1980.

Porath, C. L. & Pearson, C. M. (2000, August). Gender differences and the behavior of targets of workplace incivility: He 'dukes' it out, she 'disappears' herself. Paper presented at the annual meeting of the Academy of Management, Toronto, Ontario, Canada.

Porath, C. L. & Erez, A. (2007). Does rudeness really matter? The effects of rudeness on task performance and helpfulness. *Academy of Management Journal, 50,* 1181–1197.

Putnam, R. D. (2000). *Bowling Alone: The Collapse and Revival of American Community.* New York: Simon & Schuster.

Rawlins, W. K. (1985). Stalking interpersonal communication effectiveness: Social, individual or situational integration? In T. W. Benson (ed.), *Speech Communication in the Twentieth Century* (pp. 109–129). Carbondale: Southern Illinois University Press.

Skarlicki, D. P. & Folger, R. (1997). Retaliation in the workplace: The roles of distributive, procedural, and interactional justice. *Journal of Applied Psychology, 82,* 434–443.

Schneider, B. (1987). The people make the place. *Personnel Psychology, 40,* 437–453.

Simons, T. (2002). Behavioural integrity: The perceived alignment between managers' words and deeds as a research focus. *Organization Science, 13,* 18–35.

Spitzberg, B. H. & Cupach, W. R. (eds) (1998). *The Dark Side of Close Relationships.* Hillsdale, NJ: Erlbaum.

Sutton, R. (2007). *The No Asshole Rule.* New York: Warner Business Books.

Sypher, B. D. (2004). Reclaiming civil discourse in the workplace. *Southern Communication Journal, 69,* 257–269.

Tepper, B. J. (2007). Abusive supervision in work organizations: Review, synthesis, and research agenda. *Journal of Management, 33,* 261–289.

Thau, S., Crossley, C., Bennett, R. J. & Sczesny, S. (2007). The relationship between trust, attachment, and anti-social work behaviours. *Human Relations, 60,* 1155–1179.

Tracy, S. J., Lutgen-Sandvik, P. & Alberts, J. K. (2006). Nightmares, demons, and slaves: Exploring the painful metaphors of workplace bullying. *Management Communication Quarterly, 20,* 148–185.

Tracy, K. & Tracy, S. J. (1998). Rudeness at 911:Re-conceptualizing face and face-attack. *Human Communication Research, 25,* 225–251.

Troester, R. L. & Mester, C. S. (2007). *Civility in Business and Professional Communication.* New York: Peter Lang.

Vardi, Y. & Weitz, E. (2004). *Misbehaviour in Organizations.* Mahwah, NJ: Lawrence Erlbaum.

Vickers, M. H. (2006). Writing what's relevant: Workplace incivility in public administration – A wolf in sheep's clothing. *Administrative Theory & Praxis, 28,* 69–88.

Wanous, J. P., Reichers, A. E. & Austin, J. T. (2000). Cynicism about organizational change. *Group and Organization Management, 25,* 132–153.

Watzlawick, P., Beavin, J. H. & Jackson, D. D. (1967). *Pragmatics of Human Communication: A Study of Interactional Patterns, Pathologies, and Paradoxes.* New York, NY: W. W. Norton & Company.

Winters, A. M. & Duck, S. (2001). You ****!: Swearing as an aversive and a relational activity. In R. Kowalski (ed.), *Behaving Badly: Aversive Behaviours in Interpersonal Relationships* (pp. 59–77). Washington, DC: American Psychological Association.

Zauderer, D. (2002). Workplace incivility and the management of human capital. *Public Manager, 31*(1), 36–42.

10
Narcissism at Work: The Narcissistic Personality and Organizational Relationships

Adrian Furnham

This chapter is predicated on four fundamental axioms. The *first* is that self-esteem at both the global (facet) and specific (domain) level is normally distributed in the population. Like nearly all human characteristics and traits, from creativity to conscientiousness, and integrity to intelligence, there is, in the general population, a bell curve (normal) distribution with a few people with very high self-esteem and a few with very low self-esteem. Further it has trait-like qualities being stable over time and relatively consistent across social situations.

The *second* is that the relationship between self-esteem and social adjustment is possibly more curvilinear than linear. That is, too much is as bad as too little self-esteem. Optimal self-esteem, combined with optimal self-insight, is related to healthy, productive and stable social relationships at, and outside, work. Having little self-esteem and self-confidence can inhibit the development of relationships while too much self-esteem (narcissism) can equally impair social relationships. It should be noted that Sedikides, Rudich, Gregg, Kumashiro and Rusbull (2004) argued, and demonstrated, that 'normal' narcissists are psychologically healthy but admit that extreme levels may be associated with psychological disturbance and illness.

The *third* axiom is that self-esteem has a powerful influence on the success individuals have in their ability to initiate, maintain and benefit from social relationships in and out of the workplace. Many factors determine the quality and quantity of their social relationships, but self-esteem plays an important part.

Fourth, the causal relationships between self-esteem and overall success at work in both the social and output sense is bi-directional leading to *virtuous* and *vicious* cycles. It is misleading to believe that the direction of causality is from self-esteem to work success therefore implying that enhancing self-esteem has a simple causal relationship on work-related behaviour. Indeed, there may well be circumstances when the primary causal relationship is the other way around. That is, teach people to become successful at work and their self-esteem goes up. Successful people feel good about themselves: i.e., it is not that teaching self-esteem leads to success, but rather success at work enhances self-esteem.

There is a vast literature on 'self' words in psychology such as self-esteem, self-confidence, self-worth and self-awareness. The idea is that people make assessments and evaluations about themselves, particularly in their abilities and personality and also about their motives, their physical attractiveness and their 'potential'. Whilst these self-assessments are inevitably subjective they can be measured at least against the judgement of others. Further it is assumed that the more accurate these assessments against objective, observatory or even reputational criteria the more healthy and adapted the individual. On the other hand low accuracy implies the possibility of delusions. Self-awareness is thus seen as a crucial index of mental health and adaptation.

It is common to see talented, attractive and conscientious people at work underachieve or perform because of their low self-esteem. Through their primary or secondary socialization as well as the simple lack of opportunity or accurate feedback certain individuals hold views about themselves which inhibit their behaviour. They seem never to explore or exploit their potential. Some seek help and can benefit from attempts to appropriately bolster their self-esteem.

One definition of narcissism is where a person's assessment of some aspect of their self (ability, appearance, motives, personality) is different from, (i.e. greater than) the subjective but aggregated rating of others or by valid, objective test results. In this sense, narcissists are simply not self-aware. Further, this lack of self-awareness can have considerable effect on a narcissist relationship with others who clearly do not share their perceptions.

There is a great deal of research on self-awareness, starting from early work in multi-source now called 360 degree feedback (Furnham & Stringfield, 1994; Furnham, 2007). A more recent and perhaps more relevant literature has examined people's beliefs about self assessment of their own intelligence (Furnham, 2001). Various studies on the correlations between estimated own intelligence and 'actual' intelligence (as measured by validated psychometric tests) indicate correlations of between $r = .3$ to $r = .5$. Further there is evidence of specific and interesting groups of outliers characterized by two very different groups. The *humility* group often over-represented by females give low self-estimates compared to their test score. They underestimate their cognitive ability. The *hubris* group, over-represented by men, on the other hand, show the opposite pattern. They overestimate their score as manifest by the ability test. In this sense they may be thought of as cognitively narcissistic.

Thus one way to possibly detect narcissism in the workplace is to seek out managers who show large discrepancies in their 360 degree, multisource feedback with self-ratings being consistently and significantly higher then ratings of peers, superiors or subordinates. In other words those who show a self-enhancement bias (Paunonen, Lonqvist, Verkasalo, Levkas & Nisswen, 2006).

This hypothesis was tested by Judge, Le Pine and Rich (2006) who looked at narcissist self-ratings and other ratings of leadership, workplace deviance, contextual and task performance. They found evidence to support all their ideas namely that narcissism is positively related to enhanced self-ratings, but negatively related to other-ratings. They also predicted, and found, that the narcissism score of an individual is more strongly and negatively related to other ratings of contextual rather than task performance. Thus narcissists see themselves as particularly altruistic, courteous and virtuous as well as being seriously job outcome focused. Further they found Narcissism had incremental validity over the 'Big Five' in predicting ratings, particularly in other ratings. The more open and conscientious the person the higher their self ratings, but narcissism contributed unique variance.

All self-other rating differences are of course interesting and predictive but where they originate and how they are maintained is most interesting. Judge et al. (2006) argue that self-aggrandizing typically denigrates others and deprive them of *their* self-esteem. Further self aggrandizers may make bad decisions and have distorted views of the world because of their brittle ego which also punishes those giving negative or threatening feedback.

This chapter will focus on those with too much self-esteem: those effectively with narcissistic personality disorder. Whilst many people (adolescents in particular) may appear too full of arrogance and hubris at times, one only 'qualifies' for the diagnosis for the disorder if various criteria are met. These will be outlined later in the chapter.

There is a potential paradox with this personality disorder which indeed distinguishes it from other personality disorders like the antisocial personality disorder. That is, narcissists may at first be beneficial at work or in social relationships. People are attracted to those with self-confidence; no doubt because they believe they have something to be self-confident about. Narcissists assume their experience has taught them that they have been successful in the past (at many things) and will no doubt therefore be successful in the future. Indeed self-confidence in others maybe particularly attractive to those who struggle with it in themselves. Highly self-confident people do well at job interviews and can inspire considerable trust in others. The problem arises when self-confidence 'spills over' into arrogance and narcissism. Further there may be a very thin line between healthy self-confidence and unhealthy narcissism. However it should always be born in mind that for high self-confidence to be healthy it should be based on actual criteria. It may not reach the 'criteria' of full blown narcissism, but may still be maladaptive. At the core of the problem is a keen and accurate self-awareness of one's abilities, attributes and preferences.

The narcissism myth and legend

Several versions of the myth of Narcissism survive. They are warnings about hubris and pride. Most rely on the Ovid version of the myth: Narcissus was the son of Cephissus, the river god, and the nymph Leiriope. By the time he was 16 everyone recognized his ravishing beauty, but he scorned all lovers – of both sexes – because of his pride. The nymph Echo was hopelessly in love with Narcissus but she was hindered by her inability to initiate a conversation. Eventually Narcissus rejected her. She wasted away in her grief to a mere voice. A young man, similarly spurned, prayed that he would love himself unremittingly. The goddess Nemesis answered this prayer by arranging that Narcissus would stop to drink at a spring on the heights of Mount Helicon. As he looked in the water he saw his own reflection and instantly fell in love with the image. He could not embrace his reflection in the pool. Unable to tear himself away he remained until he died of starvation. But no body remained – in its place was a flower.

An earlier version has been more recently discovered; a similar but subtly different version. In this story Ameinias, a young man, loved Narcissus but was scorned by him. To tell off Ameinias Narcissus gave him a sword as a present. Ameinias used the sword to kill himself on Narcissus' doorstep and prayed to Nemesis that Narcissus would one day know the pain of unrequited love. This curse was fulfilled when Narcissus became entranced by his reflection in the pool and tried to seduce the beautiful boy, not realizing it was himself he was looking at. He only realized it was his reflection after trying to kiss it. Completing the symmetry of the tale, Narcissus takes his sword and kills himself from sorrow. His corpse then turns into a flower. Thus Narcissus died because he could only love his image at the expense of himself.

Poets, painters and moralists have been intrigued with the myth seeking to interpret its meaning. The Freudians found the myth beguiling and sought intrapsychic and psychopathological interpretations. There have also been various illuminating psychological accounts of famous plays like Miller's (1949) *Death of a Salesman* as being a prototypic story of narcissism (Tracy & Robins, 2007).

At the heart of the myth is the caution of misperception and self-love: the idea that inaccurate self-perceptions can lead to tragic and self-defeating consequences. There appears to be a moral, social and clinical debate about Narcissism. The moral issues concern the evils of hubris; the social issue of the benefits (or otherwise) of modesty; the clinical debate is about the consequences of misperceptions. This chapter focuses on how narcissism 'plays out' in the workplace.

Psychologists have also attempted to measure narcissism and to distinguish it from simply being a form of 'high self esteem'. The most established measure is probably the Narcissistic Personality Inventory which appears to have four identifiable factors (Emmons, 1984; Raskin & Hall, 1981).

- Exploitativeness and Entitlement: the complete belief that one is very good at and entitled to manipulate people for one's own end.
- Leadership and Authority: the belief that one is extremely talented at leadership and all authority roles.
- Superiority and Arrogance: the belief that one is a 'born leader' and quite simply better than others.
- Self-Absorption and Self-Admiration: a belief that one is special and worth adoration and respect.

Narcissistic culture

Is it possible that narcissism is sanctioned, or indeed encouraged, by an organizational or national culture? Can whole cultures endorse or encourage narcissism to make it appear normal, even desirable? Observers have noted a change in the puritan, service-above-self, value system to the 'me-culture' that appears almost narcissistic.

Many commentators on contemporary culture have attempted to discern trends and patterns that trace the waxing and waning of movements, ethics, or cults. One influential analysis of American culture has been that of Lasch (1979), who argues that the dominant American culture of competitive individualism has changed into the pursuit of happiness and a narcissistic preoccupation with self. Central to Lasch's (1979) thesis is the decline of the Protestant Work Ethic (PWE) and what he calls 'changing modes of making it'. In doing so he very succinctly describes the PWE as it underpinned American culture.

'Until recently the Protestant work ethic stood as one of the most important underpinnings of American culture. According to the myth of capitalist enterprise, thrift and industry held the key to material success and spiritual fulfilment. America's reputation as a land of opportunity rested on its claim that the destruction of hereditary obstacles to advancement had created conditions in which social mobility depended on individual initiative alone. The self-made man, archetypical embodiment of the American dream, owed his advancement to habits of industry, sobriety, moderation, self-discipline and avoidance of debt. He lived for the future, shunning self-indulgence in favour of patient, painstaking accumulation; and as long as the collective prospect looked on the whole so bright, he found in the deferral of gratification not only his principal satisfaction but an abundant source of profits. In an expanding economy, the value to investments could be expected to multiply with time as the spokesman for self-help, for all their celebration of work as its own reward, seldom neglected to point out'. (pp. 52–53).

For Lasch (1979) the *Puritan* gave way to the *Yankee*, who secularized the work ethic and stressed self-improvement (instead of socially useful work) that consisted of the cultivation of reason, wisdom and insight as well as money. Wealth was valued because it allowed for a programme of moral self-improvement and was one of the necessary preconditions of moral and intellectual advancement.

The spirit of *self-improvement*, according to Lasch (1979) was debased into *self-culture* – the care and training of the mind and body through reading great books and healthy living. Self-help books taught self-confidence, initiative, and other qualities of success. The management of interpersonal relations came to be seen as the essence of self-advancement. People were told that they had to sell themselves in order to succeed. The new prophets of positive thinking discarded the moral overtones of Protestantism. The pursuit of economic success was now accepted along with the need to exploit and intimidate others and to ostentatiously show the winning image of success.

The new mind-set meant that people preferred admiration, envy and the excitement of celebration, to being respected and esteemed. People were less interested in how people acquired success – defined by riches, fame, and power – than in that they had 'made it'. Success had to be ratified and verified by publicity. The quest for a good public image lead to a confusion of successful completion of the task with rhetoric that is aimed to impress or persuade others. Thus impressions overshadow achievements and the images and symbols of success were more important than the actual achievements.

It became important, according to Lash's historical analysis, to get on with others; to organize one's life in accordance with the requirements of large organizations; to sell one's own personality; to receive affection and reassurance. The dominant perception was that success was dependent on the psychological manipulation of one's own and other's positive and negative emotions and social behaviours.

The pursuit of self-interest, formerly identified with the accumulation of wealth, had become a search for pleasure and psychic survival. Social conditions approximate the vision of republican society conceived by the Marquis de Sade at the very outset of the republican epoch (Lasch, 1979).

For Lasch (1979) the cult or ethic of narcissism has a number of quite distinct features:

- *The waning of the sense of historical time.* The idea that things are coming to an end means that people have a very limited time perspective, neither confidently forward nor romantically backward. The narcissist lives only in, and for, the present.
- *The therapeutic sensibility.* Narcissists seek therapy for personal well-being, health and psychic security. The rise in the human potential movement and the decline in the self-help tradition have made people dependent on experts and organizations to validate self-esteem and develop competence. Therapists are used excessively to help develop composure, meaning and health.
- *From politics to self-examination.* Political theories, issues, and conflicts have been trivialized. The debate has moved from the veridical nature of political propositions to the personal and autobiographical factors that lead proponents to make such suppositions.
- *Confession and anticonfession.* Writers and others attempt simple self-disclosure, rather than critical reflection, to gain insight into the psycho-historical forces that lead to personal development. But these confessions are paradoxical and do not lead to greater, but rather lesser, insights into the inner life. People disclose, not to provide an objective account of reality, but to seduce others to give attention, acclaim, or sympathy and, by doing so, foster the perpetual, faltering sense of self.

- *The void within.* Without psychological peace, meaning, or commitment people experience an inner emptiness which they try to avoid by living vicariously through the lives of others, or seeking spiritual masters.
- *The progressive critique of privatism.* Self-absorption with dreams of fame, avoidance of failure, and quests for spiritual panacea means that people define social problems as personal ones. The cult suggests a limited investment in love and friendship, avoidance of dependence and living for the moment.

Lasch (1979) argues that psychological insights into the narcissistic personality of our time miss the social dimension of this behaviour pattern such as pseudo self-insight, calculating seductiveness and nervous, self-deprecating humour.

The narcissism, or the ethic of self-preservation, appears to many people to be the best way of coping with the tensions, vicissitudes, and anxieties of modern life. The traits associated with this ethic – charm, pseudo-awareness, promiscuous pan-sexuality, hypochondria, protective shallowness, avoidance of dependence, inability to mourn, dread of old age and death – are, according to Lasch who does not provide evidence, learnt in the family, reinforced in the society but are corruptible and changeable. Ultimately the paradox of narcissism is that it is the faith of those without faith; the cult of personal relations for those who are disenchanted with personal relations.

This cynical view of the change of the work ethic into the narcissism ethic is an analysis from a socio-historical view of current America. To what extent it is generally or specifically true is uncertain or, indeed, if it applies to other countries with similar political and economic systems. Perhaps because profundity is always associated with pessimism, Lasch's (1979) analysis has failed to reveal much good about this ethic. It could be argued that Lasch's analysis understates the problem as it appeared in the decade of the last century (and millennium) where me-values and narcissism thrived in the west. In other words Lasch's analysis is fundamentally correct but out-of-date.

It may also be that norms and values in the workplace condone and promote narcissism. It is therefore possible that many organizational cultures take on board narcissistic values which are trumpeted. Organizations may therefore have selected, sought and praised those with self-esteem bordering on narcissistic personality disorder. In this sense narcissism can be seen as the property of culture as well as individuals.

The social psychology of modesty and self-enhancement

Judo-Christian teachings advocate the virtue of modesty, of being moderate, unassuming or even reticent in estimating and describing one's abilities. Modesty is freedom from such things as boastfulness, vanity or self-assertion. Modesty is valued for being unpretentious and non-deceptive. It can be seen in people's attitudes, dress and social conduct. However at the core of the definition is the idea of perceptual accuracy. Modest people do not underestimate their achievements, abilities or merits but neither do they overestimate them. They are quietly, unpretentiously aware of what they can or cannot do.

The problem of an accurate portrayal of one's abilities is particularly problematic with those outside the normal range. For those, say within one standard deviation of the mean, there should be no particular problems with accurate disclosure about abilities. The problem lies for those over two standard deviation above or below the norm. The question becomes: is it healthy or indeed acceptable to present oneself as very inadequate and well below average with few abilities or desirable characteristics? Equally can it be acceptable to 'show off' when one believes one's self to be in the top 2% of the population. Can humility and hubris be acceptable because they are accurate reflections of ability?

If being honest about one's abilities is desirable then self-enhancement should be thought of as undesirable. Yet there remains an interesting paradox. Self-enhancement is both pervasive and often thought of as socially and clinically desirable. Sedikides, Gregg and Hart (2007b) list various related psychological constructs which all attest to the same issue:

- *the better than average effect:* people think they are all better than average at most things.
- *self-serving bias:* people are happy to claim credit for their success of any type but reject taking responsibility for their failures.
- *Anemic neglect:* people actively and selectively forget feedback that shows their shortcomings.
- *over-optimism:* people see their, but not their peers, future as unrealistically bright and positive.
- *moral hypocrisy:* consistent and conspicuous attempts to appear highly moral without actually being so.

They argue that self-enhancement is pervasive and potent and pose the question: Can it be curtailed or at least modestly induced? They suggest that this is possible because self-enhancement is partly malleable and controllable. This can be achieved by modifying moods by close relationship and by introspection (Sedikides et al., 2007a). Social psychologists in contrast to personality theorists always stress situational, rather than stable trait, predictors of behaviour. Thus they strive to demonstrate that such things as narcissism are simply reactions to particular social forces. Equally they argue that situations can be contrived or manipulated to either increase or decrease incidents of narcissistic behaviour. Sedikides et al. (2007a) conclude thus: modesty may bestow minimal mental health gains in the short-run, but intrapersonal and interpersonal benefits in the long-run. Alternatively, modesty and self-enhancement may be associated with different types of mental health gains. For example, self-enhancement may be linked most strongly with resilience and modesty with life satisfaction. Likewise, modesty and self-enhancement may be associated with different types of social benefits. For example, self-enhancement may promote advancement to glamorous and high-status social positions (e.g., actor, politician), whereas modesty may promote advancement to useful and moderate-status positions (e.g., civil servant, nurse). Future research would do well to focus on untangling this complex interplay of factors. Both modesty and self-enhancement may be critical to attaining different aspects of optimal human functioning.

Harmful effects of high self esteem

For nearly 30 years it has been an accepted fact in psychology that low self-esteem was the root cause of many social problems particularly among young people. Thus everything from teenage pregnancy to suicide and delinquency to school failure was due to low self-esteem. Hence the development and proliferation of the self-esteem movement which attempted through a variety of crypto-clinical and educational interventions set out to raise the esteem of various targeted groups. The assumption was because self-esteem has such powerful causal power it was the most efficient way to improve the lot of various groups that experienced a variety of social problems.

Millions were poured into this industry which was sanctioned by many different groups. Studies in many of the social, medical and clinical sciences seemed to suggest the link was clearly established. Well over 1000 popular books in the self-help tradition endorsed the message. A few, often moral, voices were raised about the issue of the disconnect between praise and achievement and the possible implications of the pervasive discourse of constant affirmation. Indeed Twenge (2006) argued that individuals born between 1970–1990 were the 'Generation Me' cohort with elevated feelings of egotism, entitlement and self-centredness. It is an argument for the consistent secular increase in narcissism. These findings have been empirically challenged (Trzesniewski, Donnellan & Robbins, 2008a).

However over the last few years social psychologists have challenged many of these assumptions and found them wanting. One challenge came from Emler (2005) who did a careful, critical evaluation of the literature. His conclusion was essentially that there is little evidence for the *causal power* of low self-esteem causing social problems or for that matter, of the efficacy of programmes that attempted to raise it. The research drew a number of specific conclusions:

- Relatively low self-esteem is *not* a risk factor for delinquency, violence toward others (including child and partner abuse), drug use, alcohol abuse, educational under-attainment or racism.
- Relatively low self-esteem is a risk factor for suicide, suicide attempts, depression, teenage pregnancy and victimization by bullies. However in each case it is only one among several related risk factors.
- Although the causal mechanisms remain unclear, relatively low childhood self-esteem also appears to be associated with adolescent eating disorders and, among males only, with low earnings and employment problems in young adulthood.
- Young people with very high self-esteem are more likely than others to hold racist attitudes, reject social pressures from adults and peers and engage in physically risky pursuits, such as drink-driving or driving too fast.
- The most important influences on young people's levels of self-esteem are their parents – partly as a result of genetic inheritance and partly through the degree of love, concern, acceptance and interest they show their children.
- Personal successes and failures also influence self-esteem. But despite the attention given to the effects on high or low achievement in school, the degree of influence of self-esteem is relatively small.
- Children's self-esteem can be raised by parenting programmes and other planned interventions, but knowledge of why particular interventions are effective is limited.

Emler in fact argued that low self-esteem could have beneficial motivational characteristics while high self-esteem could lead to arrogant, conceited, self-satisfied behaviour rather than provide specific benefits.

In addition to reviews, experimental studies began to show the negative effects of high self-esteem. That is, they appeared to show that people with high self-esteem pose a greater threat to themselves and others than those with low self-esteem.

Baumeister's (Baumeister, Campbell, Krueger & Volis, 2003; Bustiman & Baumeister, 1998) imaginative studies have probably provided the best empirical evidence that there is no causal relationship between low self-esteem and life success though this conclusion has been disputed. Some recent longitudinal studies suggest otherwise (Trzesniewski et al., 2008c). In fact if anything the opposite is true. Still others have shown that self-esteem can have both positive and negative consequences. If people derive their self-esteem from external factors like physical appearance they maybe prone to eating disorders (Crocker & Wolfe, 2001).

The essence of the argument is that we need to be accurate in self-evaluation of our competencies with both a spirit of acceptance and realism. To be self-accepting we need to take responsibility for our actions. Hence there is a difference between authentic or genuine self-esteem and external or false self-esteem. The former is internal and under our control, the latter external and under the control of others which may be insecure and fickle.

Similarly it is important to try to distinguish between unhealthy narcissism with all its ego-inflatedness and self-absorbed vanity, and genuine, correct and appropriate high self-esteem. Those with narcissism are dependent on others to affirm them. In this sense they are highly vulnerable and addicted to their positive affirmations. Thus the genuine narcissist keeps seeking personal validation but this is never enough to convince them of their own adequacy. Because they do not have genuine high self-esteem they strive to fake it.

As will be noted there have been various attempts to make differentiations in the narcissism literature which spans psychiatry and psychology. It has been conceived as a type, a trait and even a psychological process. There have been studies on overt (more exhibitionistic and aggressive) vs covert (anxious, defensive, vulnerable) narcissists (Otway & Vignoles, 2006) and many attempts to differentiate healthy, productive narcissism from unhealthy, destructive narcissism. Indeed there appears to be some differences when there is a 'clinical' vs 'non-clinical' account of narcissism (Campbell, 2001). This problem may be resolved by the trait concept whereby it is possible to locate everybody on the self-esteem–narcissistic trait. Clinicians may see only extreme cases that are recommended for therapy while personality and organizational psychologists see less 'extreme cases' who appear 'relatively' well adjusted. However, there is a considerable and fascinating psychiatry on the Narcissistic Personality Disorder.

Narcissistic personality disorder

Oldham and Morris (2000) have noted that narcissists never seem defensive or embarrassed about their ambition and remain supremely confident. However, because they are so aware of, comfortable with and grateful for their strengths they are easily and profoundly wounded by any suggestion that they have serious weaknesses or shortcomings.

At work they tend to be high-energy, outgoing and competitive. They seem instinctively drawn to office politics and how to find and use power. They will charm those in authority or those from whom they believe they have something to gain.

This disorder apparently occurs in only 1% of the population. It is also called a disorder of arrogance or self-confidence. The website www.personalityresearch.org/pd.html suggests that the word SPECIAL is a helpful way to diagnose the narcissistic personality disorder:

S: Special (believes he or she is special and unique).
P: Preoccupied with fantasies (of unlimited success, power, brilliance, beauty, or ideal love).
E: Entitlement.
C: Conceited (grandiose sense of self-importance).
I: Interpersonal exploitation.
A: Arrogant (haughty).
L: Lacks empathy.

The DSM-IV manual has nine diagnostic features. Narcissists are boastful, pretentious and self-aggrandising, over-estimating their own abilities and accomplishments while simultaneously deflating others. They compare themselves favourably to famous, privileged people believing their own discovery as one of them is long overdue. They are surprisingly secure in their beliefs that they are gifted and unique and have special needs beyond the comprehension of ordinary people. Paradoxically, their self-esteem is fragile, needing to be bolstered up by constant attention and admiration from others. They expect their demands to be met by special favourable treatment. In doing so they often exploit others because they form relationships specifically designed to enhance their self-esteem. They lack empathy being totally self-absorbed. They are also envious of others and begrudge them their success. They are well-known for their arrogance and their disdainful, patronizing attitude. As managers their difficult-to-fulfil needs can lead them to have problematic social relationships and make poor decisions.

The manual points out that they are exceptionally sensitive to setbacks, feeling both degraded and humiliated. They mask this with defiant counter-attacks and rage. They may withdraw from situations that lead to failure or try to mask their grandiosity with an appearance of humility. Those diagnosed with Narcissistic personality disorder tend to be male.

There are also many issues with differential diagnosis i.e., distinguishing what is unique about the disorder. The most useful feature in discriminating Narcissistic Personality Disorder from Histrionic, Antisocial and Borderline Personality Disorders is that the latter is characterized by interactive styles (being respectively coquettish, callous and needy). Narcissistic Personality Disorder, on the other hand, can be distinguished by *grandiosity* characteristics. The relative stability of self-image as well as the relative lack of self-destructiveness, impulsivity, and abandonment concerns also help distinguish Narcissistic Personality Disorder from Borderline Personality Disorder. Excessive pride in achievements, a relative lack of emotional display and disdain for other's sensitivities help distinguish Narcissistic Personality Disorder from Histrionic Personality Disorder. Although individuals with Borderline, Histrionic and Narcissistic Personality Disorders may require much attention, those with Narcissistic Personality Disorder specifically need that attention to be admiring. Individuals with Antisocial and Narcissistic Personality Disorder will share a tendency to be tough-minded, glib, superficial, exploitative and unempathetic. However, Narcissistic Personality Disorder does not necessarily include characteristics of impulsivity, aggression, and deceit. In addition, individuals with Anti Social Personality Disorder may not be as needy of the admiration and envy of others, as persons with Narcissistic Personality Disorder (p. 661).

At work narcissistic individuals have a grandiose sense of self-importance (for example, they exaggerate their achievements and talents and expect to be recognized as superior without commensurate achievements). Inevitably they believe they rightly deserve all sorts of markers of their specialness: bigger offices and salary; inflated job titles, a bigger budget dedicated to their needs; more support staff; and greater liberty to do as they wish.

Most individuals with Narcissistic Personality Disorder are preoccupied with fantasies of unlimited success, power, brilliance and money. They believe that they are 'special' and unique and can therefore only be properly understood by, or should associate with, other special or high-status people (or institutions). They may try to 'buy' themselves into exclusive circles. They often require excessive admiration and respect from people at work for everything they do. This is their most abiding characteristic. They usually have a sense of entitlement – that is, unreasonable expectations of especially favourable treatment or automatic compliance with their manifest needs. Worse, they take advantage of others to achieve their own ends, which makes them inefficient and disliked as managers. They are unsupportive but demand support for themselves. All are unwilling to recognize or identify with the feelings and needs of others in and out of work. They have desperately low Emotional Intelligence though are apparently unaware of this. Indeed they may assume they have superior emotional intelligence. Curiously they are often envious of others and believe that others are envious of them. In this sense they are deluded. They show arrogant, haughty behaviours or attitudes all the time and everywhere at work (and home) (Hogan, 2007).

Narcissists are super-self-confident: they express considerable self-certainty. They are 'self-people' – self-asserting, self-possessed, self-aggrandizing, self-preoccupied, self-loving – and ultimately self-destructive. They seem to really believe in themselves: they are sure that they have been born lucky. At work they are out-going, high energy, competitive and very 'political' depending of course on their normal (big five) trait profile. Thus the extraverted conscientious narcissist may be rather different from those more neurotic and open. They can make reasonable short-term leaders as long as they are not criticized or made to share glory. They seem to have an insatiable need to be admired, loved and needed. This can appear amusing or pathetic to outside observers. They are often a model of the ambitious, driven, self-disciplined, successful leader or manager. The world, they believe and demand, is their stage.

But narcissism is a *disorder* of self-esteem: it is essentially a cover-up. People with NARCISSISTIC PERSONALITY DISORDER self destruct because their self-aggrandisement blinds their personal and business judgement and managerial behaviour. At work they exploit others to get ahead yet they demand special treatment. Worse their reaction to any sort of criticism is extreme, including shame, rage, and tantrums. They aim to destroy that criticism, however well-intentioned and useful. They are poor empathisers and thus have low emotional intelligence. They can be consumed with envy and disdain of others, and are prone to depression as well as manipulative, demanding and self-centred behaviours; even therapists don't like them.

Many researchers have tried to 'unpick' the essence of the paradoxical, fragile self-esteem of the narcissist. The narcissist's self-esteem is at once unstable and defensive. It seems their self-esteem is utterly contingent on others' feedback. Further, it is dissociated between explicit (overt) and implicit (covert) views (Tracy & Robins, 2007).

Hogan and Hogan (2001) call these types 'arrogant' 'the lord of the high chair' a two-year-old, sitting in its high chair demanding food and attention, and squealing in fury when his or her needs are not met. Narcissists expect to be liked, admired, respected, attended to, praised, complimented and indulged. Their most important and obvious characteristic is a sense of entitlement, excessive self-esteem and quite often an expectation of success that often leads to real success. They expect to be successful at everything they undertake, they believe that people are so interested in them that books will be written about them, and when their needs and expectations are frustrated, they explode with 'narcissistic rage'.

What is most distinctive about the narcissists is their self-assurance which often gives them charisma. Hogan and Hogan (1997) note that they are the first to speak in a group and they hold forth with great confidence, even when they are wrong. They so completely expect to succeed, and take more credit for success than is warranted or fair, that they refuse to acknowledge failure, errors or mistakes. When things go right it is because of their efforts; when things go wrong, it is someone else's fault. This is a classic attribution error and leads to problems with truth telling because they always rationalize and reinterpret their failures and mistakes usually by blaming them on others.

Narcissists can be energetic, charismatic, leader-like and willing to take the initiative to get projects moving. They can be relatively successful in management, sales and entrepreneurship, but usually only for short periods. However, they are arrogant, vain, overbearing, demanding, self-deceived and pompous yet they are so colourful and engaging that they often attract followers. Their self-confidence is attractive. Naively people believe they have to have something to be so confident about.

Narcissists handle stress and heavy workloads badly but seemingly with ease; they are also quite persistent under pressure and they refuse to acknowledge failure. As a result of their inability to acknowledge failure or even mistakes and the way they resist coaching and ignore negative feedback, they are unable to learn from experience. In a more accessible, almost self-help book written as a collaboration between psychiatrist and a journalist Oldham and Morris (2000) chose the more neutral term self-confidence.

Oldham and Morris (1991, p. 80) note nine characteristics of these types they call 'Self-Confident':

1. Self-regard: Self-Confident individuals believe in themselves and in their abilities. They have no doubt that they are unique and special and that there is a reason for their being on this planet.
2. The red carpet: They expect others to treat them well at all times.
3. Self-propulsion: Self-Confident people are open about their ambitions and achievements. They energetically and effectively sell themselves, their goals, their projects and their ideas.
4. Politics: They are able to take advantage of the strengths and abilities of other people in order to achieve their goals, and they are shrewd in their dealings with others.
5. Competition: They are able competitors, they love getting to the top and they enjoy staying there.
6. Dreams: Self-Confident individuals are able to visualise themselves as the hero, the star, the best in their role, or the most accomplished in their field.
7. Self-Awareness: These individuals have a keen awareness of their thoughts and feelings and their overall inner state of being.
8. Poise: People with the Self-Confident personality style accept compliments, praise, and admiration gracefully and with self-possession.
9. Sensitivity to criticism: The Self-Confident style confers an emotional vulnerability to the negative feelings and assessments of others which are deeply felt, although they may be handled with this style's customary grace.

More importantly they note four tips for working with narcissists:

1. Be absolutely loyal. Don't criticize or compete with them. Don't expect to share the limelight or to take credit. Be content to aspire to the number-two position.
2. Don't expect your self-confident boss to provide direction. Likely he or she will expect you to know what to do, so be sure you are clear about the objectives before you undertake any tasks. Don't hesitate to ask.
3. You may be an important member of the boss's team, but don't expect your self-confident boss to be attentive to you as an individual. Don't take it personally.
4. Self-confident bosses expect your interest in them, however. They are susceptible to flattery, so if you're working on a raise or a promotion or

are trying to sell your point of view, a bit of buttering up may smooth the way (Oldham & Morris, 2000, p. 85).

This is advice for those working with narcissists. It clearly taken an optimistic perspective never considering that a narcissistic boss could be both an abusive and deeply incompetent.

Miller (2008), in another popular book about personality disorders describes narcissistic bosses and employers as 'preeners' and gives advice to those who may be either. For bosses, he suggests documenting your credentials, being realistic about what you can be proud of and to treat all employers with respect. He suggests to the potentially narcissistic employee to take an honest self-inventory (to gain insight); to emulate the successful and present ideas appropriately.

There remains considerable debate about the treatment of, and prognosis for, each of the personality disorders. Until relatively recently it was argued that they were particularly difficult to treat and that prognosis was therefore poor.

The business world often calls for (and rewards) arrogant, self-confident and self-important people. These individuals seek out power and abuse it. They thrive in sales roles and those where they have to do media work. But, as anyone who works with and for them knows, they can destabilize and destroy working groups by their deeply inconsiderate behaviour (see also Chapter 9). Management and self-help books stress how to cope with clinical or subclinical narcissism. Few take a very negative view or report case studies where narcissists personally destroy whole organizations.

The two sides of narcissism

Paunonen et al. (2006) have identified two strands in the narcissistic leadership literature. The first is that although many narcissists are described as charismatic their egotistical Machiavellianism derails them in the end. But in contrast to this *dark* view there is a *bright* view. This suggests that narcissists have low depression and anxiety, and high subjective wellbeing. Further their obviously strong needs for achievement, control, power and status serve them well to obtain leadership positions, but their inward focus usually leads in the long-term to self-destruction.

Clearly the exploitative, entitlement-obsessed narcissist who manipulates those around him/her for his/her ends is unlikely to be successful in the long run. However, Paunonen et al. (2006) are happy to distinguish between the benign and pathological narcissist. Further they are happy to think of narcissism as a trait (not a type) which consists of a constellation of distinct inter correlated traits on a continuum.

In their study of narcissism and leadership Paunonen et al. (2006) measured egotism which they took to represent the bright side of narcissism and Machiavellianism as the dark side. They also measured two aspects of impression management: the conscious version and the less conscious delusion version. Their study was a peer-rating study of military cadets who rated five factors: leadership, popularity, benevolence, aggression and honesty. Their results supported their theory notably that the highest rated leaders had the bright side narcissism profile, high in egoism and self-esteem but low in manipulativeness and impression management. Indeed they conclude by arguing that they are 'hard pressed' to think of any situation where dark side narcissism would not threaten the leader-followership relationship to lead it to soon collapse.

Many writers on leadership narcissists contrast the upside-bright or downside-dark traits of narcissistic leaders. This helps resolve the apparent conflict of ideas that narcissistic managers can (perhaps only in the short term) be good managers. Rosenthal (2007) notes a number of the problematic intercorrelated dark-side traits and the leaders with whom they are most associated:

- Feelings of inferiority – the need to be surrounded by flattering syco-phants (Mao Tse-Tung, Krushchev).
- An insatiable need for recognition and superiority – unrelenting quest to gain power to show potency (Saddam Hussein).
- Hypersensitivity and Anger – intense, vengeful, hostile rage when crossed (Kennedy, Castro).
- Lack of empathy – idiosyncratic, self-centred, hubristical behaviour (Bush).
- Amorality – cruel acts justified to others (Saddam Hussein).
- Irrationality and inflexibility – over-confident, fantasy-thinking and decision-making.
- Paranoia – seeing enemies everywhere.

It may well be that certain organizations at certain points in their history attract narcissists who do well. Those that consistently court attention through PR, those in crisis or those that crave 'strong leadership' may seek out those dangerously narcissistic.

On the other hand Rosenthal (2007) sees narcissism as being crucial in a crisis. Narcissists can have great vision and take dramatic action. They not only appear to be, but are larger than life figures described as 'productive narcissists'. These are the PR hungry CEOs driven to gain power, glory and the admiration of others. They can be visionaries and risk takers seeing the big picture while down playing rules, laws and conventions which handicap them. When they have some insight and self-awareness into their preferences and abilities and which organization forces are in place to restrain them they can act as great forces for positive change and advancement.

The narcissistic manager

It should not be assumed that narcissism is necessarily a handicap in business. Indeed the opposite may be true. If a manager is articulate, educated and intelligent as well as attractive his/her narcissism may be seen to be acceptable.

Bright side Narcissists can be good delegators, good team builders and good deliverers. They can be good mentors and genuinely help others. However subordinates soon learn things go wrong if they do not follow certain rules:

- Everyone must acknowledge who is boss and accept rank and hierarchical structure.
- They must be absolutely loyal and never complain, criticize or compete. They should never take credit for something but acknowledge success is primarily due to the narcissists talent, direction or insights.
- They should not expect the narcissist to be very interested in their personality, issues or ambitions but they must be very interested in the narcissist's issues.
- They have to be attentive, giving and always flattering. They need to be sensitive to the whims, needs and desires of the narcissistic manager without expecting reciprocity.
- Narcissistic managers can be mean, angry or petulant when crossed or slighted and quickly express anger, so subordinates have to be careful when working with them.
- They must ask for help, directions and clarity about objectives when they need it.
- They need to watch out that a narcissistic manager's self preoccupation, need for approbation and grandiosity does not impede their business judgement and decision-making.

- They need to find ways of giving critical feedback in such a way that the manager both understands it but does not get offended.

The dark side narcissistic manager tends to have shallow, functional uncommitted relationships. Because they are both needy and egocentric they tend not to make close supportive friendship networks in the workplace. They can often feel empty and neglected as a result.

Narcissistic leaders may have short-term advantages but long-term disadvantages because the narcissist's consistent and persistent efforts are aimed at enhancing their self-image which leads to group clashes. Campbell, Bush, Brunell and Shelton (2005) note that narcissistic leaders often maintain positive feelings around the self with high positive and low negative affect, as well as high self-esteem. However they bring 'costs' because of their need to distort reality into a form conducive to self-enhancement. They also have the need to seek out positive social feedback while attacking or disparaging negative feedback. Further, they experience long-term performance deficits because their illusion of success interferes with them obtaining real success. Narcissists also trade interdependence and closeness for individual status and esteem. Finally, they adopt strategies that, while showing gains at the individual level, show losses at the group level. That is, they may gain themselves short-term advantage by looking skilful or tough or insightful while these decisions actually have long-term disastrous consequences. Thus radical re-engineering may improve short term profitability but lead to long-term chaos and collapse.

Kets de Vries (2006) argues that a certain degree of narcissism is an essential prerequisite for leadership. He offers a psychoanalytic interpretation for the aetiology of narcissism which is inevitably bad parenting. It is seen as problems associated with two related issues – how they perceive themselves as well as salient others; more specifically how they come to cope with reality that one is neither omnipotent or omniscient nor that parents are powerful and perfect. The child's lifelong quest for admiration and approbation is often a mask for self-doubt or hatred or feeling one is never properly loved for one's own sake alone.

Inevitably with psychoanalysis both the neglected and the pampered child (too much and too little of a good thing) can lead to the development of narcissism. The indulgent, all praising, pampering parents lead to exactly the opposite of what they want or expect. Excessive praise leads to feelings of superiority and destined greatness which, whilst being beneficial for really talented individuals, only serves to undermine those who cannot understand why the world does not react like their doting parents. The narcissist does a lot of transference – the unconscious redirection of early feelings (to the parent) to other people. The psychological imprints of early care-givers are thus manifest throughout adult life.

Whilst a 'touch' of narcissism can be good for leaders it can be problematic in the long run particularly if the problem is severe. Because of their selfishness and egocentrism, narcissistic managers are more committed to their own welfare than that of their team or indeed the whole organization. Kets de Vries (2006) also distinguishes between constructive and reactive narcissism.

The healthy constructive narcissist (that is the person with high self-esteem) does take advice, accepts feedback and responsibility for both success and failure. Their energy, zeal and larger-than-life enthusiasm and theatrics can be precisely what it takes to transform organizations. On the other hand the reactive narcissist has a defective sense of identity and self-esteem. They can be troubled by feelings of anger and inadequacy as well as lingering but intrusive thoughts of both deprivation and emptiness. Their whole aim is to compensate for this sense of inadequacy and insecurity. Hence the constant, pervasive and insistent need for praise. The childhood memories of being ignored, belittled or maltreated can, it seems, only be overcome by success in adulthood.

To some extent one can see the narcissistic urges as highly motivational. If narcissistic managers have a very high need for praise and recognition this may well drive them to work hard to achieve worthy goals. In this sense they can learn to earn recognition. But that need can turn to envy, spite, greed and vindictiveness.

When things are going well the narcissistic manager can be good news. They can be upbeat and their sense of wellbeing spreads to others. However even slight and temporary set backs can cause disproportionate negative reactions. This might lead to outbursts of rage followed by feelings of dejection, depression and lethargy. However the narcissist is a master at finding others to blame. They rationalize, they project and they explain away. Some get vindictive attempting to 'get even' with those who they perceive to have slighted them. The major problem is that they do not learn from their mistakes.

Kets de Vries (2006) uses political and business examples because both business and power provide a wonderful stage to see the vicissitudes of narcissism acted out. The short-term expediency, the opportunism, the self-righteousness and self-centredness of the narcissist lead to bad business decisions, poor problem-solving and low morale.

However one really important feature in the narcissism at work scenario is the complicity of followers. It is said that we get the leaders we deserve. That is, that if our expectations are unrealistic we tend to get very disappointed. Often particularly in situations of difficulty or crisis people at work have unrealistic expectation of their leaders. They want them to be superhuman and to ensure success and continuity.

Followers, according to Kets de Vries (2006) encourage two types of behaviours in narcissistic leaders which are very bad for both leader and follower. First, there is the process of *mirroring*, where followers use leaders to reflect what they want to see. Narcissists get the admiration they crave and there occurs mutual admiration. The problem is that managers can take their eye off the ball being more concerned with policies and procedures which make them look good rather than serving the best interests of all stakeholders. Second, there is idealization in which followers project all their hopes and fantasies onto the leader. Thus leaders find themselves in a hall of mirrors which further decreases their grip on reality.

Where narcissistic leaders become aggressive and vindictive Kets de Vries (2006) claims some followers in order to stave off their anxiety do identify with the aggressor. Followers impersonate the aggressor becoming tough henchman of the narcissistic manager. Inevitably this only exacerbates the problem and begins to explain the vicious cycle of narcissistic management failure.

The central question for the work psychologist is how they can set up processes, apart from careful selection, that help prevent narcissistic induced management failure occurrences.

Can one reduce the possibility of appointing, promoting or encouraging narcissistic managers? Clearly this has a great deal to do with selection policies. However Kets de Vries (2006) offers three others strategies which may help to 'downsize the narcissist'.

- Ensure distributive decision-making to guarantee checks and balances. Thus do not combine roles like CEO and chairman.
- Educate the CEO and board to look out for signs of narcissism and to have strategies to put in place when they do spot the signs. This involves clear systems of accountability and involving shareholders in crucial decisions.
- Offering coaching and counselling to those clearly identified as reactive narcissists although few seem willing to accept help because

they, by definition, rarely take personal responsibility for their failure.

Perhaps certain organizations attract narcissists more than others. It therefore is highly recommended that these organizations become aware of the psychological processes associated with narcissism and be willing and able to do something about them.

There are comparatively few empirical studies on narcissistic leaders though a great deal has been written about them. Chattèrjee and Hambrick (2007) however, in a unique and important study, attempted to correct this omission. They argued the paucity of research into this topic occurred essentially for three reasons: first, because narcissism was considered a lay, non-scientific concept with no way of measuring it; second, the problems associated with reliable and accurate data collection on the topic, and third, because the reluctance of organizational researchers to recognize the practical or theoretical importance of executive narcissism.

They note the psychological and psychiatric literature identifies both cognitive and motivational components of narcissism. Cognitively it concerns confidence in abilities and other agentic facets. Motivationally it is about affirmation and admiration. This, they argue, leads narcissistic leaders to engage in 'bold, quantum, highly visible initiatives rather than incremental elaborations on the status quo' (p. 357). They may be too prone to risky, attention-seeking decisions, that lead to big wins (and losses) and hence highly fluctuating personal, board and organizational performance. They also note, as have others, the distinction between healthy (reactive, optimal) and unhealthy (destructive, excessive) narcissism. Narcissism, like self-esteem, (and practically every other human characteristic) can be plotted on a dimension.

Their analysis of CEO narcissism led to the testing of five hypotheses. They were interested in seeing if the greater the narcissistic tendencies of the CEO – the (a) the greater the dynamism of the company's strategy, (b) the greater the number and size of the acquisitions, made by the company, (c) the more extreme the company's performance and (d) the greater the CEO's fluctuation in the company's performance.

In their study of 111 CEOs they chose four unobtrusive measures (1) the prominence of the CEO's photograph in the company's annual report (2) their prominence in positive press releases (3) the use of first person singular pronouns in interviews and (4) cash compensation relative to the second-highest-paid firm executive (the number two). They found these different measures were all highly correlated. The measures of organizational performance included strategic dynamism, changes in resource allocation indicators like advertising, R & D, administration and financial debt; acquisitions, performance extremes and fluctuations.

Naturally they had to attempt to control various factors like CEO age and tenure as well as stock owned by the CEO. They attempted to control issues around the firm like resource availability, asset/liabilities ratio and the prior years' performance. They controlled for the sector the firm was in as well as endogeneity which is the idea that narcissistic CEOs are drawn to certain situations or conditions that allow or indeed encourage them to demonstrate their tendencies. Finally they selected for sample bias.

The results provided clear support for a number of the hypotheses. There was a dramatic linear increase in both size of acquisitions and Return on Assets (ROA) extremes as a function of CEO narcissism. However Chatterjee and Hambrick (2007) did address the most obvious questions from both an employee and a investor perspectives: *Does a company overall perform better or worse with a narcissistic CEO?* Their results showed *no* significant differences. However this could be dependent on the state of the economy.

They pondered over the question of whether the 'combustible combination' of CEO narcissism and recent company performance would trigger many aggressive acts of hubris. They also questioned whether narcissism changes in the sense that it is modified by experience, and whether other traits may interact with it to influence CEO behaviour. Finally they felt the effect of CEO narcissism on the board's dynamics worth investigating.

This was an interesting and important study in a much neglected area of research.

Unanswered questions

Rosenthal (2007) has suggested that the topic of the narcissistic leader is well worth exploring and identified seven areas to examine:

1. The line between narcissism and healthy, optimal self-confidence and self-esteem. This differentiates between the so-called 'bright-side', 'charismatic', 'constructive' or 'productive' narcissists and those 'dark-side', 'destructive' narcissists. This is about drawing the line between confidence and arrogance, healthy and unhealthy, normal or

abnormal. The question is whether those demarcations can be made accurately and whether they are situationally appropriate.

2. Whether there are optimal conditions for narcissistic leadership. That is, are there times in organizational life when narcissistic leadership is both desirable and effective? Thus in times of crisis or rapid growth this style of leadership may be highly efficient while in steady state times, when building sustained relationships and trust is important, it is much less so. Indeed it is very debatable as to whether the narcissist is really capable of building sustained, trusting relationships.

3. Whether narcissistic leadership is effective only in the gaining, but not the maintaining of power. That is, are they prone to a rapid rise-and fall-scenario because their self-defeating behaviour which soon overwhelms their supposed charisma? In this sense they are, from a stakeholder perspective, only very superficially attractive and desirable.

4. What is it about followers that they choose narcissistic leaders? Is the aggressive, confident charismatic type exactly what people want and expect from their leaders? Is it because of their superhuman confidence that they appear so appealing? It has been suggested that a mirroring takes place in that narcissistic followers choose narcissistic leaders. Thus organizations, indeed nations, may choose leaders to 'sooth their own narcissistic insecurities' and even create other narcissistic enemies. However it is likely that followers soon rebel against those they have elected and blame them for living up to their quite obviously unrealistic expectations. Indeed for both parties – narcissistic leaders and followers – self-loathing is projected onto the other with highly negative consequences.

5. Whether a criteria of productive or destructive narcissistic leaders is the extent to which they sacrifice all personal relationships (home and work) for 'success'. Many successful leaders have impaired personal relationships (multiple divorces; fractured broken families), but a central question is whether this is necessarily a sign of narcissism.

6. What can or should be done to prevent productive narcissists' destructive behaviour leading to serious 'organisational damage'. Thus one may have a stable, non narcissistic deputy or 'side-kick' or one might encourage coaching for the narcissistic leader. Other possibilities include having various procedures which act as checks and balances to the narcissist's power hungry and sometimes rash decision making.

7. Most importantly a good deal of this research is justified by finding historical examples to justify ideas. The best test is that of predic-

tive validity; namely being able to accurately make predictions about individuals that can be verified by research data.

Conclusions

It has only been comparatively recently that work psychologists have begun to take an interest in personality disorders. Of all the personality disorders it is no doubt the antisocial or psychopath that is of most interest. Recent work by Babiak and Hare (2006) has explored the successful psychopath. More recently attention has focused on the other disorders, particularly the narcissistic disorder (Hogan, 2007).

Recruiters, as a result, are now as interested in 'selecting out' criteria as 'selecting in' criteria and the use of instruments that help identify those who will prove problematic in management roles (Hogan & Hogan, 2001). Thus they need to actively look for traits, dispositions and attitudes they do not want and select them out.

Many researchers have pointed out the paradox of narcissism at work being that many traits and processes associated with narcissism can seem positive and beneficial while others are the precise opposite. This paradox has been 'solved' by trying to distinguish between the adaptive and maladaptive narcissist though it is not clear whether this is merely a linguistic tautology. Could one call a constructive narcissist a narcissist? In this sense it is also an oxymoron.

Conceiving narcissism as a self-esteem trait disorder does imply, as many personality psychologists have argued, that there is a clear continuum between healthy and unhealthy. The issue remains however where to draw the line.

It is also important to bear in mind the perspective of social and work psychologists who stress how situational and cultural variables moderate narcissism. That is, organizations may unwittingly reinforce narcissism thus leading to their own destruction. They may indeed encourage or discourage certain processes (like performance appraisals) which make the problems of narcissists much worse.

They may agree to disband committees and allow narcissistic managers to make decisions on their own. They may allow and encourage expensive privileges for people once they achieve certain levels. They may inhibit upward or negative feedback reaching senior managers.

Certainly narcissists create friends and enemies in organizations and can be a major contributing factor to the dysfunctional workplace (Langan-Fox, Cooper & Klimoski, 2007). They certainly provide a serious management challenge to ensure their pathology works for, as against, the fortunes of the organization.

References

Babiak, P. & Hare, R. (2006). *Snakes in Suits*. New York: HarperCollins.

Baumeister, R., Campbell, J., Krueger, J. & Volis, K. (2003). Does high self-esteem cause better performance, interpersonal success, happiness and healthier lifestyles? *Psychological Science in the Public Interest, 4*, 1–44.

Bustiman, B. & Baumeister, R. (1998). Threatened egoism, narcissism, self-esteem and direct and displaced aggressions. *Journal of Personality and Social Psychology, 75*, 219–229.

Chatterjee, A. & Hambrick, D. (2007). It's all about me: Narcissistic Chief Executive Officers and their effects on company strategy and performance. *Administrative Science Quarterly, 53*, 351–386.

Crocker, J. & Wolfe, C. (2001). Contingencies of self worth. *Psychologist Review, 108*, 593–623.

Campbell, W. (2001). Is narcissism really so bad? *Psychological Inquiry, 12*, 214–216.

Campbell, W., Bush. C., Brunell, A. & Shelton, J. (2005). Understanding the social costs of narcissism. *Personality and Social Psychology Bulletin, 31*, 1358–1368.

Emler, N. (2005). The costs and cause of low self-esteem. Unpublished paper. London School of Economics.

Emmons, R. (1984). Factor analysis and construct validity of the Narcissistic Personality Inventory. *Journal of Personality Assessment, 48*, 291–300.

Furnham, A. (2001). Self estimates of intelligence. *Personality and Individual Differences, 31*, 1381–1405.

Furnham, A. & Stringfield, P. (1994). Congruence of self and subordinate ratings of managerial practices as a correlate of supervisor evaluation. *Journal of Occupational and Organisational Psychology, 67*, 57–67.

Furnham, A. (2007). Multi source feedback and personality. Unpublished.

Hogan, R. (2007). *The Fate of Organisations*. New York: Erlbaum.

Hogan, R. & Hogan, J. (1997). Manual for the Hogan Development Survey. Tulsa, OK: Hogan Assessment Systems.

Hogan, R. & Hogan, J. (2001). Assessing leadership: A view from the dark side. *International Journal of Selection and Assessment, 9*, 40–51.

Kets de Vries, M. (2006). *The Leader on the Couch*. New York: Jossey-Bass.

Judge, T., Le Pine, J. & Rich, B. (2006). Loving yourself abundantly. *Journal of Applied Psychology, 91*, 762–776.

Langan-Fox, J., Cooper, C. & Klimoski, R. (eds) (2007). *Research Companion to the Dysfunctional Workplace*. Cheltenham: Edward Elgar.

Lasch, C. (1979). *The Culture of Narcissism*. New York: Norton.

Miller, A. (1949). *Death of a Salesman*. New York: Penguin.

Miller, L. (2008). *From Difficult to Disturbed*. New York: Amacom.

Oldham, J. & Morris, L. (2005). *The New Personality Self-Portrait*. New York: Bantam Books.

Otway, L. & Vignoles, V. (2006). Narcissism and childhood recollections. *Personality and Social Psychology Bulletin, 32*, 104–116.

Paunonen, S., Lonqvist, J-E., Verkasalo, M., Levkas, S. & Nisswen, V. (2006). Narcissism and emergent leadership in military cadets. *Leadership Quarterly, 17,* 475–488.

Raskin, R. & Hall, C. (1981). The narcissistic personality inventory. *Journal of Personality Assessment, 45,* 159–167.

Rosenthal, S. (2007). *Narcissism and Leadership. A Review and Research Agenda.* Working Paper: Centre for Public Leadership, Harvard University.

Sedikides, C., Rudich, E., Gregg, A., Kumashiro, M. & Rusbull, C. (2004). Are normal narcissists psychologically healthy? *Journal of Personality and Social Psychology, 87,* 400–416.

Sedikides, C., Horton, R. & Gregg, P. (2007a). The why's the limit: Curtailing self-enhancement with explanatory introspection. *Journal of Personality, 75,* 783–824.

Sedikides, C., Gregg, A. & Hart, C. (2007b). The importance of being modest. In C. Sedikides and S. Spencer (eds) *Frontiers in Social Psychology – The Self.* New York: Psychology Press.

Tracy, J. & Robins, R. (2007). 'Death of a (Narcissistic) Salesman'. An integrative model of fragile self esteem. *Psychological Enquiry.*

Trzesniewski, K., Donnellan, M. & Robins, R. (2008a). Is 'Generation me' really more narcissistic than previous generations? *Journal of Research and Personality.* In Press.

Trzesniewski, K., Donnellan, M. & Robins, R. (2008b). Do today's young people really think they are extraordinary? *Psychological Science.* In Press.

Trzesniewski, K., Donnellan, M., Moffit, R., Robins, R., Poulton, R. & Caspi, A. (2008c). *Low Self-Esteem During Adolescence Predicts Poor Health, Criminal Behaviour, and Limited Prospects During Adulthood.* Paper under review.

Twenge, J. (2006). *Generation Me.* New York: Free Press.

11

The Dark Side: Relationships with Psychopaths at Work

Giles St. J. Burch and Iain McCormick

What started out to be a promising career as customer services manager at a large manufacturing company turned into a nightmare for Stephen Jackson. After six months in the job, Stephen had serious regrets because his boss, Nick, was a psychopathic bully. He would get angry, and yell and scream, and at other times he would give Stephen the silent treatment and not talk to him for days. Stephen worked nine or ten hours a day but Nick was never satisfied. Stephen had never had any poor feedback from his international customers, yet Nick often hinted 'darkly' that he knew of bad comments and would use these against Stephen if he had to. Steven felt utterly enraged by the allegations but felt powerless, as he had no idea how to tackle this issue. He found himself feeling 'depressed' about his situation, and would often get drunk with friends on weeknights, a pattern he found disturbing. There was no point in talking to Nick's boss, Helen, as she seemed enamoured of Nick. What was Stephen to do?

The above vignette highlights the negative impact that working with a psychopath can have. Relationships with psychopaths in the workplace, be they an individual's superior, peer or even subordinate, can be very concerning and destructive, and can have a major impact on people in terms of psychological wellbeing, physical health, and work-related performance, as well as in other domains of their life. The impact of having psychopaths in the organization, though, goes beyond the individual victims, and can have serious consequences for the team and wider business. The literature describing personality psychopathology in the workplace (more commonly referred to as the 'dark side' of personality) has been attracting particular attention over the past few years, both with the public and from psychologists. Indeed, within the academic literature, Burch and Anderson (2008, in press) have recently suggested that research into the dark side of personality should have a central role within research investigating personality at work issues. The authors went on to highlight the importance of personality psychopathology in the workplace by incorporating it into their generic causal model of work-related behaviour and performance, alongside 'normal' personality. Although Burch and Anderson recognized that personality psychopathology may represent the extreme end of normal personality, they separated these dimensions out in order to highlight the need for research into the dark side of workplace personalities, in a field of research dominated by what has been referred to the 'bright side' of personality (e.g., Hogan, Curphy & Hogan, 1994). This developing literature into the dark side is concerned with a range of dysfunctional personalities, for example, antisocial, narcissistic, schizotypal, borderline, histrionic, and so forth (see for example: Burch, 2006; Goldman, 2006; Judge, LePine & Rich, 2006; Khoo & Burch, 2008; Hogan & Hogan, 2001; Moscoso & Salgado, 2004). However, in this chapter we are specifically concerned with relationships with psychopaths or those with psychopathic personalities. We therefore firstly define the concept of psychopathy and briefly consider the possible causes of this disorder, before discussing the impact that relationships with such people can have on individuals and the wider organization, and finally considering the best possible ways in which organizations can mitigate the damage and destruction left by psychopaths.

Psychopathy defined

One question that is asked of us on a regular basis is, 'What actually is a psychopath?' This is an important question as the term 'psychopath' tends to mean more to psychologists and psychiatrists than it does to the layperson – although, as Claridge and Davis (2003) have pointed out, 'the label "psychopath" itself has suffered greatly in the hands of psychiatrists and psychologists, who over the years have defined and re-defined and subcategorized it in various ways' (p. 75)! While the DSM-IV-TR (American Psychiatric Association, 2000) provides the diagnostic criteria for antisocial personality disorder (APD), which includes such criterion as deceptiveness, impulsiveness, aggressiveness, nonconformity, recklessness, and a lack of remorse, there are no specific diagnostic criteria for psychopathy *per se*. In the literature, the terms APD and psychopathy are sometimes used interchangeably; however, more typically psychopathy is regarded as comprising a broader set of personality and clinical criteria than that for APD (e.g., Babiak & Hare, 2006; Hare, Hart & Harpur, 1991; Harpur, Hart & Hare, 2002).

For example, Babiak and Hare (2006) have pointed out that the difference between psychopathy and APD is that psychopathy includes traits such as lack of empathy, shallow emotion and grandiosity, which are not part of the criteria for diagnosis for APD. Additionally, research has also suggested that there are two types of psychopaths, first, *primary psychopaths*, characterized by manipulation, callousness, lying, and low levels of anxiety and empathy, and second, *secondary psychopaths*, whose behaviour is more impulsive and less characterized by the traits associated with primary psychopathy (Cleckley, 1976; Newman, MacCoon, Vaughn & Sadeh, 2005; Karpman, 1948).

The concept of psychopathy, as we use it, can be traced back Cleckley (1941) who provided a thorough clinical description of this disorder and, although Cleckley's definition was included in the DSM-II, subsequent editions have deviated away from that definition with the introduction of the diagnostic criteria for APD (see Hare, 1996; Harpur et al., 2002; Salekin, 2002). Subsequently, the work of Robert Hare, who estimates that one percent of the population are psychopaths, has been particularly influential, especially with the development of the Psychopathy Checklist (PCL; e.g., Hare, 1991), in providing as alternative set of criteria for assessing and diagnosing psychopathy (Harpur et al., 2002) (see Table 11.1).

In the previous chapter, Adrian Furnham described the impact of working with narcissistic personalities at work, from which we can see

Table 11.1   The revised psychopathy checklist (PCL-R; Hare, 1991)

Factor 1	**Personal and Emotional Traits**
	Glibness/superficial charm
	Grandiose sense of self-worth
	Pathological lying
	Conning/manipulative
	Lack of remorse or guilt
	Lack of empathy
	Shallow affect
Factor 2	**Lifestyle**
	Need for stimulation/proneness to boredom
	Parasitic lifestyle
	Early behavioural problems
	Lack of realistic, long-term goals
	Impulsiveness
	Irresponsibility
	Juvenile delinquency
	Revocation of conditional realise

that there are a number of similarities between these two types of 'disorder'. Indeed, the literature often refers to the 'dark triad of personality' (e.g., Jakobwitz & Egan, 2006; Paulhus & Williams, 2002), that is, narcissism, psychopathy and Machiavellianism, where Machiavellianism refers to a manipulative/political personality originally described by Niccolò Machiavelli in his sixteenth century classic work *Il Principe* (The Prince). Recent research highlights that these three constructs are distinct but overlapping, with the strongest observed relationship being between narcissism and psychopathy with a reported correlation coefficient of .50 (Paulhus & Williams, 2002). Despite the similarities, the distinction between psychopaths and narcissists has been usefully described by Maccoby (2007; pp. xxi–xxii) when he stated that:

> Both psychopaths and narcissists can be extremely seductive when they need something from people. Both can be glib, charming, manipulative, deceitful, and ruthless. Both use people, squeeze them like oranges, and throw them away once they've drunk the juice. The difference then is that psychopaths, unlike some productive narcissists, always operate at the lowest level of moral reasoning with no concern for the common good, much less remorse or guilt for self-serving actions that harm other people. Psychopaths can be brilliant, but they build no lasting relationships. Narcissists sometimes do.

The literature in relation to psychopaths at work has developed more recently than that regarding narcissists and the workplace, in particular that relating to narcissistic leaders (see for example: Kets de Vries, 1985; Lubit, 2002; Rosenthal & Pittinsky, 2006; Sankowsky, 1995). However, the recent publication of a number of popular books on workplace psychopaths (e.g., Babiak & Hare, 2006; Clarke, 2005) has raised the profile of this topic amongst academics, consultants, managers and the general public, and there is now a growing acceptance of the existence of psychopaths in the workplace and greater understanding of how they operate.

At this point it is important to note that there are two approaches to understanding personality psychopathology. First, that of a disease-based approach, in which an actual 'diagnosis' is made – consistent with the DSM-IV-TR, and second a dimensional approach, which regards personality psychopathology to be at the extreme end of a continuum of 'normal' personality (e.g., Claridge, 1997, in press; Hogan & Hogan, 1997, 2001; Hogan, Hogan & Barrett, in press). Indeed, in relation to psychopathy more specifically, Zuckerman (2007) suggested that psychopathy could represent the extreme end of the personality factor of 'Impulsive Unsocialized Sensation Seeking' or the personality factor of 'Psychoticism'. However, Zuckerman went on to point out that while most psychopaths are sensation seekers, not all sensation seekers are psychopaths. Meanwhile, in relation to the 'Big Five' factors of personality, Harpur et al. (2002) and Miller and Lynam (2003) suggested that high Extraversion, and low Neuroticism, Agreeableness, Openness and Conscientiousness scores are indicative of psychopathy. Whichever approach is taken, it can be seen from the above descriptions of psychopathy that the term should not be restricted to the axe-wielding murderer (as may be the common conception held by the lay-person) and that psychopaths can exist anywhere and everywhere. As Millon and Davis (2000, p. 108) have pointed out:

> In everyday life, they flourish in the form of the smooth-talking businessman and the less-than-forthcoming used-car salesman. Their damage to society is not as vivid as that of the murdering psychopath, but is more common and just as great, and constitutes an important reminder that any scientific theory of the antisocial personality must span normality and pathology.

Causes of psychopathic personality

We will not provide a complete and comprehensive review of the epidemiology of psychopathy; however, it is important for those working alongside psychopaths to have some understanding of the possible causation of this disorder. One question asked of personality psychologists on a regular basis is whether personality is determined by nature or nurture – this is the best starting point for our discussion. Current thinking generally assumes a combination of both genetic and social/cultural factors. There is certainly evidence that there is causal relationship between DNA and personality/personality disorder (see Carey & Goldman, 1997; Ebstein, Benjamin & Belmaker, 2003), and neurobiological mechanisms and personality disorder (e.g., Depue & Lenzenweger, 2005). One neuro-biological account with particular relevance here is the late Jeffery Gray's Reinforcement Sensitivity Theory (RST; Gray, 1982; Gray & McNaughton, 2000; see also Corr, 2004, 2008; McNaughton & Corr, 2004), a theory of basic emotion and motivation, the individual outputs of which make up what we know as 'personality'. In its simplest form, RST postulates that different brain structures underpin individual sensitivity to both aversive and appetitive stimuli, resulting in two orthogonal personality dimensions, impulsivity and anxiety (Gray, 1970). More recently, Gray and McNaughton (2000) suggested that the biological substrates underlying these dimensions are the Behavioural Approach System, the Behavioural Inhibition System and the Fight-Flight-Freeze System (FFFS). The Behavioural Approach System responds to appetitive stimuli, initiating and controlling all reward-seeking behaviour, the FFFS responds to all aversive stimuli, with the FFFS and Behavioural Approach System feeding information into the Behavioural Inhibition System, which is responsible for resolving conflicts between approach–avoidance, avoidance–avoidance, and approach–approach (Gray & McNaughton, 2000). There is currently a great deal of research being carried out into RST, and interest is developing in the application of RST to the workplace (see Burch & Anderson, 2008; Furnham & Jackson, 2008; Hutchison, Burch & Boxall, in press; Jackson, 2001). While much of the research into RST has focused on normal personality, there is also a body of literature describing the relationship between personality psychopathology and RST, including psychopathy (e.g., Levenson, Kiehl & Fitzpatrick, 1995; Ross et al., 2007). For example, a recent study found evidence that primary (but not secondary) psychopathy is positively related to the Behavioural Inhibition System, while both primary and secondary psychopathy have been shown to be related to the Behavioural Approach System in a sample of noninstitutionalized young adults (Ross et al., 2007; although see also: Poythress et al., 2008). Meanwhile, Newman et al. (2005) found evidence that primary psychopathy is associated with a weak Behavioural Inhibition System and a normal Behavioural Approach System while secondary psychopathy is associated with a strong Behavioural Approach System. These findings therefore highlight the link between neurobiological mechanisms and psychopathy, alongside of which there is also evidence that RST's Behavioural Inhibition System and Behavioural Approach System are heritable and genetically stable (e.g., Takahashi, Yamagata, Kijima, Shigemasu, Ono & Ando, 2007).

Having considered the possible role of biology in the causation of psychopathy, it is now important to consider possible psychological factors. Psychoanalytic theory suggests that psychopathic or antisocial personality is derived from a domination of the id and the pleasure principle, along with a lack of development of the super-ego (i.e., conscience) (Friedlander, 1945; Millon & Davis, 2000). This is illustrated by Millon and Davis (2000) who point out that 'just as classical psychoanalytic theory holds that the id is completely centred on its own immediate needs, antisocials impulsively and egocentrically violate shared standards of social living' (p. 118). The cognitive interpretation of psychopathy suggests that antisocials hold beliefs that they are 'entitled to *break* rules; others are patsies, wimps; others are exploitative' (Pretzer & Beck, 2005, p. 67), with such beliefs subsequently mediating behaviour. Meanwhile, learning models have suggested that psychopaths have been inappropriately reinforced in their development, and desensitized to emotional stimuli (Eron, 1997; Salekin, 2002). Finally, Levenson (1992) proposed a more philosophical approach to understanding psychopathy in suggesting that 'psychopathic tendencies toward the trivialization of others and an extreme self-centeredness can be seen as the product of postmodernist philosophy in which the other is treated as inherently meaningless, and thus lacking in essential value (p. 68)'. At this juncture it is important to take note of Burch and Anderson's (2008) generic causal model of work-related behaviour and performance which highlights the interplay of biological, social, cultural, situational, contextual, and cognitive-affective meditating that determine our behaviours in the workplace – including those of psychopaths – highlighting the complexity of these relationships (see Figure 11.1).

Psychopaths at work

People with psychopathic personalities are everywhere, including in our workplaces (Hare, 1993). These people are functioning within 'normal' society (including organizations), and often with apparent success (Babiak & Hare, 2006; Hare, 1993). Thus, when we talk of psychopaths, we refer not only to those who have been imprisoned or hospitalized, but also those who are operating at a sub-clinical or sub-criminal level, before they are 'found out', as has been illustrated by other authors who have referred to the high-profile cases of *inauthentic* transformational leaders, Enron's Jeff Skilling and Worldcom's Bernie Ebbers (e.g., Sosik, 2006). It is important to note here, though, that the presence of psychopaths is not restricted to those in the most senior positions; after all, managers and leaders had to rise there from somewhere. Psychopaths have the potential to be everywhere in the organization. While clinicians have stated that psychopaths represent their worst fears, stereotyping all that is 'bad' in personality disorder (Walker & Hayward, 2007), the same sentiments should be expressed by organizational psychologists, consultants, and managers in relation to the psychopath in the workplace – psychopaths stereotype all that is bad in the workplace!

Perhaps the first place to start when considering this continuum of behaviours is with workplace bullying. While bullying is certainly a characteristic of psychopathic personality, not all bullies are necessarily

Figure 11.1 A generic causal model of work-related behaviour and performance

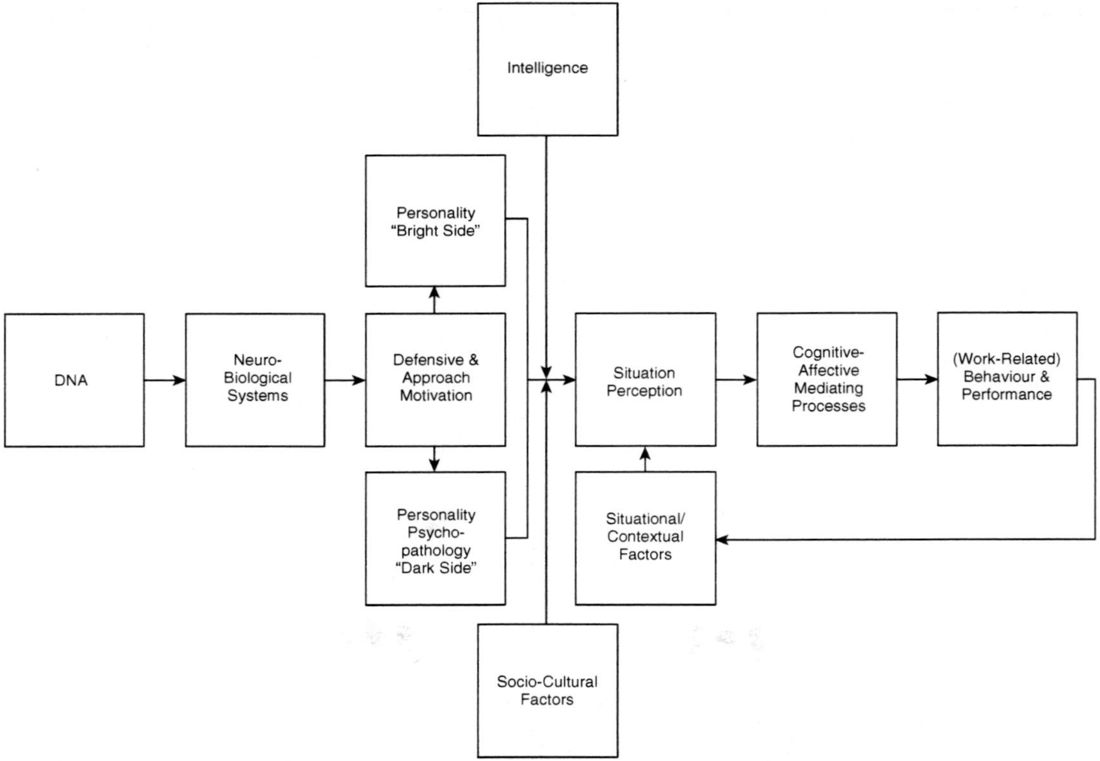

Source: From Burch & Anderson (2008, p. 293)

psychopaths (Namie, 2007); however, it is the bullying behaviours of the psychopath that are those most often observed in the workplace. Namie (2007) identified four different types of bullying behaviour in the workplace: (1) *The Screaming Mimi* – the stereotypical bully, who screams, yells, swears and threatens, scaring and humiliating people; (2) *The Constant Critic* – the nit-picker who behind closed doors targets those seen as incompetent. This behaviour leads to long-term damage and ultimately destroys their careers as it greatly lowers the self-esteem of the victims; (3) *The Two-Headed Snake* – the superficially charming character that destroys others with malicious rumour and uses divide and conquer tactics to paralyse work teams; and (4) *The Gatekeeper* – who controls others by withholding resources necessary to succeed or reach targets. He or she takes the credit for others' work, then isolates and torments the victims. These are all types of bully that we are likely to have been exposed to in our own organizations, a number of whom will most certainly be psychopaths. As Namie (2007) went on to point out, the workplace is often a breeding ground for bullies, and suggested three reasons for this. First, the workplace often fosters bullying by allowing aggressive competition between individuals and between teams. Management often indicates that success is best achieved by cut-throat aggression. Second, a toxic mix of personalities is created in some workplaces with highly ambitious individuals who will exploit each other to get their own way; helpful, cooperative types are thus forced out of the workplace. Third, employers provide positive reinforcement for aggression with these individuals gaining pay rises and promotion. These three factors are likely to also foster a psychopathic's behaviour in the workplace, including charm, charisma, manipulation, pathological lying, impulsive non-conformity, sensation-seeking, egocentrism, low empathy and lack of inhibition, remorse, guilt or loyalty (Babiak & Hare, 2006; Hare, 1993). While it would be expected that such individuals would be detected easily enough within the organization, the ever-changing nature of contemporary workplaces provides an environment without the controls necessary to pick on the presence of a psychopath, where they can, in actuality, thrive (Babiak, 1995). This would appear particularly so when we consider some of the characteristics displayed by corporate psychopaths, such as charisma, a smooth and fast-talking style, self-assurance, social confidence, coolness when under pressure, ruthlessness, and a lack of concern about a possibility of being caught when engaging in 'bad practice' (Babiak & Hare, 2006; Hare, 1993). These are traits that may be considered similar to those regarded as typical of good leadership (Hare, 1993; Sosik, 2006). As we stated earlier, such people exist in all of the organizations that we work in, albeit with a varying degree of psychopathic traits. Accepting that such people do exist in the workplace is the first step in being able to understand the nature of our relationships with such people and their subsequent impact on the workplace.

Impact on the workplace

The presence of psychopaths in the workplace, demonstrating the types of traits as described above, will clearly impact other employees, the team and the wider organization, and are likely to result in a range of serious problems. These have been illustrated by Giacalone and Greenberg (1997, pp. 7–8) who have usefully listed a number of antisocial behaviours that are displayed in organizations, and Boddy (2006, pp. 1468–1470) who lists a number of effects from the presence of psychopaths in managerial positions in organizations (see Table 11.2).

Table 11.2 Antisocial behaviours displayed in organizations and effects of psychopaths in management positions

Antisocial Behaviours Displayed in Organizations (Giacalone & Greenberg, 1997, pp. vii–viii)	Effects of Psychopaths in Management Positions (Boddy, 2006, pp. 1468–1470)
Arson	Corporate failure
Blackmail	Fraudulent activities
Bribery	Unnecessary employee redundancies
Discrimination	Exploited workforce
Espionage	No sense of corporate social responsibility
Extortion	Disheartened workforce
Fraud	Political decision making
Interpersonal violence	Workplace bullying
Kickbacks	Short-term decision-making
Lawsuits	Disregarded investor interests
Lying	Lost economies of expertise
Sabotage	Environmental damage
Sexual harassment	Decisions of questionable legality
Theft	Business partnerships with organizational psychopaths
Violations of confidentiality	
Whistle-blowing	

Namie (2007) asserts that epidemiologists and occupational health researchers have linked exposure to an abusive work environment with a range of negative health consequences. Thirty years of research has indicated that an increase in workload and a decrease in personal control over work tasks can damage the cardiovascular system. The risk of cardiovascular disease (e.g., hypertension, stroke or heart attack) is 30% more likely when workers believe their workplace is unjust (Namie, 2007). The psychopath will create and maintain great injustices. Unrelenting stress from a toxic workplace causes anxiety and clinical depression in 39% of respondents and post-traumatic stress disorder in 30% of female and 21% of male targets (Namie, 2007).

Table 11.3   The impact of the psychopath on business, employees, and customers/suppliers/joint venture partners

Impact on the business	Impact on individual employees	Impacts on customers, suppliers and joint venture partners
Deteriorating profit margins or profit growth, perhaps even insolvency.	Feelings of victimisation and fear.	Lost sales.
Decreased morale among employees.	Stress and anxiety.	Lost supply contracts.
Increased absenteeism.	Decreased work motivation.	Joint ventures destroyed.
Increased employee turnover.	Decreased career interest.	Reduced revenue and profits.
Decreased productivity.	Depression and withdrawal.	Besmirched company reputation.
Slow sales.	Increased sickness levels.	Brand value reduced or destroyed.
Increased customer complaints.	Loss of self confidence.	
Increased employee stress levels.	Suicidal ideation and even suicide.	
Decreased levels of employee engagement, trust & satisfaction.		

The damage caused by the presence of psychopaths in the workplace is potentially huge and impacts the business as a whole, individual staff members, and also the organization's customers, suppliers or joint venture partners (see Table 11.3).

What can be done?

Having identified the issues associated with psychopaths at work, we now consider how to deal with a psychopath, which will depend on whether the individual is an employee, peer, manager or even the CEO.

What can individuals do?

When faced with the impact of the deception inflicted by the psychopath many victims are stunned and disabled by the experience. Yet there are things that an individual can do to help themselves when they find themselves working with a psychopath.

1) Know what to look for

No one should consider labelling another individual a psychopath in a flippant or light-hearted manner. This is a very serious and profound claim that should only ever be made after considerable thought (Burch & McCormick, 2006; McCormick & Burch, 2005). Understanding the key signs and symptoms exhibited by the psychopath is critical. There is general agreement on the typical symptoms that are exhibited by the psychopath (Babiak, 1995; Babiak & Hare, 2006; Boddy, 2006; Furnham & Taylor, 2004; Hare, 1993; McCormick & Burch, 2005; Morse, 2004). To aid the memory for the 'symptoms', they have been grouped using the mnemonic **PSYCHOPATH** (see Box 11.1).

2) Understand the severity of psychopathic behaviour

One of the complexities of dealing with psychopathic behaviour is to understand that it is not a simple single entity. It covers a wide spectrum from the devious manipulative bullying behaviour of an employee who is a high achiever and very sought after by management – to the compulsively violent behaviour of a hardened criminal. Psychopaths are increasingly common in business – the so-called 'successful' psychopaths (Babiak & Hare, 2006). They are attracted to, and retained in, highly competitive workplaces, by unwitting companies who reinforce their behaviours by promoting them.

Box 11.1   Symptoms of the PSYCHOPATH

Practiced and skilful at lying, typically highly articulate, even charismatic.

Shallow emotionally, devious, often egocentric and sometimes grandiose, yet highly competent, even brilliant in a technical or narrow business sense.

Yearns for excitement, challenge, competition and is unable to tolerate routine or monotony.

Compulsive in the need to control and criticise others around them in order to maximise their own power and influence.

Holds deep prejudices and typically makes up his or her mind before the facts are known.

Obsequious, ingratiating and smooth; yet is highly results driven and often ruthlessly achievement orientated.

Plausible and convincing to supervisors, managers and the Board of Directors who often see the person as a "natural leader".

Adept at creating conflict between those who would otherwise collaborate.

Trust is absent in almost all of their relationships.

Harass and bully others without remorse or guilt.

3) Decide if the problem is you

The impact of the psychopath on an unsuspecting victim is often so deep and profound that it is natural for the victim to ask, 'Is it me or is it him (her)?' This important question deserves serious consideration. We all come across people at work from time to time, who are difficult, devious and troublesome but are they psychopathic? Perhaps the problem lies with the troubled victim and not the troublesome perpetrator? Almost every victim will wonder if he or she is being too sensitive or thin-skinned in the face of a forceful driving achiever. The path out of this dilemma is to ask the following three sets of questions:

- Am I usually emotionally stable? Am I able to withstand the typical stresses of work life without getting too upset or distressed? Or am I a sensitive individual who feels emotions, particularly breaches of trust, very deeply?
- Is this a rare occasion for me to come across someone who is this extreme in their vindictive control? Or am I the sort of the person who frequently feels extremely hurt and even devastated by the behaviour of someone at work?
- Is the destructive behaviour of the individual something that is widely acknowledged in the workplace or even in the wider community? Or is the behaviour something that would be described by others as assertive, robust and forceful?

If the individual sees the troublesome behaviours as set out in the previous section and if he/she is generally an emotionally stable individual, the behaviour is something you have rarely seen, and the destructiveness is observed by others in the same way as you, then it is almost certain the perpetrator has psychopathic tendencies. This therefore leads us to the question of what to do if faced with a psychopath.

A range of actions have been suggested in dealing with a psychopath in the workplace (e.g., Babiak & Hare, 2006; Boddy, 2006; Clarke, 2005; Lubit, 2002; McCormick & Burch, 2005). First, it is important for the victim to understand his or her own reaction, an important initial step of which is self-awareness. Appreciate that disbelief and deep-seated frustration are the normal and natural outcomes of dealing with a psychopath. The victim typically feels a sense of unreality at the blatant and wilful harm. Most victims experience intense and sometimes prolonged symptoms as a result of the glib deception. Insomnia, intense self-doubt and mild depression are very common experiences. In more severe cases chronic anxiety, depression, despair and even suicidal ideation can result from the destruction of jobs, careers, joint ventures or businesses. Given these effects, it is important that the victim should find an outside coaching psychologist to talk to, someone who has a full and qualified understanding of personality psychopathology in general and psychopathy specifically. Seeking help from someone who does not have a qualified understanding of psychopathy could actually end up being counterproductive as the coach may encourage the coachee to engage in inappropriate strategies and behaviours in dealing with the psychopath. The victim should explore his or her own weaknesses and areas of vulnerability because these can be ruthlessly exploited by the psychopath. The victim should get support and encouragement to deal with the situation. Self blame is a common reaction to victimization by a workplace psychopath. This is unfortunate and victims need to understand that it is very unlikely that they have personally brought on the attacks.

Power is often the only language the psychopath understands and responds to, so it can be useful to establish a power-base by quietly talking to the manager of the psychopath about the troublesome behaviour and to request the strictest confidentiality in the matter. If the victim is a peer or subordinate of a psychopath then he or she is unlikely to be able to have any major influence. The most senior managers in the organization must deal with serious manipulation and gross irresponsibility. However, while power may be the only language the psychopath understands, wielding this power against such an individual is typically filled with difficulty. Only managers with a great deal of resilience and ego strength should undertake such a task.

What not to do

Individuals dealing with psychopaths often try to use logic and rationality. These types of tactics are useless. Even worse, they can be turned against the unsuspecting individual who is trying to resolve a situation. It is important therefore not to try to reason with the psychopath. Likewise, the victim should not try to plead with the psychopath as it can very easily be interpreted as a sign of weakness and be exploited. Likewise, it is important for the victim not to try to negotiate, because the psychopath will typically be very unwilling to reason. Indeed, the psychopath will often insist that the victim only has two or three totally unacceptable alternatives to choose from. Finally, the victim should not fight head on, as a favourite tactic of the psychopath is to set individuals and groups against each other. The benefits are that the psychopath gets a large amount of gratification from provoking the hostility, and it ensures that other people's attention is diverted from the real cause of the conflict. Directly fighting a psychopath is likely to be futile.

Managing the psychopathic staff member

What can a manager do if he or she comes to realize that a staff member is psychopathic? Clearly many of the suggestions above for the individual will be relevant. However, in addition, the manager should understand that the psychopath is typically very astute at managing upward. This means the psychopath may use flattery or manipulation to ensure that the manager sees him or her in a good light. This may blind the manager to the devastation that the person is causing in the team. It is very important to listen to a range of views from team members about problems and challenges and not to be taken in by flattery. Managers are often more aware of their strengths than their vulnerabilities or weaknesses. A psychopath will use a weakness such as a dislike of conflict to manipulate a manager to get what he or she wants. Managers also need to be aware that psychopaths are often very technically competent. This does not mean that they are good team players or that their manipulation of others is justified. The astute manager should report his or her concerns about bullying or psychopathic behaviour at an early stage to senior management and to the human resources department. Such reports should be based on facts and observed behaviours, and never contain a diagnosis. Finally, the manager should seek professional advice and support from a coaching psychologist to deal with his or her own emotions and to deal with the perpetrator. Further suggestions can be found in the section below, 'What the organization can do'.

Dealing with the psychopathic peer or colleague

The psychopath can be found in any area of work from the simplest manual role to high-powered professions such as banking, law, consultancy or the media. It has been suggested that one out of every 100 people is a 'subclinical psychopath' (Hare, 1993) These individuals will almost certainly dominate and exploit others while gaining approval from management for their action orientation or 'just getting on with it'. Becoming aware of the existence of psychopathic peers is important and if done early enough it can stop others becoming their next victim. The psychopath will often be looking for a 'feeding ground' and so reporting their behaviour early is critical.

The practical steps that any individual can take when faced with a psychopathic peer or colleague include the following. Firstly, it is vital to understand the behaviour patterns of the psychopath (see Box 11.1). When the full nature of the behaviour is understood, the victim must be very careful not to arouse the anger or hostility of the psychopath. Certainly trying to confront an individual like this is unwise. The victim should find practical ways to build their own resilience and mental toughness. The victim can best do this with the assistance of a professional psychologist, executive coach or counsellor. Books such as *The Resilience Factor: 7 Keys to Finding Your Inner Strength and Overcoming Life's Hurdles* by Karen Reivich and Andrew Shatte can be very helpful to victims (Reivich and Shatte, 2002). Gaining emotional support from friends and family is also very helpful and can reduce the degree of hurt and frustration experienced by the victim. In some cases, it may be possible for the victim to get organizational support from their manager or from the human resource management department, however great care needs to be taken in case the psychopath finds out about this situation and seeks revenge. As a last resort, the victim should look to find an internal transfer or change jobs entirely.

Coping with the psychopathic boss

Clarke (2007) claims that workplace psychopaths have the same psychological make-up as killers; however, the major difference is that they have the ability to hide their psychopathic tendencies. As many corporate psychopaths are highly technically competent, they are often promoted to senior positions with power. Field (1996) suggests that while psychopaths may seem to be working efficiently for the organization they are typically only interested in power, control, domination and subjugation. The psychopathic boss will often target one individual while being friendly and charming to everyone else in the team. The victim will be isolated from supporting peers and then be publically humiliated until they leave the workplace or break down. Field claims that female psychopaths are more dangerous than males as they are more socially skilful in their manipulation. They will often recruit male colleagues to undertake the worst of the cruelty. Females are less likely to be violent and so are less likely to get engaged in criminal behaviour. Field suggests that if someone believes that his or her manager is a psychopath the only thing to do is resign before too much damage is done. The greatest problem in dealing with a psychopathic boss is that the individual has both positional and psychological power over the victim so doing anything effective to counter him or her is very unlikely to work.

Dealing with the psychopathic CEO when you are a board member

Individual directors sitting on governance boards are particularly vulnerable to manipulation by psychopathic CEOs. By necessity boards do not get involved in the day-to-day management of the business, and they typically see the financial, customer and business process reports that are presented by the CEO. The evidence of the destructive personality is thus well-hidden below the glossy reports and compelling presentations. If this is the case how can board members ever know the CEO is psychopathic? There are a number of tell tale signs:

1) **Staff turnover** – the board needs to carefully monitor the level of staff morale, loyalty and turnover. High and persistent turnover

may indicate that staff are being unfairly treated by a psychopathic CEO.

2) *Customer and supplier dissatisfaction* – the board must regularly review the level of customer and supplier complaint and dissatisfaction. An elevated and continual level of complaint may indicate that these stakeholders are being manipulated by a psychopathic CEO.

3) *Beware of 'collective responsibility'* – lists of responsibilities for directors can specify that once decisions are made by boards then all members must abide by them. The psychopathic CEO can cleverly use this responsibility to control the board. Directors may receive an impassioned plea from the CEO for a particular decision which, once made, cannot easily be overturned and must be abided by. Sometimes this plea can be for restricting board member communication with stakeholders. Yet the restricted communication may provide a cloak and enable free rein for the CEO to destroy the reputation of staff, suppliers, customers or joint venture partners. Such pleas for restricting communication are an important warning sign that should be noted by directors.

So, what can be done? First, while directors should not get involved in the day-to-day running of any organization, it is entirely appropriate for them to have input from sources other than the CEO. Presentations from other senior management team members, meetings with key suppliers, customers and alliance or joint venture partners are appropriate. At the very least directors should undertake site and customer visits. Second, all boards should take the opportunity to meet on a regular basis without the CEO being present – this is simply good practice and provides a time for members to speak openly on issues which impact the CEO directly. This can be extremely valuable for critically reviewing the performance of the CEO and, if needed, terminating employment in the case of a psychopath. Thirdly, directors must pursue the truth with persistence – when confronted by any hint of wrongdoing the psychopathic CEO will often skilfully twist the accusation, evade any challenge, change the subject and leave out important facts in order to put the directors off the trail. It is critical for the board to quietly and persistently check out the facts and be aware that in every explanation by the psychopathic CEO there will be a grain of truth inserted to try to reassure the directors of the validity of the argument. Fourthly, critically review media coverage – the typical psychopathic CEO has a deep and enduring hunger for attention and fame, even if generated by fear and loathing from others. Board members should examine the press coverage and ask the question, 'Is the aim of the articles to build the company brand or simply to provide glory for the CEO?' The CEO will, of course, argue that the two are intertwined, and there is some truth in this. However if the board has its suspicions about the morality of the CEO they need to gather evidence wherever they can – media coverage can be an important source. Finally, it is necessary that there be a strong chairperson on the Board. Removing a psychopathic CEO from the board will take courage, particularly on the part of the chairperson. If the current chairperson does not have the fortitude to undertake this task, then the board should look for someone who is willing to do it.

What the organization can do in relation to psychopathic employees

Namie (2007) suggests that to stop bullying and psychopathic behaviour the organization must critically examine its response to aggression and institute a zero tolerance policy that punishes any indication of bullying or unreasonable manipulation. The organization should not try to alter the behaviour of psychopathic individuals; it should simply remove them. McCormick and Burch (2005) have suggested a range of actions that can be taken by organizations.

Protect the victims

The damage done by a psychopath in any organization can adversely affect many people. It is not only the primary victims of manipulation who suffer but also the colleagues, families and friends of these unfortunate individuals. Sensitive acknowledgement by the organization of the issue and caring support may be necessary for a range of different victims.

Recruitment and selection

Organizations can find that, once recruited, psychopathic individuals can be very difficult to remove and are likely to become highly abusive and litigious when threatened with job termination. Therefore, it is important that great care and rigour are applied when recruiting and selecting staff into an organization. McCormick and Burch (2005) have suggested a number of useful tactics when recruiting individuals into the organization in order to minimize the risk of bringing psychopathic individuals into the business. For example, McCormick and Burch highlight that recruiters need to be aware of the concept of psychopathology in the first place. As Barr and O'Connor (2002) have pointed out, those responsible for organizational selection often do not have the necessary experience of psychopaths or any training in recognizing the signs of psychopathy. This is particularly important when potential employees present excellent references, which may not indicate a competent executive, but rather the desire by the current organization to transfer a troublesome employee somewhere else. Additionally, the initial charm, confidence and self-assurance of the psychopathic interviewee can be very convincing, and often seduces HR and line managers into the offer of a job. However, once successfully appointed to the job, it is not long before the true nature of the psychopath becomes apparent.

The routine use of valid personality questionnaires in selection processes has a clear benefit as psychopathy can be identified from the profile. For example, measures of the 'Big Five' factors of personality can provide an indication of psychopathic personality, that is, high Extraversion scores, coupled with low Neuroticism, Agreeableness, Openness and Conscientiousness scores (e.g., Harpur et al., 2002; Miller & Lynam, 2003). There are also a number of tools specifically available for measuring personality psychopathology/disorder; however, these may not have face validity when completed within the organizational context. However, one tool that shows particular promise as a measure of dysfunctional dispositions is the Hogan Development Survey (HDS; Hogan & Hogan, 1997), which was developed for explicit use within the organizational setting. Within this questionnaire, there is a measurement scale of Mischievous (i.e., antisocial personality), defined as 'enjoying risk-taking and testing the limits; needing excitement; manipulative, deceitful, cunning and exploitative' (Hogan & Hogan, 1997, p. 5), which could also be a particularly useful indicator of psychopathic personality. Additionally, the Hare Psychopathy Checklist: Screening Version (PCL: SV), an abbreviated version of the PCL-R (Hare, 1991), can be used for screening for psychopathy in non-forensic populations. While personality profiling can have a clear use in identifying those with psychopathic personalities, it is essential that only qualified practitioners, in accordance with the test publisher's guidelines and protocols, use such measures.

Not only should care be taken in relation to recruitment and selection, but also when it comes to internal promotion. The superficial charm and apparent decisiveness of the psychopath can easily be mistaken for leadership unless careful promotion processes are used. It is important that before making any promotion decisions managers cross check with individuals who know the candidate well and who have real working experience with them over a prolonged period. If there is evidence of unreasonable manipulation, the promotion should not take place. Using 360° appraisal feedback that is completely anonymous is clearly a useful way to evaluate important dimensions such as impulsivity, recklessness and lack of responsibility. Astute human resource managers should also look for major differences in 360° feedback ratings between the individual's managers, where strong positive ratings can be common, and the individual's subordinates where negative ratings are very likely.

Also be aware that large ranges in subordinates' ratings may mean that the psychopathic individual is being predatory or parasitic with one or two individuals. In addition to the use of 360° appraisal, the use internal and external customer satisfaction surveys, when completed over a number of time points, can indicate that the individual has a superficial charm initially in the relationship, but is unable to sustain customer relationships and satisfaction in the longer term. This is a classic sign of psychopathic personality.

Organizations with a suspected psychopath can support individuals who want to talk to an outside coach or to their manager about the manipulative individuals. It is often more junior employees who first notice the manipulation because these people have least power in the organization and so are the easiest victims. It is therefore important to encourage openness with all levels of employees, and as Lubit (2002) succinctly points out: 'Share information with people. Don't keep information to yourself out of embarrassment' (p. 73).

A final note on the 'treatment' of psychopaths

While the previous section was devoted to strategies for managing employees' relationships with psychopaths, as well as the impact of the psychopath on the organization, one thing that the reader will have noted was that there was no discussion on how to coach the psychopath, which may be considered curious given the current popularity of workplace coaching interventions. However, this is an area that is complicated, and our warnings should be heeded carefully as any suggestion of 'therapy' is likely to be received very poorly by the psychopath and, of even more concern, as pointed out by Lubit (2002), psychopaths will probably use what they have learned in coaching or therapy against other people. Even at a clinical level, it has been suggested that psychopaths may actually become 'worse' as a consequence of treatment (e.g., Rice, Harris & Cormier, 1992). However, this being said, intense individual psychotherapy has been found to be an effective intervention method for psychopathy, with the most successful interventions being cognitive-behavioural (mean p success rate = 0.62) and psychoanalytic (mean p success rate = 0.59) (Salekin, 2002). However, we strongly suggest that engaging someone with a psychopathic personality in therapy, counselling or coaching is not something that should be taken lightly, and certainly not by a coach or therapist who has not been trained in this type of work. If this is the chosen route, the individual concerned must *want* to seek help and be motivated to work constructively with the coach or counsellor, which of course, is very often not the case! It is therefore necessary to ascertain the reasons as to why the individual seeks help in order to understand their motivation, and be clearer about who has referred them for intervention. Clear boundaries must be maintained within the therapeutic relationship, and it is imperative that the coach seeks regular supervision from a qualified supervisor who also understands the nature of psychopathy.

Conclusion

Psychopaths are highly destructive and manipulative individuals who have no remorse for their actions, which can result in a range of serious issues for organizations and the people within those organizations. In this chapter, we have considered the nature of psychopaths in the workplace and ways in which employees and organizations can best act in order to minimize the impact of the organizational psychopath. Consider the words of Winston Churchill (Churchill & James 1974):

> The truth is incontrovertible; malice may attack it, ignorance may deride it, but in the end, there it is (p. 2421).

References

American Psychiatric Association. (2000). *Diagnostic and Statistical Manual of Mental Disorders*. Washington DC: American Psychiatric Association.

Babiak, P. (1995). When psychopaths go to work: A case study of an industrial psychopath. *Applied Psychology: An International Review, 44*, 171–188.

Babiak, P. & Hare, R. D. (2006). *Snakes in Suits: When Psychopaths Go to Work.* New York, NY: HarperCollins.

Barr, K. N. & O'Connor, B. P. (2002). Antisocial personality disorder. In J. C. Thomas & M. Hersen (eds), *Handbook of Mental Health in the Workplace.* Thousand Oaks, CA: Sage Publications, Inc.

Boddy, C. R. (2006). The dark side of management decisions: Organizational psychopaths. *Management Decision, 44*, 1461–1475.

Burch, G. St. J. (2006). The creative-schizotype: Help or hindrance to team-level innovation. *The University of Auckland Business Review, 8*(1), 43–51.

Burch, G. St. J. & Anderson, N. (2008). Personality as a predictor of work-related behaviour and performance: Recent advances and directions for future research. In G. P. Hodgkinson & J. K. Ford (eds), *International Review of Industrial and Organizational Psychology*, Vol. 23 (pp. 261–305). Chichester: John Wiley & Sons.

Burch, G. St. J. & Anderson, N. (in press). Personality at work. In P. J. Corr & G. Matthews (eds), *Handbook of Personality*. Cambridge: Cambridge University Press.

Burch, G. St. J. & McCormick, I. A. (2006). Minimising the impact of the workplace psychopath. *People and Organizations at Work*. Spring Edition 8–9. British Psychological Society, Division of Occupational Psychology.

Carey, G. & Goldman, D. (1997). The genetics of antisocial behaviour. In D. M. Stoff, J. Breiling, J. D. Maser (eds), *Handbook of Antisocial Behavior*. New York, NY: John Wiley & Sons.

Churchill, W. & James, R. R. (1974) *Winston S. Churchill: His Complete Speeches, 1897–1963*. London: Chelsea House Publishers, p. 2421.

Claridge, G. (1997). Theoretical background and issues. In G. Claridge (ed.), *Schizotypy: Implications for Illness and Health* (pp. 3–18). Oxford: Oxford University Press.

Claridge, G. (in press). Personality and psychosis. In P. J. Corr & G. Matthews (eds), *Handbook of Personality*. Cambridge: Cambridge University Press.

Claridge, G. & Davis, C. (2003). *Personality and Psychological Disorders*. London: Arnold.

Clarke, J. (2005). *Working with Monsters: How to Identify and Protect Yourself from the Workplace Psychopath*. Sydney: Random House Australia.

Clarke, J. (2007). *Pocket Psycho*. Random House Australia.

Cleckley, H. (1941). *The Mask of Sanity.* St. Louis, MO: Mosby.

Cleckley, H. (1976). *The Mask of Sanity (5th edition)*. St. Louis, MO: Mosby.

Corr, P. J. (2004). Reinforcement sensitivity theory and personality. *Neuroscience and biobehavioural reviews, 28*, 317–332.

Corr, P. J. (2008) Reinforcement sensitivity theory: Introduction. In P. J. Corr (ed.), *The Reinforcement Sensitivity Theory of Personality*. Cambridge: Cambridge University Press.

Field, T. (1996). Bully in sight. How to predict, resist, challenge and combat workplace bullies. *Success Unlimited*, Monday 7 November 2005.

Depue, R. A. & Lenzenweger, M. F. (2005). A neurobehavioural dimensional model of personality disturbance. In M. F. Lenzenweger & J. F. Clarkin (eds), *Major Theories of Personality Disorder* (2nd ed.). New York, NY: The Guildford Press.

Ebstein, R. P., Benjamin, J. & Belmaker, R. H. (2003). Behavioural genetics, genomics and personality. In R. Plomin, J. C. DeFries, I. W. Craig & P. McGuffin (eds), *Behavioural Genetics in the Postgenomic Era*. Washington DC: American Psychological Association.

Eron, L. D. (1997). The development of antisocial behaviour from a learning perspective. In D. M. Stoff, J. Breiling, J. D. Maser (eds), *Handbook of Antisocial Behaviour*. New York, NY: John Wiley & Sons.

Friedlander, K. (1945). Formation of the antisocial character. *Psychoanalytic Study of the Child, 1*, 189–203.

Furnham, A. & Jackson, C. (2008). Reinforcement sensitivity theory in the workplace. In P. J. Corr (ed.), *The Reinforcement Sensitivity Theory of Personality*. Cambridge: Cambridge University Press.

Furnham, A. & Taylor, J. (2004). *The Dark Side of Behaviour at Work*. Basingstoke: Palgrave Macmillan.

Giacalone, R. A. & Greenberg, J. (1997). *Antisocial Behaviour in Organizations*. CA: Sage Publications, Inc.

Goldman, A. (2006). High toxicity leadership: Borderline personality disorder and the dysfunctional organization. *Journal of Managerial Psychology, 21,* 733–746.

Gray, J. A. (1970). The psychophysiological basis of introversion-extraversion. *Behavioural Research Therapy, 8,* 249–266.

Gray, J. A. (1982). *The Neuropsychology of Anxiety: An Enquiry into the Functions of the Septo-Hippocampal System.* Oxford: Oxford University Press.

Gray, J. A. & McNaughton, N. (2000). *The Neuropsychology of Anxiety: An Enquiry into the Functions of the Septo-Hippocampal Syste, 2nd Edition.* Oxford: Oxford University Press.

Hare, R. (1991). *The Hare Psychopathy Checklist – Revised, Manual.* Toronto: Multi-Health Systems, Inc.

Hare, R. (1993). *Without Conscience: The Disturbing World of the Psychopaths Among Us.* NY: Guilford Press.

Hare, R. (1996). Psychopathy and antisocial personality disorder: A case of diagnostic confusion. *Psychiatric Times, 13*(2), www.psychiatrictimes.com

Hare, R. D., Hart, S. D. & Harpur, T. J. (1991). Psychopathy and the *DSM-IV* criteria for antisocial personality disorder. *Journal of Abnormal Psychology, 100,* 391–398.

Harpur, T. J., Hart, S. D. & Hare, R. D. (2002). Personality of the psychopath. In P. T. Costa & T. A. Widiger (eds), *Personality Disorders and the Five-Factor Model of Personality.* Washington DC: American Psychological Association.

Hogan, R. & Hogan, J. (1997). *Hogan Development Survey.* Tulsa, OK: Hogan Assessment Systems.

Hogan, R. & Hogan, J. (2001). Assessing leadership: A view from the dark side. *International Journal of Selection and Assessment, 9,* 40–51.

Hogan, R., Hogan, J. & Barrett, P. (in press). Good judgement: The intersection of intelligence and personality. In G. Bedney (ed.), *Ergonomics and Psychology: Developments in Theory and Practice.* London: Taylor & Francis.

Hogan, R., Curphy, G. J. & Hogan, J. (1994). What we know about leadership: Effectiveness and personality. *American Psychologist, 49,* 493–504.

Hutchison, A., Burch, G. St. J. & Boxall, P. (in press). Reinforcement sensitivity theory and workplace motivation. In S. Boag (ed.), *Personality Down Under: Perspectives from Australia.* New York: Nova Publishers.

Jackson, C. (2001). Comparison between Eysenck's and Gray's models of personality in the prediction of motivational work criteria. *Personality and Individual Differences, 31,* 129–144.

Jakobwitz, S. & Egan, V. (2006). The dark triad and normal personality traits. *Personality and Individual Differences, 40,* 331–339.

Judge, T. A., LePine, J. A., & Rich, B. L. (2006). Loving yourself abundantly: Relationship of the narcissistic personality to self- and other perceptions of workplace deviance, leadership, and task and contextual performance. *Journal of Applied Psychology, 91,* 762–776.

Karpman, B. (1948). The myth of the psychopathic personality. *American Journal of Psychiatry, 104,* 523–534.

Kets de Vries, M. (1985). Narcissism and leadership: An object relations perspective. *Human Relations, 38,* 583–601.

Khoo, H. S. & Burch, G. St. J. (2008). The 'dark side' of leadership personality and transformational leadership: An exploratory study. *Personality and Individual Differences, 44,* 86–97.

Levenson, M. R. (1992). Rethinking psychopathy. *Theory & Psychology, 2,* 51–71.

Levenson, M. R., Kiehl, K. A. & Fitzpatrick, C. M. (1995). Assessing psychopathic attributes in a noninstitutionalized population. *Journal of Personality and Social Psychology, 68,* 151–158.

Lubit, R. (2002). The long-term organizational impact of destructively narcissistic managers. *Academy of Management Executive, 16,* 127–138.

Maccoby, M. (2007). *Narcissistic Leaders: Who Succeeds and Who Fails.* Harvard: Harvard Business School Press.

McCormick, I. A. & Burch, G. St. J (2005). Snakes in suits: Fear and loathing in corporate clothing. *New Zealand Management,* November, 34–35.

McNaughton, N. & Corr, P. J. (2004). A two-dimensional neuropsychology of defense: Fear/anxiety and defense distance. *Neuroscience and Biobehavioural Reviews, 28,* 285–305.

Miller, J. D. & Lynam, D. R. (2003). Psychopathy and the five-factor model of personality: A replication and extension. *Journal of Personality Assessment, 81,* 168–179.

Millon, T. & Davis, R. (2000). *Personality Disorders in Modern Life.* New York, NY: John Wiley & Sons, Inc.

Morse, G. (2004). Executive psychopaths. *Harvard Business Review, 82,* 10, 20.

Moscoso, S. & Salgado, J. F. (2004). 'Dark side' personality styles as predictors of task, contextual, and job performance. *International Journal of Selection and Assessment, 12,* 356–362.

Namie, G. (2007). The challenge of workplace bullying. *Employment Relations Today, 24,* 43–51.

Newman, J. P., MacCoon, D. G., Vaughn, L. J. & Sadeh, N. (2005). Validating a distinction between primary and secondary psychopathy with measures of Gray's BIS and BAS constructs. *Journal of Abnormal Psychology, 114,* 319–323.

Paulhus, D. L. & Williams, K. M. (2002). The dark triad of personality: Narcissism, Machiavellianism, and psychopathy. *Journal of Research in Personality, 36,* 556–563.

Poythress, N. G., Edens, J. F., Landfield, K., Lilienfeld, S. O., Skeem, J. L. & Douglas, K. S. (2008). A critique of Carver and White's (1994) behavioural inhibition scale (BIS) for investigating Lykken's (1995) theory of primary psychopathy. *Personality and Individual Differences, 45,* 269–275.

Pretzer, J. L. & Beck, A. T. (2005). A cognitive theory of personality disorders. In M. F. Lenzenweger & J. F. Clarkin (eds), *Major Theories of Personality Disorder (2nd ed.).* New York, NY: The Guildford Press.

Rice, M., Harris, G. & Cormier, C. (1992). An evaluation of a maximum-security community for psychopaths and other mentally disordered offenders. *Law and Human Behaviour, 16,* 399–412.

Reivich, K. and Shatte, A. (2002). *The Resilience Factor: 7 Keys to Finding Your Inner Strength and Overcoming Life's Hurdles.* New York: Broadway Books.

Rosenthal, S. A. & Pittinsky, T. L. (2006). Narcissistic leadership. *The Leadership Quarterly, 17,* 617–633.

Ross, S. R., Moltó, J., Poy, R., Segarra, P., Pastor, M. C. & Montañés, S. (2007). Gray's model and psychopathy: BIS but not BAS differentiates primary from secondary psychopathy in noninstitutionalized young adults. *Personality and Individual Differences, 43,* 1644–1655.

Salekin, R. T. (2002). Psychopathy and therapeutic pessimism: Clinical lore or clinical reality? *Clinical Psychology Review, 22,* 79–112.

Sankowsky, D. (1995). The charismatic leader as narcissist: Understanding the abuse of power. *Organizational Dynamics, 23,* 57–71.

Sosik, J. J. (2006). Full range leadership: Model, research, extensions, and training. In R. J. Burke & C. L. Cooper (eds), *Inspiring Leaders.* New York, NY: Routledge.

Takahashi, Y., Yamagata, S., Kijima, N., Shigemasu, K., Ono, Y. & Ando, J. (2007). Continuity and change in behavioural inhibition and activation systems: A longitudinal behavioural genetic study. *Personality and Individual Differences, 43,* 1616–1625.

Walker, J. & Hayward, P. (2007). Personality disorder – treatment. In S. Lindsay & G. Powell (eds), *The Handbook of Clinical Adult Psychology, 3rd Edition.* London: Routledge.

Zuckerman, M. (2007). The sensation seeking scale V (SSS-V): Still reliable and valid. *Personality and Individual Differences, 43*(5), 1303–1305.

Index